The World of

DUKE

ELLINGTON

M

The World of

DUKE

ELLINGTON

by Stanley Dance

A Da Capo Paperback

Library of Congress Cataloging in Publication Data

Dance, Stanley.
  The world of Duke Ellington.

  (A Da Capo paperback)
  Reprint of the 1970 ed. published by C. Scribner's
Sons, New York.
  Discography: p.
  Includes index.
  1. Ellington, Duke, 1899-1974. 2. Jazz musicians—
United States—Biography. I. Title.
  [ML410.E44D3 1981] 785.42′092′4 [B]   80-29358
ISBN 0-306-80136-1

"An Afternoon with Ben Webster," "An Interview with Billy Strayhorn," "The Art Is in the Cooking" "Cat Anderson: Trumpet Astronaut," "Ellington Marches On," "The Independent Lawrence Brown," "The Immutable Cootie Williams," "Jimmy Jones," "On the Boardwalk with Johnny Hodges," "Organ-ic Formation," "Putting on the Pots and Pans" and "Warm Root: Ray Nance" are reprinted by permission of *Down Beat Magazine.*

"Clark Terry," "Conversation with Paul Gonsalves," "Harold 'Shorty' Baker," "Harry Carney," "Johnny Hodges," "Mitchell Wood" and "The Story of Suit Thursday" are reprinted by special permission of Robert Asen, publisher of *Metronome.*

"In Those Days" from the booklet, *The Ellington Era,* is reprinted by courtesy of Columbia Records.

Other articles or interviews appeared first in *Jazz Journal, Jazz, Music Journal* and *Saturday Review.* Copyright © 1964, 1965, 1968 Stanley Dance.

This Da Capo Press paperback edition of *The World of Duke Ellington* is an unabridged republication of the first edition published in New York in 1970. It is reprinted by arrangement with Charles Scribner's Sons.

Published by Da Capo Press, Inc.
A Subsidiary of Plenum Publishing Corporation
233 Spring Street, New York, New York 10013

TO MY WIFE

whose Irish patience was never quite exhausted

Contents

EVENTS & OCCASIONS

DISCOGRAPHY, CHRONOLOGY, INDEX

Foreword

Stanley is well informed about my activities and those of my associates. He has been a part of our scene for a long time, maybe longer than he cares to remember. However, I am sure he has not revealed more than he ought!

He and his wife, Helen, are the kind of people it is good to have in your corner, the kind of people you don't mind knowing your secrets. In other words, they are friends—and you don't have to be careful with friends.

Let them introduce you to my mad world.

February 20, 1970

Introduction

This book is neither a history, a biography, nor an all-inclusive survey. It is addressed primarily to those who have already experienced and been fascinated by the musical world of Duke Ellington, and it seeks to present different views of this world as seen by the inhabitants. That their views overlap, confirm, and sometimes contradict, goes without saying, and the more distant past is probably magnified by memory as often as it is diminished.

The man at the center of this world is a creative force of exceptional energy and drive. His capacity for hard, unrelenting work was not recognized for a long time by those who, assessing him in show-business terms, were more conscious of his appetite for life and its pleasures. Eventually, of course, the sheer volume of the work he accomplished—quite apart from its quality—made a formidable impression on the twentieth century. Much of his inspiration came from those around him, a *comédie humaine* he viewed with affectionate tolerance even when its sins and sorrows affected him adversely. Essentially, however, his achievements were due to a highly original mind, one that looked acutely at every subject from a distinctly personal viewpoint. Had this mind been applied to painting or playwriting, for both of which he has demonstrated remarkable gifts, a similarly distinguished career would undoubtedly have resulted. What makes his musical triumphs the more remarkable in retrospect is the circumstances under which they were won. No other composer of note in any field has ever worked or traveled so incessantly while continuing to lead a band of acknowledged, and temperamental, virtuosi. Again and again he has mastered time, meeting the challenge of deadlines under impossible conditions, producing the fresh and unexpected, and confounding the prognostications of his critics.

Behind the artistic ability is an abiding faith in God. As a child, Ellington went to church twice on Sundays, first to his mother's Baptist church, and then to his father's Methodist church. "Later on," he said, "I read the Bible completely four times, and after that I began to understand what I had learned in school." Although he never paraded it, his intimates were well aware of his belief, and not merely because he wore a gold cross around his neck and was meticulous about saying grace before meals. When he was invited to present a sacred concert in Grace Cathedral, San Francisco, he welcomed the opportunity, and was gratified to be accepted "on the team" of ecumenically minded people. "Now," he said, "I can say loudly and openly what I've been saying to myself on my knees." This concert and the greater second edition in the Cathedral Church of St. John the Divine, New York, were followed by performances throughout the United States and Europe that brought him deep satisfaction. "This is the greatest thing I have done," he has said on many occasions.

Blessed with a strong constitution, he is often prodigal of energy, but he pays careful attention to most aspects of his health. He gave up drinking years ago, when it was still a major occupational hazard. "I retired undefeated champ," he explained wryly. He walks fast when obliged to walk, but doesn't exercise, and professes a fear of "fresh-air poisoning." Conversely, he mistrusts air conditioning and likes to have the windows open when he sleeps, which he does without a pillow. He often conducts interviews from his bed with his feet high on the wall above the headboard, while presumably reversing the blood flow beneficially. His diet is rigorous, even monotonous, consisting mostly of grapefruit juice, steak, and salad. An old passion for ice cream has been very strictly controlled, and he smokes only a modest quantity of unfiltered cigarettes. His medicine bag, which accompanies him on all journeys, was a present from Billy Strayhorn and is marked *Dr. E.K.E.*, a partly humorous reference to one of the many honorary degrees Edward Kennedy Ellington has received from universities. In it are a variety of vitamin pills and protein tablets, with which he doses himself liberally and regularly. Members of his band and entourage are also given remedies from this bag in emergencies. Wherever he is, he is pleased to see his friend and doctor, Arthur Logan. "Take my pulse," he will insist in the middle of the most hectic activity. "One never knows how one feels until one has been advised by one's doctor."

Women are a source of unending fascination to Ellington, just as he is to them. His exceptional conversational skills are never deployed so imaginatively as when he is in their company, and his wit and charm are completely democratic. He derived memorable pleasure from conversing with Queen Elizabeth II, and he can be stimulated and even inspired by an exchange of banter with a pretty airline stewardess. For him, women represent the gracious element in life, on the horizon and in the atmosphere, and his interest is not confined to the smart, elegant, and beautiful. He is quickly aware of inner qualities, inner beauty, that others, less sensitive, might miss. Needless to add, women have, in general and in particular, inspired some of his most famous compositions.

Nearly all the interviewing and writing in this book was done during the 1960s, so that everywhere the perspective really belongs to that decade—a disastrous one in music generally, but an extraordinarily eventful and exciting one in Ellington history.

Ellington himself is interviewed in the first part of the book. The second and third sections are devoted to his aides and musicians. The last contains descriptions of events that I have witnessed. Some of the great figures in the Ellington pantheon had died before 1960, so men like Bubber Miley, Artie Whetsol, Joe "Tricky Sam" Nanton, Wellman Braud, and Jimmy Blanton appear here only in the words of their colleagues. The pieces on Alice Babs, Toby Hardwick, and Cootie Williams were written by my wife, and here our occasional collaborative roles were reversed.

The length of Ellington's career has resulted in a body of work as enormous as it is unique. Fortunately, it has nearly all been recorded, and during the 1960s the major record companies have recognized its significance with extensive reissue programs. Much, however, remains to be reissued, and much has never been issued at all. As he repeatedly affirms, Ellington likes to hear his music performed as soon as possible after it has been composed, and when this does not coincide with the policies of the record companies, he goes ahead and records it at his own expense. A treasure house of experimental music and spontaneous, small-group improvisations awaits posterity—or the attention of a record company as much concerned with music as with money.

Suggestions are often made that Ellington should re-record all the masterpieces of his library. Overlooked is the fact that most of his compositions have been written for specific performers, some of whom are no longer with him. It would probably be more fruitful to encourage the continuous publication of his new material without delays. The various transcription series and wartime V–Discs, the release of which could surely be negotiated, would in any case provide attractive alternative versions of the basic repertoire. Excellently recorded, these offer such illuminating contrasts as Jimmy Hamilton playing roles originally created by Barney Bigard.

Several discographies furnish details of the Ellington band's personnel changes and recorded history. They include: Brian Rust's *Jazz Records, 1897–1931* and *Jazz Records, 1932–1942*, both published in England; Benny H. Aasland's *The Wax Works of Duke Ellington*, published in Sweden; Jorgen Grunnet Jepsen's *Jazz Records, 1942–1965, Vol. III*, published in Denmark; Luigi Sanfilippo's *General Catalog of Duke Ellington's Recorded Music*, published in Italy; and *Duke Elling-*

ton's Story on Records, 1925–1945 in five volumes by Luciano Massagli, Liborio Pusateri and Giovanni M. Volonté, also published in Italy. Another exhaustive work, *The Duke Is on the Air, 1937–1947* by Benny H. Aasland and Jerry Valburn, is scheduled to appear in Sweden well before publication of this book. It is significant that all these discographies originate in Europe, where Ellington's recorded work is also available in much greater profusion.

To suggest, however, that Ellington is a prophet without honor in his own country would be to exaggerate, for he has received many great honors here, culminating with the celebration of his seventieth birthday at the White House in 1969. The four walls of his trophy room are covered with tributes in every form from all over the world, but the majority have come from the hands of his countrymen. Newspaper reporters, trying to provoke him into controversial utterances, have often retired discomfited when they found he was not merely an American conscious of his place in American society, but an unabashed patriot, too.

STANLEY DANCE

Rowayton, Connecticut
1969

Patient television performer

Critical listener

Conductor in record studio

THE MAESTRO

Duke Ellington's frequently expressed impatience with categorization extends to the term "jazz" itself. Neither his band nor his music belongs under any of the flags of convenience that have flown on the angry seas of jazz criticism.

Dixieland, Traditional, Chicago Style, Hot, Swing, Kansas City Style, Bop, Progressive, Modern, Cool, West Coast, East Coast, Mainstream, Hard Bop, Funky, Third Stream, and Avant Garde are some of the terms critics have employed through the years, in communicating with the public, as labor-saving reference tags. Sometimes, too, these tags have served as rallying cries, or as slogans in calculated and systematic promotions.

To Ellington, and many other musicians, they represent divisions, illdefined and indefensible, which tend to restrict the artist's prerogative of freedom. "If 'jazz' means anything at all, which is questionable," he has said, "it means the same thing it meant to musicians fifty years ago—freedom of expression. I used to have a definition, but I don't think I have one anymore, unless it is that it is a music with an African foundation which came out of an American environment."

The first piece in this section voices his concern with categorization, but it incorporates a wide range of his opinions on the musical field in which he has played so big a part. In the second, he continues with reflections of a general nature, while the third and fourth derive from what was perhaps the most unusual and important foreign tour he ever made—that of the Middle East, India, and Ceylon for the U.S. State Department in 1963.

The Art Is in the Cooking

"People are told that they must never drink anything but a white wine with fish or a red wine with beef. The people who don't know, who've never been told that, who've never been educated along those lines—they drink *anything!* I suspect they get as much joy out of their eating and drinking as the other people.

"It's just like people who listen to music. They don't necessarily *know* what they're listening to. They don't have to know that a guy is blowing a flatted fifth or a minor third, but they enjoy it, and this I consider healthy and normal listening. A listener who has first to decide whether this is proper form when a musician plays or writes something—that's not good. It's a matter of 'How does it sound?' and, of course, the sound is modified by the taste of the listener.

"One listener may like things that are pretty, what we consider pretty or schmaltzy. Another may like a graceful melodic line, with agreeable harmony under it and probably a little romantic element. A third may like subtle dissonance, while a fourth may go for out-and-out dissonance. A fifth may have a broad appreciation and enjoy all kinds. But what is really involved here, I think, is personal taste rather than categories.

"Music itself is a category of sound, but everything that goes into the ear is not music. Music is music, and that's it. If it sounds good, it's good music, and it depends on who's listening *how* good it sounds! Now let me put this right. Music can sound good to somebody who likes nothing but cacophony, but it doesn't necessarily have to sound good to the man sitting next to him. There are quite a few people around who really dig distortion. Everybody in the world doesn't like pretty. Everybody in the world doesn't like sweet. There are some people who don't like either one ever, but they are all entitled to their likes and dislikes. Some people, you know, don't even like to get along with others. They're not happy unless they're fighting all the time. Some people are a little sadistic, shall we say, and some are a little masochistic. I've ofter suspected, when people have said some-

3

thing about others, that they've said it deliberately, expecting them to come back with something ugly, so that they could get their kicks.

"Now let's consider this imaginary customer of yours who goes into the restaurant. As I understand you, he looks at the menu and finds the dishes classified under such headings as fish, fowl, and meat. That's a convenience for him. Right? He orders steak, but, after a few minutes, here comes the waiter with a plate of fish. When he complains, the chef—and the chef is the important cat!—comes out of the kitchen with a big carving knife in his hand. The chef tells him to eat up, because it's good food, because if he were starving he wouldn't care if it were fish *or* steak. So you mean the question is more than one of just good food or the other kind, eh?

"Well, if a man has some very hungry ears for what he considers jazz, or for a pleasant noise that makes him feel he wants to swing (and we have there possibly a reasonable definition of jazz), then almost anything would suffice. At least, if he were starving he would tolerate it for one take. But if he were not starving, and if he were now like a gourmet in a gourmet restaurant, and he ordered fish, and they brought him fish, and the minute he tasted it he said, 'No, this is not cooked by Pierre! Who is the chef today? This is not the way I like it. I like it the way Pierre cooks it.' What then?

At U. S. Embassy,
Buenos Aires, 1968

"This is not a matter of categories. This is personal. He wants his fish cooked a particular way, just as some people want their trumpet played by Louis Armstrong, some by Dizzy Gillespie, some by Harry James, some by Miles Davis, and some by Maynard Ferguson. And I know a lot of people who like to hear Ray Nance play trumpet!

"Some people have been raised on nothing but fish. There's been nothing else available where they live. Some people have been raised on nothing but beef, because sheep aren't allowed in their territory. Some people have been raised on fowl, because it's the only thing they can get, and they have to shoot it down. Each of these people may develop a taste for the food they've been accustomed to, and when they experience one of the others they may find it strange and distasteful. They may possibly decide that beef hasn't the delicacy of fish, but maybe they don't put it down. Maybe they say, 'This is something new. This is something I never tasted before, and I like it.' And they acquire a taste for it.

"Now I don't really regard these three—fish, fowl, and meat—as three different categories of food. Maybe I'm too basic, too primitive! They're all prey. Maybe I still think in terms of killing the animal and eating it a half-hour later. (I must admit I never caught a fish in my life!)

"You could divide up the meat section of that menu under beef,

Listening to record playback

Welcoming visitors

lamb, pork, and so on, under hot and cold, or according to the way they were cooked—grilled, roasted, baked, boiled, etc.—and maybe that's a service to the customer, but to multiply divisions that way in music, in my opinion, merely multiplies confusion. Fish, fowl, and meat may provide us with a parallel, but never forget that *the art is in the cooking.* And what is convenient for the listener, or the critic, is not necessarily helpful to the musician.

"I'm sure critics have their purpose, and they're supposed to do what they do, but sometimes they get a little carried away with what they think someone *should* have done, rather than concerning themselves with what he did.

"Those trumpets we mentioned don't come out of the same egg. It isn't that at all. If you like what Louis Armstrong plays, you like that on trumpet. If you like what Dizzy Gillespie plays, you like that on trumpet. So this is more a matter of personal identification, which means that you like not a category, but Louis Armstrong trumpet, and that anyone else who plays like Louis Armstrong should be labeled 'Imitation of Louis Armstrong.' And anyone who plays like Dizzy Gillespie should be labeled 'Imitation of Dizzy Gillespie' This is a matter of imitation, not category. When a guy has invented a style, or become identified with a style, somebody else cannot come along and be a great member of this democratic world of sound which he has created. It's *his* world. Anyone else who uses his creation is an imitator and should be labeled as such. We'll come back to the modifications, but this, I feel, completely destroys the category business. It's a matter of *personal* sound.

"It's the same even where you have bands and clusters of sounds. A certain sound comes out of a big band. It may be the character given it by a large brass section, or by a particularly skillful group of saxophones. The minute you change the men in the section, it doesn't sound the same, although you may have the same arranger. What happens to the category? The arranger can continue to write in the same style, and someone else who has studied his scores can copy the style, but that brings us back to imitation.

Imitation, influence, and inspiration? Where do you draw the lines now? That's one thing I'd like to know. Yes, just about everybody has been inspired by another musician, has adopted characteristics of his style and clothed them in his own personality. Some people have done it very skillfully and deliberately. Others have done it, you might say, grabbing at a straw! It may surprise you, but I think those who have done it, grabbing at a straw, are the ones who have come up with the *nearest* thing to something new.

"Imitation, influence, and inspiration! We haven't finished with them!

"Well, take the people you hear playing plungers in the band. They derive their styles in part from Bubber Miley and Tricky Sam, but Charlie Irvis was first. Nobody ever really picked up on Charlie Irvis. He used an object that was very effective, and he played in a different register of the horn. There was a kind of mute they built at that time to go into the trombone and make it sound like a saxophone, but he dropped his one night and the darn thing broke into a million parts. So he picked up the biggest part that was left and started using it. This was *his* device and it was greater than the original thing. He got a great, big, fat sound at the bottom of the trombone—melodic, masculine, full of tremendous authority. I wish I could find someone to do it now. When he was with me we weren't making many records, and I don't know if he was on those with Bubber Miley and Mae Barnes. The same Mae Barnes. She's still wailing!

"But Bubber and Tricky were the first to get really wide recognition for the plunger thing. They had such beautiful teamwork together. Everything they played represented a mood, a person, a picture. As a matter of fact, everything we used to do in the old days had a picture. We'd be riding along and see a name on a sign. We used to spend a lot of time up in New England, around Boston, and we'd see this sign, "LEWANDO CLEANERS," and every time we saw it we'd start singing:

"Oh, Lee—wan-do!"

Out of that came *East St. Louis Toodle-oo.* Probably it would have been better if we had called it *Lewando* and got some advertising money from it. Everything was like that then. The guys would be walking up Broadway after work and see this old man coming down the street, and there was the beginning of *Old Man Blues.* Everything had a picture or was descriptive of something. Always.

"A lot of guys heard and listened to Bubber and Tricky's thing. When Cootie Williams first came into the band, taking Bubber's place, he picked up the plunger and became *so* expert. He did things with a greater range than Bubber. Tricky was there all through this and he was followed by Tyree Glenn.

"Tyree, to me, is a very beautiful trombone player. He plays real good legit trombone, and when he applied the plunger to it his tone remained very precise and clean, so that you were tempted to like it better than Tricky's, because it was so clean. But then Tricky's was so very plaintive. Tyree is a very agile-minded musician and he always wants to do a lot of things. I'm sure he had enjoyed Tricky before. He must have, because he couldn't have done the plunger work so well if he hadn't enjoyed doing it. He still uses the plunger and he is one of the most effective plunger trombones I have ever heard.

The Cotton Club Band, 1929

"After Tyree came Butter (Quentin Jackson), and he returned us to a little of Tricky's plaintiveness. Then there was Booty Wood, and he had more of a gutty thing in his playing.

"Some people hesitate to take the plunger role. Maybe they've heard it for years and they have a thing in their minds, and it all seems mysterious to them. But those who have come in and picked up on it have really done it from a *gracious* point of view, of carrying on where someone else has left off. It has to do with conforming to a character and styling, which they obviously enjoy doing. It is sometimes considered a traditional device with us, both as regards the growl solo and the section with plungers, which we call the 'pep' section. A lot of guys come in and they know the part before they get here. They don't need an arrangement and, if they did, in most instances there wouldn't be one anyway.

"We've been very fortunate that way, to find guys in there who wanted to be there. You take Paul Gonsalves. When he came into the band, the first night, he played Ben Webster's solos, every solo, identical with Ben's. He knew them all. He knew everything in the book. But he's no imitator. You hear him today. That was a matter of his musicianship and ear.

"Of course, if I said everyone who has adopted some of Louis Armstrong's things was an imitator, I would be damning a whole lot

8

With Louis Armstrong

Ray Nance, Rex Stewart, Joe Nanton,
Harry Carney, Sonny Greer

of wonderful people. Certain modifications can be made to that. I
don't even think the imitators of Louis form a specific category,
because they divide up by personalities. If someone took one of these
big, fat IBM machines and worked it down (with time, I'm sure it
could be done), you could say that so-and-so had a style based on
Louis Armstrong's to a certain point, to 75.439 percent blah-blah-
blah, beyond which he developed a new perspective that now boils
down to nineteen figures with a decimal point. This is so-and-so, but
it all comes back to individual people. There is no category. There is
one of every style. *If two people are playing identically the same, one
is an imitator.*

"Some people really don't give much credit to the creative element. I've known them to say the imitation was better than the
original. Are you going to say the son has better blood than the
father?

"You're right, it is possible, because it's not all the father's blood.
The mother can raise the quality! And certain parts of the blood's
potency may not have come forward until possibly the third genera-
tion, so the father never enjoyed it, yet he had it all the time. Things
like that are in the Bible. (You haven't read the Bible lately? Then
you've got to start reading it again this year!)

"Anyway, I think we've solved our problem. I think it's some-

9

thing I've been trying to say for a long time. You cannot say that two performers who play in an identical way are out of the same mold. What you can say is that of these two, one is an imitator.

"Yes, there were some very good Lester Young imitators. Lester was one of the very potent influences. Charlie Parker had plenty of imitators. Johnny Hodges, too. And there was a time when there was hardly a tenor player in the world who didn't try to sound like Coleman Hawkins. But we mustn't leave out the greatest—Bechet! The greatest of all the originators, Bechet, the symbol of jazz!

"I heard him before I left Washington. He always played the same way—the same way then as just before he died. I remember hearing him play *I'm Coming, Virginia* in 1921—the greatest thing I ever heard in my life. I'd never heard anything like it. It knocked me out.

"He played clarinet back in New Orleans, and later on he still played it occasionally, but when he got on soprano he wouldn't get off it. He was just as great a clarinet player. He had a wonderful clarinet tone—all wood, a sound you don't hear anymore. The New Orleans guys absorbed something down there along with the Albert system.

"I consider Bechet the foundation. His things were all soul, all from the inside. It was very, very difficult to find anyone who could really keep up with him. He'd get something organized in his mind while someone else was playing, and then he'd play one or two choruses—or more—that would be just too much.

"He played with us in 1926, when I had a band up in New England. Johnny learned a lot from him, particularly on soprano. We had Toby Hardwick, Bubber Miley, Tricky Sam, Sonny Greer, and the tuba player, Mack Shaw. The police, gangsters, or somebody had caught Mack out in Chicago, beaten his face in and broken up all the bones. This cat would be blowing his tuba and blow out a loose bone. He had a whole lot of loose bones in his face, and he'd just put them together again and continue blowing! We had a terrific band then.

"It had to be terrific in those days, because that was when Mal Hallett had a band up in New England and you had to play alongside him. The big dance territories were in Massachusetts and Pennsylvania. Charlie Shribman put on dances and they'd have battles of music. All these big bands used to come up from New York and Mal Hallett would blow them right out over the Charles River. He just played big, fat arrangements of dance music, and most of his guys were legit, but they'd open up with a flag-waver, and that was *it!* Paul Whiteman came up there with twenty-eight pieces one night, but Mal was too much for him with his novelties and everything.

"We had a six-piece band and we used to play him contrast-wise.

He'd know we were coming on and he'd blow up a storm and lift the roof off. Then we'd crawl up there with our six pieces and begin softly, and develop it, so that when we did play loud it would seem as though we were playing louder than we actually were.

"That was a long time ago. Then as now, it's hard if you don't keep with it. If you just stay home for a while and listen tò what the other kids are doing out there on the battlefield, you may see where this one made a lot of mistakes, or where that one missed a great opportunity, but on the other hand you get more fears. You may read where so-and-so lost this particular battle and so many men were washed away, and it's all a little terrifying. If you come out from home cold—bang!—and all the other cats have been roaming around the jungle, fighting the different animals who're growling with their plungers, honking with their tenors, screeching with their flutes and clarinets, then these animals can sound pretty wild after the comforts of home. . . .

"You see the time? I've got to go and marshal the front-line forces over at Basin Street right now!"

[*1962*]

It's Really a Twisting World

"There was a tendency a few years ago for a lot of guys to say, 'We only play concerts.' It got to the stage where everybody was giving concerts, so that none made much of an impression. We did them for eleven years at Carnegie Hall, and there was always something new written specially each time. Those concerts were very big for a while and a point was reached where we had to do two nights instead of one. When Django Reinhardt was brought over, he played with us and was given to the audience almost unannounced, as a sort of bonus.

"I've always preferred to mix dances and concerts, to play high-brow stuff in the concert hall—like the engagements we did with the Cleveland Symphony, the National Symphony, etc.—and the next night to play a prom. Sometimes we play for the Elks club or the Moose club, and it's *Melancholy Baby* all night, but I love it, because I like the change of pace in going from one extreme to another. We have so much stuff in the book, and not only jazz.

"I like to play theatres, too. But how many theatres are there now? The Apollo, the Howard in Washington, and the Regal in Chicago. The Royal in Baltimore is too small. Then we've played two or three debutante parties this year and have a couple more coming up. They're interesting. I like all of it.

"When you play a military base, you soon start getting requests, and you can get them all night. We had to play *Suite Thursday* at one the other night where the second line was twenty deep. They were so full of requests that some of the dancers came up to beef. They just wanted to twist. *Schwiphti* was too fast for that, but it was during the fourth movement that they complained.

"At any affair like that, I think you can have your biggest success by fulfilling as many requests as possible. It means something to the people who make the requests, and you're there for the purpose of making them happy. In one night, we can have in the audience those who identify us with the Newport Festival and Paul Gonsalves' performance of *Diminuendo and Crescendo*, and others who romanced and married to *Mood Indigo*, and we'll play music that goes all the way back to 1927 and all the way up to 1962. Youngsters sometimes ask us to play *Black and Tan Fantasy*. We play it, but I don't know how they came to like it or where they ever heard it, because we haven't made a record of it for a long time. Sometimes, too, these requests have resulted in our putting numbers in the book which have become extremely popular parts of our repertoire—not music we've written ourselves, but tunes like *All of Me*. There is also a public, created mainly through records, which wants to hear numbers we hardly ever play. We may reach in the book for them occasionally and play something with apologies for its being 'unprepared.'

"When you play a prom nowadays, you don't know who the chaperones are, because *everybody* is doing the Twist. It's not like it used to be. We used to get a big bang out of the first hour, playing nice, smooth music, what they called 'danceable' music. What we played in that first hour to impress the chaperons was a little 'businessman's bounce' and a little slow, romantic stuff, but now they want to twist from the first number!

"People used to dance more back in the '30s, and there were more really popular songs for them to dance to, which resulted in more variations in the programs. The Twist is bringing people back to dancing, which I think is a very good thing, but I don't know how much it is benefiting jazz groups generally. Some of them may not bend to conform to it. It seems to me that with everyone in the whole world doing the Twist, you're out of step if you don't do it. I do it. I don't like to be odd.

12   "Before the Twist, there hadn't been a dance craze for some

time. The last was for the cha-cha-cha, the mambo, and that stuff. Further back there were dances like the Lindy Hop and the Charleston, but none has ever been so big as the Twist. None captured so many different kinds of people. Society people are doing it. The kids are doing it, the rich people and the poor people, the fancy and the frumpy—everybody!

"The Twist has brought me out. It's actually an old wallflower's dance. You know who used to do it years ago when the floor was full of people dancing? The guys who hadn't anyone to dance with. They'd be on the sidelines with a glass or a bottle in one hand. They'd be doing the Twist!

"I used to be a pretty good dancer at one time. I think it's very important that a musician should dance. Of course, I don't do the Twist very violently myself. I know a few steps in the Latin American dances, too. I'm the type of ham who displays one or two Sunday-punch steps. When you get the audience, then you leave them! 'He's a great dancer,' they think, but what you did was your whole, dramatically paced to get favorable audience reaction.

"Yes, dancing is very important to people who play music with a beat. I think that people who don't dance, or who never did dance, don't really understand the beat. What they get in their minds is a mechanical thing not totally unacademic. I know musicians who don't and never did dance, and they have difficulty communicating.

"They used to have great dancers up at the Ritz, Bridgeport. Every now and then you go into a ballroom like that where they have great dancers. It's a kick to play for people who really jump and swing. On two occasions up there we were using a substitute drummer, but we didn't have to worry about him because the dancers were carrying the band and the drummer. You start playing, the dancers start dancing, and they have such a great beat you just hang on!

"Shows used to call for a big variety of tempos, but so did ballrooms. We used to have dancers years ago who danced really fast, but they would also dance very, very slow things. The waltzes were extremely slow, but the two-step and the one-step could be so fast. They took on different names. You remember what a galop the Lindy Hop was? When we get a request for a waltz now, what we usually play is a head, but we also have a vocal waltz, the song from *Moulin Rouge.*

"We've been doing these jazz waltzes all the way back. There was that waltz with a beat in the *All American* record. One of the first things I wrote when I came to New York was a jazz waltz called *Come Back to Me.* I sold it outright. There was a terrific one in *Jump for Joy,* and there's a jazz waltz in *Black, Brown, and Beige,* in the Harlem

13

scene—*Sugar Hill Penthouse*. There's a jazz waltz in *Paris Blues,* too.

"We have our Latin American specialties as well. When Tizol was in the band, he was always suggesting them and helping us along with them. I remember once, when we were playing the Coronado Hotel, St. Louis, that I had a kind of hand drum. We didn't call it a tom-tom, a conga, a bongo, or anything. I'd had a cylinder made of a kind of plastic board, and taken a tambourine and nailed it on the head after removing the tingle things. I was playing it in *Pyramid* when Gene Krupa came by. He saw it and had his whole band set up like that, so that everyone in it had a drum. I didn't have it merely for appearance. We'd begin that number with just rhythm section and Tizol playing melody on trombone. Recently, we got into something else on a date we did with Coleman Hawkins. We recorded some *Limbo Jazz* for the benefit of the limboists.

"With the new music that already is, and what is coming, there's no predicting what effect the disassociation from dancing will have in the future, but my own idea is that it is going to make a big fat curve and come right back to where it was, except that it will be on a slightly higher musical plane. I think there will be more of a oneness in American music. The guys who compose will get more into what I'll call the 'legitimate' forms of music, and they'll write for larger orchestras. I don't know who's going to play them, but they'll write

Recording with Symphony Orchestra, Paris, 1963

them and they'll get them played somehow. This will be a big jump from what was. Years ago, a guy who studied in a conservatory and got to the stage where he could write a big orchestral work often never got to hear it, because no symphony would play it. He never knew what it sounded like, although he knew what it should sound like.

"So far as strings are concerned, you have to remember they are like the other instruments: a lot depends on who is playing them. I hear people say, 'I *love* a *string* section!' What does that mean? A string section is great when you have people playing strings who play strings. Strings in the wrong hands can be pretty bad.

"Now, I've never written or attempted this, but it is said by some good musicians that anything that can be done with strings can be done with percussion. You know, with the various mallets. That's what they claim, that there's no effect you get with strings that you cannot get with mallets. From one who is really a master, you can get a roll with the mallets which is as fine as drawing a bow across the violin. A mallet is so seldom used like that. Someday, I think I shall experiment in that field. Certainly, you'd have to get a big collection of percussion instruments—vibraphones, xylophones, marimbas, glockenspiels, and one or two others—but look what big collections of strings they use! When you've got lightweight strings, you've got

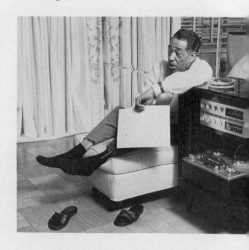

Working at home

With Boston friends in the '30s

practically nothing. You need a whole lot of strings to achieve a good musical effect. With the mallets you would have to have real great people playing them, as expert as the people you hear playing strings.

"We had Moe Goldenberg playing the melody on tymps in our record of *Tymperturbably Blue*. We had nine tymps on that and he was running around from one to the other playing melody. That was in an album called *Jazz Party*—a good album, I thought. But I guess there were too many different types of things in it.

"Times have changed. People used to say, 'I love chocolate cake, but I can't eat it three times a day.' Today, people who like chocolate cake eat it five times a day. They want it all the way. It's the same in music. Everything has to be aimed at one audience. If you have an audience that likes *One O'Clock Jump*, you have to play *One O'Clock Jump*, or everything like *One O'Clock Jump* with the same tempo and beat. In the same way, we've had to play *Sophisticated Lady* six times in one evening. They particularly don't want that beat to change.

"But there's certainly nothing demeaning to my mind in playing music for dancing. Isn't music supposed to have begun as an accompaniment for dancing? The idea some people have that dance music has no artistic value reminds me of an article by Ian Fleming on 'How to Write a Thriller' in *Show*. I found something he had to say in there very important. He said he just wrote for pleasure and money. He disclaimed any attempt at art, yet what came out was a form of art. So there *is* a kind of relationship between art and popular taste. I don't believe in a lot of elaborate plans and preparations either. Just pour it out as it comes, and then maybe do some reshaping afterwards."

[*1962*]

Orientations

"We were appointed by the Cultural Committee—one of President Kennedy's favorite projects—to represent our country in the East on a long tour last fall under the sponsorship of the State Department. We were accepted, as some people put it, as "ambassadors" of the United States of America in Syria, Jordan, Afghanistan, India, Ceylon, Pakistan, Iran, Iraq, and Lebanon, and we everywhere met with grace, warmth, hospitality, and generosity from U.S. ambassadors, consuls, and officials of U.S.I.S. We were also in Kuwait, Cyprus, and Turkey, but we did not play there because of the assassination of the President. In Turkey, everything was flying high. There was a reception at the ambassador's residence—and I was always in the receiving line at such receptions—but immediately after this one the whole thing blew up because of the tragedy in Dallas.

"The tour was a great adventure for us on what is indeed the other side of the world. Sometimes I felt it was *this* world upside down. The look of the natural country is so unlike ours and the very contours of the earth seem to be different. The smell, the vastness, the birds, and the exotic beauty of all these countries make a great impression. I remember the astonishing little lizards on the ceilings in India. They are harmless and they eat the insects. We saw chameleons, too, in Madras, and then there were the elephants, the camels, the asses, and the snakecharmers.

"The snakecharmer I think of as world champion was in Pakistan. His cobras were sleepy. He began to play his flute and when he had an audience he took the covers off his basket and slapped a cobra to get it dancing. He was a terrific showman and he had a mongoose with him. We expected to see a big battle, but the mongoose seemed to act as a chaperon or a bodyguard. He just walked around and he certainly wasn't mad with the four or five cobras the man had in his basket.

"We also saw many remarkable sunrises and sunsets. I particularly recall an extraordinary storm that came up over the sea at Bombay when we were in a hotel on the seafront. And in Calcutta we saw a completely rose sky—rose all the way up—something we had never seen before.

"I hope much of all this will go into music, but doing a parallel to the East has its problems. From my perspective, I think I have to be careful not to be influenced too strongly by the music we heard, because there is a great sameness about it, beginning in the Arabic countries and going through India all the way to Ceylon. There are many different kinds of drums, of course, and many strange instruments, and in India and Ceylon they have about ten scales, but the moment you become academic about it you are going to fall into the trap of copying many other people who have tried to give a reflection of the music. I don't think that is the smart thing to do. I would rather give a reflection of the adventure itself, though that sameness of sound may well creep into it. I cannot forget the priest who comes out on the minaret and gives the call to prayer, nor the sound of the drums which accompany the Kandy dancers in Ceylon, nor all the unusual and sophisticated instruments they have in India. At Delhi University, for instance, where they put on an entire ballet for us, there was not one instrument used by the twenty-piece orchestra that was really familiar to us in the Occident.

17

"So far as the rhythms are concerned, I don't think there is anything new there. Other musicians who had been before us had picked up on all of them. That's another reason why I didn't want to get academic about it and copy down this rhythm or that scale. It's more valuable to have absorbed it while there. You let it roll around, undergo a chemical change, and then seep out on paper in a form that will suit the musicians who are going to play it. The most work I have done so far is to *think*, and this is the most important part. Once you make up your mind, you just put it on paper. It really takes quite a bit of doing to decide what to do and what not to do; particularly when you have this big, wonderful, and beautiful world over there as a subject. You don't want to underestimate or understate it, but I have big fat plans for it!

"In one respect, I felt very neglected. Everywhere I went I asked, 'Where's the belly dancer?' I always got the same answer: 'Well, there are a couple around, but you ought to wait until you get to Beirut.' When I got to Beirut they said, 'Oh, no, man, wait until you get to Cairo!' So I've never seen the belly dancers. We were disappointed, too, not to get to Cairo, because we were looking forward to playing *Night Creature* there with the symphony.

"Though I never got to see the belly dancers, there was a piece I wrote before we ever went over there that will probably end up being called *The Dancing Girls.* I had it on tape and every time I played it in the Arabic countries ears would perk up and eyes pop open. 'What is that?' they wanted to know. They recognized it, there and in India, as their kind of music, and I told them, 'This is something I wrote in *anticipation* of the East.' I'm going to leave it that way, despite the fact that I wrote it beforehand, because as it happened it couldn't be more fitting. The rest I'll have to dream on, after thinking more on the general atmosphere of those countries.

"There was always something new and different. After more than four weeks in India, where the heat was just like a blanket, we entered the island of Ceylon during the monsoon. We came down in a huge puddle of water, so that the plane looked more like a speedboat. On arrival, as everywhere, there were little girls to put garlands around our necks. The Kandy dancers and drummers were at the airport to welcome us and there was tremendous enthusiasm.

"Our music was wonderfully well accepted. Tickets for concerts were usually sold out two or three hours after they were put on sale. For one reason or another, I found we were already quite well known. The records had been going there steadily and after thirty-five years they had to reach somebody! Some people had the old records and some had the new ones. The Maharajah of Cooch Behar had *all* of them. He flew down to Calcutta from Kashmir and brought a large proportion of his family with him.

"There was a man in Afghanistan who impressed me very much. He was the general who defended the gates of Kabul and became a national hero. He was very gracious with us and came to our concert in what I think was the ball park. He sat right in the center of the front row, and when I did that finger-snapping, head-tilting routine on *Jones*, he snapped his fingers right along. He didn't do it on the beat either, but on the afterbeat, swinging. He received me afterwards, and all the cats in the band went over and shook hands with him.

"We did practically no playing like we do normally. We'd spend a great part of the week working for the State Department and going to receptions. This was a new experience for me, and the guys in the band were wonderful representatives. They handled all of this activity gracefully, so that I was very proud of their offstage performances. The State Department paid us our fee and expenses and then arranged for local charitable organizations to take over the presentation of our concerts. These organizations benefited by the entire proceeds and this created a lot of good will.

"We became very proud of the State Department for the way they received us and the way they presented us. The ambassadors

Ellington and Harry Carney in India, 1963

Paul Gonsalves
and Ellington
in Jordan, 1963

and consuls from England, France, Holland, Germany, Japan, Russia, Yugoslavia, and many other countries would be at the receptions, and I think the tour was a success from that point of view, too. I was in the hospital for a while in Delhi and it was the Japanese ambassador who sent steaks. They are quite a rarity there, where the meat mostly eaten is lamb. After I came out of the hospital, I was a house guest of Mr. and Mrs. Chester Bowles at the embassy. In Dacca, I was a house guest of Mr. and Mrs. Jackson at the consulate, and, in the Lahore consulate, of Mr. and Mrs. Baines. They were wonderful people.

"One of the things we did everywhere, in addition to the concerts, was the lecture-demonstration. I would come out cold on the stage and talk for twenty minutes before introducing the members of the band. My subject was the American idiom that is promoted under the banner of jazz, and I would explain to the people that jazz, to me, meant having fun through freedom of expression. Before I got to the members of our band, their instruments, and what they were famous for, I spoke about some of the great musicians who preceded us, like Sidney Bechet and Louis Armstrong.

"At the press conferences, we would talk about jazz and, very often, the race situation in America. Some of them wanted information, but others wanted to discuss it from a more provocative view-

20

Ellington and admirers, India, 1963

point, and then I would have to explain that the situation of the Negro in America was more complex than we had time to clarify, but I always told them that the Negro has a tremendous investment in *our* country. We have helped to build it and we have invested blood in every war the country has fought, and this accounts for what has been happening. 'What is being done now?' they would ask, and I would reply that I was sure our leaders had strategy, but that if I knew it I wouldn't be very bright to reveal it, to cast it around for publication, because it would help our opponents to build up an even more formidable resistance than that they have now. One man asked me, 'Why hasn't the Negro artist done more for the cause?' That upset me and I said, 'If you knew what you were talking about, you wouldn't ask a question like that.' I came back to him later, after I had cooled off a bit, and explained that we had been working on the Negro situation and his condition in the South since the '30s, that we had done shows, musical works, benefits, etc., and that the American Negro artist had been among the first to make major contributions.

"I would add that apart from the time needed to discuss the Negro in America, one had to understand the values concerned, for the values here are not the same as there. Further, they would have to understand the background, to know whether it was a question of the haves and the have-nots or of the haves and the want-mores. In

21

other words, it was a matter that required a lot of pulling apart and putting together again, with everybody understanding everything that was being said, whereas a kind of halfway bouncing around is not healthy and does not help our cause. Whatever complaints we want to make about the Negro situation in America, it must be remembered that this is not an international issue but a national one, and it should be understood as such by people here in the U.S.A.— in self-defense."

[*1963*]

Press Conference, Calcutta, 1963

Q. Is a thorough musical education a help or a hindrance in jazz?

ELLINGTON. There have been people who have come into jazz with no schooling and have become very famous, and there have been others with conservatory degrees who have also become famous and done brilliant things. I think it's a good thing, no matter what kind of music you're in, to get all the training possible. It's necessary for some people to go to school to study. Others have something to say musically but don't have time to go to school to find out whether they need to study. Perhaps they're already involved, doing it, and doing it very well. In their case, the limitations vary according to the personality. The whole thing is highly personal, anyway. Years ago, back in 1914, the people who were then identified with jazz had had practically no training, but they did some very wonderful and very interesting things. I believe in the personalities very strongly, in the great personalities of jazz. But today, when you have people coming into it with tremendous academic backgrounds, I can't help feeling that the music has outgrown the word "jazz." It's necessary for some people to study, but others don't have to go to school to learn how to think. Beyond writing which is more or less elementary and that which is a little further advanced in harmonic devices and so forth, it's a matter of studying what someone else has done. If you have an inclination towards a new approach and you go to school, then in my opinion there's a risk of the original thought being modified by scholastic training, because then you're apt to apply the devices of someone in the past in order to express what you have to do. It's a matter, too, of suggestion. Sometimes people say, "You've got ability and you ought to go study." I don't know whether that's right or wrong. It depends upon who it is.

22

Q. Like Debussy, who learned all the rules before he started breaking them?

E. That's one way! And that's an instance of it turning out extremely well. Other people have attempted something like that and come out with a bad reflection because of . . . I don't want to say "taste" . . . because they've injected a certain amount of distortion which has made the result unattractive as compared with what it derived from.

Q. How have the audiences been in India as compared with those in other countries?

E. I don't think audiences vary geographically. I think audiences are the same everywhere. The audiences that come to see us want to hear us, so they don't expect anything but us, and they don't get anything but us. In Delhi, we went to the university campus and we had a lot of demonstrations of Indian instruments. We examined them quite thoroughly. We heard them played, and we sat around, and we tried them, but I'm afraid nothing happened. They're all very interesting and the great thing about them is the combinations, how they blend their tones together. The drums are wonderful in that respect, too—very unusual and very precise.

Q. Do you think Western drummers could adapt to that way of playing?

E. I suppose so. It would take quite a bit of drilling. There are a lot of quarter-tones in it, and used in quite a different way. We deal in quarter-tones, in what is known as "bending the notes," "cocked-valve" devices, and slurs, but here you have it actually in the scale. In Delhi, we saw the dancers, too, and they put on a whole ballet for us, employing a large orchestra, which was wonderful, entirely different, very effective, and a great inspiration. Though I wouldn't want to take a part of it and use it, the overall observation was wonderful. That is, to have absorbed the entire theme. Later on, something musical will come out of it, in its own form. After that experience, Billy Strayhorn said I had anticipated India in some music I did for a show in New York. It was something in the scale that resembled the Indian scales. I believe you can anticipate in that way. You may read a lot about or see pictures of a place you've never been, and you get a big, beautiful picture in your own mind. This picture is not necessarily authentic, but it's interesting. In this case, I wouldn't like to be too authentic! I'd rather just reflect it in my own refractory personality.

Q. Do you favor jazz in the concert hall?

E. The concert hall is an auditorium where people go to listen to what they want to hear. Generally, a concert is understood to be a performance or recital of one character or by one unit. People who go to the concert hall go there to do nothing but listen. It gives them a listening isolation, whereas if you go to hear a band like ours in a dancehall, you end up doing a lot of things other people with social aspirations want to do. They want to dance and embrace the girls. In a nightclub, they're probably busy drinking and smoking. But in a concert hall they do nothing but listen, which is the purpose and the virtue of it. In America, they have everything in concert halls—you name it, any kind of music you can think of.

Q. Do you think the concert hall has a cold atmosphere for jazz?

E. I don't think atmosphere has much to do with it. The performer and the listener are what is important. The architecture means nothing. It's like a city. You come to the city and it's made of concrete and steel. If you don't meet any people, you don't meet anything. You might as well be in New York as in Paris as in ... there's no personality. The people are what matter. They could turn out in a field. The music plays and you communicate. This is the only thing that is of any importance at all.

Q. Would it be more possible for Western musicians like Larry Adler, or a more rhythmic music like jazz, to blend with Indian music than with classical musicians and forms?

E. Larry Adler has a very flexible instrument. It's very close to the voice. In England, they had Menuhin play with Johnny Dankworth. I haven't yet heard what they did, but that was a long way for Menuhin, a concert man, to go. Dankworth is a highly skilled musician and very flexible, and he has dealt with a lot of different kinds of music. We've done things with the symphony and our major effort has been to make the symphony swing, which everybody says cannot be done, but I think we managed to do it very well. In fact, we have a record coming out soon by our band with ninety-two men of the Paris Opera orchestra, with eighty men of the La Scala orchestra, Milan, with the Stockholm Symphony, and with the Hamburg Symphony. And they're all on one record!

Q. Were these jam sessions or written works?

E. Oh, they were written. Some are pretty decent forms and others are (*snapping his fingers*) ... you know!

Q. What are your impressions of Indian music?

E. As I said, it's wonderful and very interesting. Of course, I don't know what's going on! Now I don't think music ever needs a name, a label, or a category, and I don't think a listener needs to know *what* he's listening to to enjoy it. I don't have to know anything about Indian music to enjoy it. I know a lot of people disagree with me on this point, but I don't have to know all the technicalities to enjoy a piece of music.

24 Q. What about notation?

E. If you have just three men, you can talk about what you want, but when you get three or four horns, or a ten-piece band, you have to go into arranging, because everyone cannot just get up and begin blowing without anything prearranged. Notation and arranging are quite different, however, because it isn't necessary to notate in order to arrange. Music can be orchestrated without being written. Notes can be given orally to the musicians. You say to one: "You play 'da-dada-da'." To the next one, "Do-dodo-da." To another, "De-deda-da." Then altogether, "Ahrrrhmmmmm!" That's arranging. We used to do it that way, and the reason was because it was easier to memorize in the days when it was not considered good showmanship to be playing on the stage with music. Thirty years ago, you never brought a music-stand on stage. We'd do it that way and the guy would remember it. Now, you give him a piece of paper and he can look at it for six months without memorizing it.

Q. How have you managed to keep a big band so long when so many others have broken up?

E. It's a matter of whether you want to play music or make money, I guess. I like to keep a band so that I can write and hear the music next day. The only way to do that is to pay the band and keep it on tap fifty-two weeks a year. If you want to make a real profit, you go out for four months, lay off for four, and come back for another

Press conference

four. Of course, you can't hold a band together that way, and I like the cats we've got. So by various little twists and turns, we manage to stay in business and make a musical profit. And a musical profit can put you 'way ahead of a financial loss.

Q. Does the popularity of, say, rock 'n' roll affect the mainstream of jazz?

E. Well, rock 'n' roll has taken from jazz, from blues, from folk, and almost everything. Rock 'n' roll has no musical mark of identification. It's a brand name that has had a bigger promotion than anything else in the world, and anything they play under that label comes out rock 'n' roll. You can play anything and call it rock 'n' roll—a waltz, anything. It used to have two or three little devices that marked it, but nothing of much significance. But nobody really loses an audience. There's still a Dixieland audience, a Swing audience, a Bop audience, and the old businessman's-bounce audience. All the audiences are still there, but the one you hear of most is the one whose music has the biggest promotion.

Q. Does it worry you that they may take some of your material and make something different of it under the rock 'n' roll label?

E. They did that with *Night Train*. They took *Happy-Go-Lucky Local*. It hurts and it's offensive. You threaten to sue, and you postpone until it's too late, and then you get real mad. You do nothing but spoil your disposition.

Q. The folk singers seem to have taken up the civil rights problem in their songs. Have you referred to it in your music?

E. In quite a lot of things. I just did an entire show in Chicago called "My People." It ran for three weeks. Its most significant social statement lay in the final song, *What Color Is Virtue, What Color Is Love?* There was another number called *King Fit the Battle of Alabam*, and quite a bit of satire. We didn't really say anything ugly about anybody, but we did insinuate here and there.

Q. I remember reading in a *New Yorker* profile that you were quite a gourmet. . . .

E. I'm afraid I came here at the wrong time. I've been eating nothing but steak and grapefruit for seven years, so I've had to scuffle. I can't eat highly seasoned food, but I've managed very well, considering. Friends have been sending me steaks, and the steak I had at the hotel today was wonderful, the best I've had since leaving New York.

[*1963*]

Dressing room rehearsal: Ellington and Billy Strayhorn

THE AIDES-DE-CAMP

Sometimes it seems that Ellington does not delegate authority as often as he should, but when he does it is with a complete and inspiring trust.

His collaboration with Billy Strayhorn from 1939 to 1967 was infinitely rewarding, and there has been nothing comparable to it in jazz. It was a perfect artistic relationship. "Whatever his comment was," Ellington said, "I was adjusted. It was like going out with your armor on instead of going out naked." Strayhorn's sympathy, understanding, and intellectuality were a source of strength to Ellington during a crucial period in his career. Some have seen his assistance as a crutch the older man did not really need. Certainly, Ellington's creativity and productivity seemed to accelerate after Strayhorn's untimely death, but how much it must have meant to have the burden shared for nearly twenty years by a capable and trustworthy colleague! Because it is indeed lonely at the top, their entente had a special meaning.

The interview with Strayhorn took place one morning a few months before he died. He was then recuperating from the first, serious operation, but he was apologetic about getting anyone up so early in the day. He felt at his most alert then, the medicines he was obliged to take making him drowsy in the afternoons. Selecting refreshment (Japanese beer) appropriate to the hour, he cheerfully proceeded to give his mind to the subjects of inspiration and interpretation.

Duke Ellington's son, Mercer, came fully into the picture after the band had endured unhappy experiences with road managers. That the latter had some cause for complaint with the temperamental and improvident musicians in their charge need scarcely be said. Besides the family name, Mercer brought charm, firmness, and intelligence to an unenviable task. Although he had previously established his independence as a bandleader, composer, arranger, and trumpet player, his chief satisfaction was now to come from playing in his father's trumpet section.

Thomas L. Whaley's seniority (he was born in 1892) permits him to express his opinions forthrightly in the Ellington camp. The leader obviously enjoys those occasions when Whaley challenges the prima donnas in the band. "Give 'em hell, Tom!" he will call encouragingly from the piano. Tom does that, and makes enemies temporarily, but his courage and honesty invariably compel admiration. He was well over seventy when he was mugged, robbed, and deposited unconscious in a New York parking lot, but he was soon back on the job, bruises and all. His appointment by Ellington as choirmaster for the sacred concerts was a source of much satisfaction to him, and an indication of trust and esteem.

Billy Strayhorn

DANCE. Should we begin by talking about what inspires musical composition?

STRAYHORN. The kind of things that provide inspiration are always those that nobody—by which I mean the public—ever considers. The public always considers that people who are inspired go off in a fine frenzy, tear their hair and all that business, and then come up with the *Fifth Symphony*. Actually, inspiration comes from the simplest kind of thing, like watching a bird fly. That's only the beginning. Then the work begins. Oh, goodness! Then you have to sit down and work, and it's *hard*. You get the inspiration, and it's only in your mind—a thought— but realizing the inspiration is work. You can't *tell* a musician a thought. You've got to elucidate, to put it on paper, *and* to communicate at the same time, which is *the* difficulty. If you could do it the way you did it in your mind, if you could just sit and think, and think it to him . . . everything would be peaches and cream. But you've got to put it on paper and preserve the freshness and spontaneity that you had in your mind. Translation, that's what it is. You have to translate it onto paper in such a way that he can reproduce what you thought.

D. He translates it back into sound?

S. Yes, but it doesn't happen too often. The skill in arranging is how well you can put this down and have it come back. It's much the same for musicians, painters, and writers. Their work is cut out for them—how to communicate. They have to communicate to a person what they want him to hear, see, read. It's the hardest thing in the world.

D. I imagine it's harder to write for an anonymous musician than for one you know, as in the case of the Ellington band.

S. Well, it's hard even for some that you know, because it's you who are saying something—or you *should* be saying something!— and he has to interpret it. So you have to get this over to him before you can get to the public. No, I don't really think it's easier with

29

someone you know than with someone you don't, although it may affect your original direction. You have someone like Clark Terry, whom you know. You know his sound and you know how he plays, so you write something you think fits him, but that's not *you*. You really need to write something that fits his sound and is *your* sound, too—a combination of what you do *and* what he does. That's what he also wants, because he can sit and play all night what *he* plays. He is an artist, and like all artists he wants to do new things.

D. In the case of the ballad-type material you write for Johnny Hodges, aren't you affected by the knowledge of how he plays?

S. "He would make this sound pretty," is what you say to yourself. When you get into it, when you write it, there may be some awkward technical aspect that he will point out to you, as concerning his performance. You don't want *that*. It's like a suit of clothes. You want it to fit. You don't want it to be baggy anywhere. I'm not a saxophone player. If he says, "This is awkward here. This is an awkward position of notes," then you say, "Is it truly? Is it impossible?" If he keeps trying it, and it is impossible, you say, "Well, all right, I'll change it."

D. Are we overlooking a division as between the composer and the arranger who envisages the treatment of the number? Or do you simultaneously conceive composition and arrangement?

S. I suppose . . . I don't really know. I don't really think of it. You get your ideas together and then you kind of define the form. You have to nail the ideas down first. Then you get the formula—how long, what key, the technical details.

D. I think what I've had in mind so far have been original compositions. Where does the inspiration come from for approaching pop tunes, *Mary Poppins*, or *Rhapsody in Blue?*

S. From your own sense of what to do. It's more a matter of morality than technique. You should say, "I wouldn't treat *this* any less carefully than I would *that*." You should treat them equally. I put the same effort into whatever I do. I try to do the best I can.

D. Well, numbers vary in quality.

S. They *differ*—not so much in quality as in variety. You have a simple tune here, a more complicated one there, or a folk tune. That's variation and it has nothing to do with quality. Or that's how I like to think about it. If I'm working on a tune, I don't want to *think* it's bad. It's just a tune, and I have to work with it. It's not a matter of whether it's good or bad.

D. I am always a bit amazed by the musicians who go around relishing challenges. It has always seemed to me that you get enough challenges in life without seeking them out.

S. (*Laughs.*) Well, an arranger is faced with arranging, and he's supposed to come through, to arrange *anything* according to what his style or talent is.

D. As compared with pop tunes and band themes, when you do something like *The Far East Suite* . . .

S. That's composition.

D. Yes, but it doesn't seem to me that there is quite the same element of challenge there, because there is the stimulus to the imagination of what was wholly new to you on the State Department tour.

S. There's challenge, too, because you're still translating. You still have to say something whether you're doing pop tunes, *Mary Poppins,* or anything else. You have to say *what* you feel about *this* tune to the people, so that when they hear it they say, "I know that's Duke Ellington. I know that sound—it's distinct and different from anybody else's."

D. Several critics thought it regrettable that the Ellington band was employed on pop tunes and band themes. They felt it should play more—or only—original material. How do you feel about that?

S. I feel it's not right for an artist to turn his back on a simple melody just because it's not a great suite or something or other. After all, Horowitz plays *Träumerei* beautifully, and why shouldn't he? Why shouldn't you play a simple melody? It's a matter of being humble. All artists are humble. All *great* artists are humble. The ones who're not are not great artists. When a little kid comes up and says, "Play *O, Say, Can You See?*," you play it. That does not mean that you have to play it the way thousands of other people have played it. You can give it your own individuality. But don't look *down* on those things, because if you look down, that's the end of you, your integrity, and everything. It's snobbery.

D. I think there's a certain amount of split-thinking involved in that attitude, too. The same people who have the highest regard for you and Duke as *arrangers* are critical when you apply your gifts as arrangers to material other than your own.

S. It's because they don't hear.

D. I think it's also a preconceived attitude, a kind of snobbery, as you said.

S. But they don't actually listen.

D. If that Beatles tune dressed in jungle colors had been issued as an original . . .

S. And it's a beautiful tune. The Beatles have done several excellent things, and we were very happy to do them. Excellent is excellent wherever you find it. It doesn't matter who did it or what the circumstances are. I don't mean that as a total endorsement, because I haven't liked *everything* they've done.

31   D. What about the *Peer Gynt Suite* and *The Nutcracker Suite?*

Billy Strayhorn

S. Well, those ... that was a difficult period. It took us quite a bit of time to consider how we were going to do them. The actual writing was nothing. You could do that overnight. It was the preparation that was tremendous. In both cases, we had to consider the composers. They're not *dead*. They're alive, and that's *their* music, and we didn't want to offend them. Arriving at the treatment we gave them was *agonizing*. The Tchaikovsky took six months. We went through it and played those pieces over and over again. We listened to them and talked about them. I flew to California and *back*. But after we decided what to use and what not to use, and how to treat it—then you could sit down and do it in a day.

D. And *Such Sweet Thunder?*

S. It was the same thing. We read all of Shakespeare!

D. But you had no musical material to work on.

S. No, but it was the same really, because we had to interpret what he said, just as we had to interpret what Tchaikovsky was saying. The only difference with Shakespeare was that we had to interpret his *words*. It took about the same amount of time, too—about six months. We had all those books we used to carry around, and all those people all over the U.S. we used to see and talk to.

D. I was only sorry that *Richard III* was left out—a good subject
32 for the blues.

S. Well, we just couldn't get everything in! We didn't do *King Lear, Coriolanus* or *All's Well That Ends Well* either. *Timon* was different, because there Duke didn't have the full burden of explaining it musically. He was only accompanying the action. In *Such Sweet Thunder* we were doing the whole job, but in *Timon* you heard the actors and saw the action.

D. Have you any new work in progress?

S. Yes, two or three pieces, but they're not really in even the discussing stage. They're nameless, and they're mostly in my head.

D. Do the titles come first or afterwards?

S. They come at various times and they usually come out of the situation or from what you're working with.

D. I asked you once about *Clementine* and *After All* when I was writing a liner note, and your attitude towards titles seemed pretty casual.

S. Actually, I think titles are very significant. They're kind of psychological. *After All* fits the first three notes, and you often get something that fits almost subconsciously. But then you have another case like *Lush Life*, which never had a title, even when the lyrics were written. How I happened to call it *Lush Life* was because that was the line everybody remembered.

D. Did you write music or lyrics first?

S. When I write lyrics, I write music and lyrics together. Because, you know, you have to bend them. Or I do. And not at the piano, but when I'm walking along the street. That's the time to polish off a phrase, when you're walking and it sings well, naturally. First of all, of course, you have to have an idea, and then you go from there, and build.

D. Where did *Take the "A" Train* get its title?

S. That's another thing. I'll tell you what I was trying to do—the original idea of *"A" Train*. I was always a great fan of Fletcher Henderson's. He wrote so many wonderful arrangement. One day, I was thinking about his style, the way he wrote for trumpets, trombones, and saxophones, and I thought I would try something like that. Now this was a case of a combination of circumstances. At the end of 1940, there was the fight between ASCAP and radio, and at the beginning of 1941 all ASCAP music was off the air. When we opened at the Casa Mañana, the third of January, 1941, we had air time every night, but could not play our library. We had to play non-ASCAP material. Duke was in ASCAP, but I wasn't. So we had to write a new library, and *"A" Train* was one of the numbers. The reason we gave it that title was because they were building the Sixth Avenue subway at that time, and they added new trains, including the "D" Train, which came up to Harlem, to 145th Street, and then turned off and went to the Bronx, but the "A" Train kept straight on up to 200-and-Something Street. People got confused. They'd take the "D" Train, and it would go to Harlem and 145th Street, but the next stop would be on Eighth Avenue under the Polo Grounds, and the one after that would be in the Bronx. So I said I was writing directions—take the "A" Train to Sugar Hill. The "D" Train was really messing up everybody. I heard so many times about housewives who ended up in the Bronx and had to turn around and come back.

D. *Raincheck* was the same year, wasn't it?

S. That was about rain, about being in California in January, February, March. . . . It was raining, and I was sitting at home in Los Angeles, and writing. . . .

D. How far back did your interest in Fletcher Henderson go? Had you always been interested in jazz?

S. No, I started out studying the Three B's—Bach, Beethoven, and Brahms. Then one day I heard Ellington! The first time I heard Fletcher Henderson's arrangements was with Benny Goodman, but I had heard of him before that. I knew of him, but I didn't hear his band when he had people like Coleman Hawkins in it. I missed his heyday. My most vivid memory of hearing Duke was when he came to Pittsburgh right after he had done *Murder at the Vanities* in 1934. He played a theatre, and he did *Ebony Rhapsody*, and that kind of shook me.

D. Andy Gibson told me the same thing.

S. Yes, I was "shook up." I got over my fears and went backstage to see him. I·didn't have anything to say and I just stood there with my mouth open. Then he came back and played a dance. By this time I was hooked, so I went, and I stood there all evening, right in front, right by the piano. He played. He played everything, including *Ebony Rhapsody*, and I was *lost*. When he came again, five years later, I went to see him about working, and then, of course, I came here, to New York.

D. Had you intended becoming a professional musician?

S. While I was in Pittsburgh, I had worked around, playing gigs, but I didn't consider myself good enough, so I hadn't decided what to do. As a teenager, I had another job and I never considered making music my living—it was an avocation, not a vocation. The money I got for gigs I regarded as just play money, and thought no more about it.

D. Had you any experience of arranging?

S. Only a little. I had done a couple of things, but I had never thought about being an arranger, I hardly knew what an arranger was, but I had a friend in Pittsburgh called Bill Esch, and he *was* an arranger. In fact, he and I came to New York together. He worked for Ina Ray Hutton and he was a great help to me. We discussed music and everything together. Even so, I wasn't particularly desirous of becoming an arranger. I came to New York because Duke liked my lyrics, but after I joined the band I was completely turned around, and I went to arranging and playing the piano.

D. How did you develop your skills?

S. More or less, you might say, by necessity. Of course, Duke is a great teacher, but not in the sense that he sits down and says, "Now you do so-and-so." He'll hand you something and say, "Do this!" And you have such faith in him that you sit down and do it! You find that you can.

[*1966*]

Mercer Ellington

DANCE. You told me once about the instruction you received from your father in 1941, when the band was playing at the Casa Mañana on the West Coast.

ELLINGTON. He would leave me problems to solve by the time he got back, and I would work at the piano while he was out. He never put a note down, but he scratched out what was in poor taste. *Moon Mist* was a number he almost wrote by omission. I had intended it for Ben Webster's tenor saxophone, but when Ben was absent on the record date it became a vehicle for Ray Nance's violin.

Before that, back in '31 and '32, I can remember nights when Ellington would come home, say around 3:30, and I'd been asleep already. I'd hear these strains being played on the piano—almost in my sleep, a kind of sublimation. Those, I think, were really my first lessons in composition—the sounds I used to emulate, and the getting used to what happened with him.

I'd done pieces of my own to ukulele chords, because that was convenient, and I'd hum things as I learned certain changes. Everything else I had learned about music had been directed more towards theory, so we didn't need any great explanations about the composition of a chord—the one, three, five, or the letters in the staff. That knowledge was assumed, and even if I hadn't had it, it wouldn't have made any difference to the way I learned from him, because at the first lesson, he said, "When you write, write something that *sounds* good." That's simple enough, but it was like telling somebody who wanted to paint to go out and paint something good.

35   He started me on harmonies. He'd pre-set a harmony and tell me

to write a melody against it, making certain that I never used any note in the harmony as part of the melody. *Moon Mist*, again, was a composition that evolved from such instructions. Then he'd leave me a project on which I was to write two songs to the same harmonies, each completely different from the other. "Make one fast and one slow," he'd say.

In a way, he worked like a psychiatrist who makes you cure yourself. He made me teach myself. "Anytime you want to, look at the scores," he told me. That is good advice for anyone. If you hear anything that interests you, check the scores out.

D. And listen to the record at the same time?

E. Yes. Another recommendation I like to make is to the works of Rimsky-Korsakov and his book on theory and arranging.

D. That's very interesting. Rimsky-Korsakov believed that certain tone colors were inseparable from a work in its creator's mind, from the very hour of its birth. Orchestration, he said somewhere, is "part of the very soul of the work." Also, like your father, he was always able to hear his works promptly performed—in his case, by the St. Petersburg Opera orchestra.

E. I think a relationship between what you might call classicists and contemporary writers might also be shown between Rimsky-Korsakov and Fletcher Henderson, in the way Fletcher separated trumpets, trombone, and saxophones. It's too bad Fletcher didn't have the facilities we have today—stereo separation and different tracks—because his music was always so complete in each area. Another reason why I cite Rimsky-Korsakov is because his music was so well documented in both sight and sound. You get an exact parallel when you seek out one in terms of the other.

D. As I remember reading, he got a lot of his skill in orchestration and knowledge of wind instruments as an inspector of naval bands.

E. Also, while actually teaching theory at St. Petersburg Conservatory. Practical experience—there's nothing like it. A man like Andy Gibson was out there at the same time as Fletcher, arranging for Charlie Barnet. Andy never wrote a score. When he did an arrangement, he wrote it down melodically. He'd write the first trumpet part, and then the second, so that it sounded good with the first, and then the third and fourth. After that, he wrote different things relative to the trumpets for the other sections. If you give it the test of your ear under repetition, it becomes good composition.

D. Andy Gibson was originally a trumpet player himself.

E. Billy Strayhorn told me, "The real test of an arrangement, after you've written it, is can you sing it?" A limited ear will write a
36   limited type of song, of course. The rock-'n'-rollers fall into that area,

and I'm not knocking any of their compositions, but you have fairly "lay" people performing now, and they have become popular mainly because the songs that they write—because they are lacking in musical information—are close to the man on the street, and he naturally relates to them. It takes conditioning to appreciate what McCoy Tyner or Dizzy Gillespie plays, to have *their* sounds fall naturally on the ear. When you get into atonal music, it takes almost a divorce from hearing. And what I object to about atonalism is that some of the composers can't remember how they *sang* it, and they have to go back and look to see what they put down. The great ones are able to improvise atonally spontaneously, but they are very few, like Bartók and Charlie Parker.

D. What contemporary developments are affecting composition?

E. One of the most important things in composition is the relationship of the song to itself. Various people have come up with descriptions of a motif, but a motif isn't a motif unless it is repeated. Many of today's songs don't repeat themselves anywhere, so you don't have motif and repetition, or anything that comes back to you ingratiatingly. The purpose of a song is entertainment, although in certain situations it may be frustrative. Suppose, for instance, it were to be used as background to a film like *The Snake Pit* for descriptive purposes. But to force an evening of frustration music on a group of people that came out for entertainment—well, that's why you have half-filled houses for well-known singers and musicians. They no longer represent entertainment.

D. They don't know how to be original *and* entertaining. But Duke Ellington has broken a few rules himself. . . .

E. I think he started breaking rules as a painter, because it was a natural tendency for him to seek individuality. Such taboos as that you can't use parallel octaves, you can't use parallel fifths, you can't let a seventh rise—he went to work on those right away, and proved they could sound good. In the last paragraph of the book I used at Juilliard, it said something to the effect that while we had been given a guide to what sounded good, we were to disregard the guide if by violating it we could find something else that sounded good. Their intention, they claimed, was not to make us follow the rules, but to produce good music.

D. Do you think jazz has been unnecessarily confined to the blues and the thirty-two bar song?

E. I don't think Ellington ever really broke away from them. In fact, I think you'll find the effect of the blues in almost everything he writes. The blues themselves were so unorthodox in terms of any

37

explained music that he took to them naturally. One of the people I feel he is more parallel to than anyone else—and not necessarily superseded by—is Schoenberg. It's just a coincidence. Schoenberg has a tendency towards more sensuousness in his music, but I'm quite sure that if he'd come along in the time of Palestrina, and somebody had said, "Don't use this because it's a passing tone," he'd immediately have gone about using it.

D. There was also the coincidence of Delius, of Ellington being likened to Delius before he had ever heard him. Do you think the influences he acknowledges, of older musicians like Will Marion Cook and Will Vodery, had anything to do with it?

E. I know that when he did hear Delius he took to him right away. But I also remember the school that came out of Washington. There was a guy down there about the same time by the name of Gump. Although he never amounted to anything in music professionally, he was affected by James P. Johnson and other greats, and it was amazing how much he and Ellington sounded alike. Music was his pastime, and he remained a chef on the Pennsylvania Railroad. He played piano, had no knowledge of theory, and couldn't read a note. Yet the two of them sounded alike, just as Johnny Hodges and Charlie Holmes did when they came out of Boston.

D. How do you account for your father's originality, or his steadily developed creativity?

E. A great deal of it had to do with the fact that he was always learning as he went along, and a great deal of the learning had to do with the individuals with whom he worked. He liked the *sound* of Toby Hardwick and Artie Whetsol. Then there was Tricky Sam Nanton, and later, Lawrence Brown. When he had these strong, individual voices, what he wrote was much more lyrical. He used to love those little, pretty things, and then have Tricky come and slop 'em up!

D. Bubber Miley was very important in this respect. . . .

E. Even long after he had left the band. You can hear the influence of Bubber in *The Gal from Joe's,* and the use of what became known as the "pep" section. The wa-wa or growl sound that he and Tricky Sam created for backgrounds by a group of horns became one of the band's identifying marks. In fact, of all the devices you might pick to define the sound of the Ellington band, the first should be that of the plunger mute.

A big step after that came with the arrival of Jimmy Blanton. He changed the sound of the rhythm section. With such a dominant personality, Ellington had to pay more attention to the bass line. From that time on, the importance of the bass developed until bassists came to regard themselves as no longer playing a rhythm instrument. They relied on the cymbal to free them, to indulge in what they probably thought of as "free composition." Sometimes, I guess, freedom can be taken too far. One result of this was that Ellington had to go back to some of his original thinking on the use of the left hand at the piano. One of the most beautiful aspects of this concern is in *Harlem*, where the band is used as a rhythm instrument to allow the bass to make a statement.

D. Ben Webster was also important.

E. Another effective device resulted from his coming into the band. In those days, a man jealously guarded his role and his part. If anyone doubled with him, or started to play along with him, he felt his position was being intruded upon. Every time Ben got up and played by ear, the whole gang jumped on him and said, "Hey, you've got my note!" So Ben decided he would get away from this and find a note nobody had. What was a four-part reed chorus in four-part harmony suddenly had five parts—in self-defense, along with great musicianship, by Ben. A semi-dissonant sound resulted from the five parts, because there was no written part for him. Ellington heard it, liked it, and learned how to apply it—another device for the orchestra.

I've mentioned what some of the notables contributed in terms of composition, but some contributed by, as it were, their very being. Harry Carney is so strong that he made Ellington compose in the midst of arranging. Everything he played cut through so much that everything written for him had to have an interesting quality. He couldn't just be the outside horn of the section, so sometimes he was taken to the inside to get a sound that was better than if he had been at the bottom. Here again Ellington violated another principle when he used the baritone above the sound of the tenors. Because of the kind of phrasing he wanted, he has also taken one of the tenors and given him the lead. Ben Webster plays lead on *Bakiff* with the altos below him. Paul Gonsalves plays lead on *Satin Doll*, but in the regular position. In Ben's case, it was like taking a contralto and having her sing above the sopranos. This came about when Ben said, in the middle of a record session, "Hey, Duke, why don't you get those cats to phrase it like this?" And then he played it, and he played it where the notes were. Ellington liked the sound, told him to stay there, and gave Johnny Hodges some different notes.

D. Wouldn't you say that many of the compositions came out of the need and the desire to write something different for the musical personalities of the men?

E. Also, to utilize the strongest contribution a man could make, whether it was his tone or his movement. For instance, Juan Tizol played a valve trombone, so for the first time he [Ellington] was able

39

to get something to move faster in the range that Tizol was in on the bottom part of the trombone. As long as you stay somewhere around, say, an F in the bass staff—the fourth-line F—you can write things the men can move fast on, because they stay in false positions and can make them at convenient distances, one note from another. When you get down below that, to the bottom of the bass staff, you can't make them move fast, because there's only one place they can play it, and that's the original position. You may have only to go for a half-tone movement from B flat to a B natural, but you've got to go from first position to seventh in order to get it. With a valve trombone, it's just a slight move, so he can go down there and make it very fast. Like on *Conga Brava,* where the trombones start very high but end up down the bottom of the staff moving very swiftly. So with Tizol, Ellington wasn't limited the way the average person was when writing for trombones. This was true of the bass horn, too, except that it wouldn't blend with the two trombones, and by this time it had gone out of the orchestra anyway.

D. I think the development of the trombone section as a separate entity was very important to the big bands of the '30s.

E. Ellington never left color when he switched from painting to music. The same tone represented a different color or shading when played by Tricky Sam, Lawrence Brown, or Tizol. The ability to get an ensemble sound that still jelled from three such diverse personalities was remarkable.

D. A lot of the compositions must nevertheless have been conceived at the piano with no special individual in mind.

E. *Satin Doll* was probably a matter of Ellington sitting at the piano, comping or fooling around, and hearing something. It wasn't written for any specific soloist. Sometimes, when he's accompanying a soloist, he plays a figure that has a complete identification of its own, and he'll either note it mentally or jot it down, and come back and make a song of it. No one person suggested it, but it suggested itself as a contribution to what was going on. Some of the questions most often asked him are, "Who is *Satin Doll?* Who is *Sophisticated Lady?*" I think at the time those numbers were written he didn't visualize any one woman. That is my opinion, although he may have different explanations. *Satin Doll* is for everybody who happens to be with a wonderful lady that night.

Of course, he can write with a purpose, too, and write very well. The show, *Jump for Joy,* was an example. He was in Salt Lake City and had one night to get into Los Angeles, and that night he wrote *Brownskin Gal, Jump for Joy,* and *I Got It Bad.* That's something I always like to mention.

Composing is often a matter of purpose. Suppose it's for a background to last fourteen minutes, to match the scenes in a film. Right away, you mark it off, scaled in relative distance, with indications of actions that need to be identified, or of something that is absolute. Then you go about figuring what sounds will suggest the moods of the picture, and finding a theme that can represent the picture as a whole. After that theme is written, it's developed in the fashion that fits the amount of time available, even if it ends up nineteen bars long, or nineteen and a half! The trick is to make it sound like something in *whatever* the distance is. Of course, when you have something like a dagger being thrown into a wall, you've got to have the brass hit, or a rimshot, or a crash of the cymbal, at the exact moment it strikes the wall. It has to be timed to that end as you watch the picture.

D. Well, those are different problems to those of the regular song.

E. Or those of a song for one particular singer. I remember writing one for Lena Horne called *Pass Me By.* I thought about her, and what she represented to me. It was a complete song, thirty-two bars, and it had to say what I thought about Lena.

D. I suppose most Ellington compositions could be divided up under three headings: songs, instrumentals for dancing and jamming, and mood pieces.

E. At the time of concept, a piece of music may be completely

Mercer Ellington with his son Edward, and his father, 1965

untitled. Suggestion plays a great part. A series of experiences can suggest a whole lot of titles. When we were in the West Indies recently, they mentioned *cascadura*, which has a euphonic sound. It's the fish of love that everybody's supposed to eat for the magic of its spell. It means you will return to Trinidad, and I guess it's something like the way a four-leaf clover is used on a wishing gimmick. When we were in South America, I thought it was unique to see a street named after the day of a month—the Ninth of July—in Buenos Aires. It spoke in terms of revolution and freedom, and where you go, what you see, speaks in terms of compositional creativity. That is reflected in *The Far East Suite* and *The Latin American Suite*.

D. Since Billy Strayhorn died, I think your father has written more prolifically than ever.

E. I think that's because he feels he has to do the total amount of work they both would have done before. Consequently, he takes on the same number of projects, and to get them done he has to sit up and work more.

D. Does that come from some feeling of responsibility?

E. No, not necessarily, because I don't think he has that. He doesn't have any obligations, or the feeling that he will stagnate if he doesn't do a certain amount of work in a certain period of time. It's a matter of development in a more individual manner.

D. Can you explain that?

E. The hotter you get, the more you can become a social recluse. He's still active mentally and physically, but he has few outlets. Some people play golf, swim, or play tennis, but his only interest is music, and he uses his energies to write.

D. The broadening experiences of the last few years have stimulated his mind?

E. Not only that, but he's fighting to get away from himself. When he first started off, he did things that were different from other composers. Now he wants to be certain he won't be accused of being old-fashioned or stereotyped. As a result, he not only wants to write something different from what others have done, but something different from what he himself has done. It calls for a lot of work, because after forty years in the business, you really have two things to fight. You have your customary way of doing, and to find something new you have to do a lot of *forgetting*.

D. Most people would be resting on their laurels.

E. An insatiability enters into the picture of creativity. You're always looking for some new realm where you'll be in a position to challenge yourself. It's like having a favorite suit. If you look at it and wear it every day, you find yourself wishing you had another to put on. We *have* to play the Ellington standards day in and day out, and as a result he has to seek something new. He can't get away from playing them, but his real satisfaction is in creating. I think all areas of musical activity are lacking if they don't have composition in them. You can't be much of an arranger if you don't do some composing.

D. Yet it seems to me that many of the best arrangers in jazz have done surprisingly little real composing.

E. Somewhere along the line they do compose, but whether they have the ability to develop a related variety is another matter.

D. I was thinking of a great talent like Benny Carter's. He has written many marvelous arrangements, but the public hardly knows him as a composer despite *Blues in My Heart, When Lights Are Low, Blue Interlude,* etc.

E. Yet you'll find that in any of the solos Benny plays on other people's songs there are segments that you could take out and develop into new songs. The same with Coleman Hawkins. You could take one of his choruses on *Body and Soul* and make a new song of that. And this most certainly applies to Louis Armstrong. After he got through stating the melody, he was composing from chorus to chorus. Spontaneous improvisation in jazz is a form of composition, and it is admired because it is done at such a fast pace and so ingeniously. The fact that musicians can think and create so fast while performing a considerable repertoire is very impressive.

D. That repertoire nevertheless doesn't contain so many compositions by jazz musicians as might be expected. The large proportion of it consists of pop songs or numbers out of musical shows, and writers as sympathetic as Gershwin and Arlen are rare. I think more Ellington works would become standards if they were repeated enough.

E. Maybe, but then I'm usually eight or nine years behind his thinking. In the extended works, I think his music tends more towards narrative than the descriptive nowadays. Of course, he always has his verbal explanation of what is taking place, as with *The Golden Broom and the Green Apple.* That's more or less a tonal painting of motion, in three sections with several motifs each. Even in a work like that, written for the symphony, he may use a common lick or riff, but when he gets through with it you won't recognize it, because it has a completely different form.

In the final analysis, I think of composition as man's attempt to lay his signature on a piece of work, whether it is composition as such, arranging, or playing a solo. It's a thought—a thought that represents his song, or his feeling about a song.

[*1969*]

Tom Whaley

DANCE. How did your career get under way in Boston?
WHALEY. When I first started playing piano in a band, the leader told me, "All I want you to do is *oompah,* and hold that tempo." His name was Lyman Jefferson and he was a violin player. There was a dancehall in Castle Square where we used to play Thursday afternoons. Then on the corner of Tremont and Camden, a fellow named Bish Hicks had a music shop with a piano in it. There'd always be music up in front, with the idea of sticking any piano player who came in. They had that in mind about me: "Tom Whaley can read so much, but we'll stick him." So one day they put up *Key to Key Rag.* "Oh, this is easy!" I said as I started playing the first page, but when I turned to the next, here were all these triplets coming up. "Oh, oh, I started too fast!" I said. They laughed and said, "We got you now!" After that, I always kept music in front of me, and I tell a lot of guys to do that today. Make sure you have the right notes in your head before you start taking liberties!
D. Who taught you originally?
W. I had a very good Russian piano teacher, and he did more for me than the nine months I spent at the New England Conservatory of Music. When I left there, I went to Suntaug Lake Inn, where I met all the great entertainers of the day, like Eddie Cantor. Caruso used to come down Sunday afternoons when he was in Boston at the opera. He'd direct the band, and we'd have to play nothing but operas and overtures with him. There'd be champagne, and at the end he'd give us a couple of hundred dollars. The rest of the time, we'd play dance music, and make as much as two or three hundred dollars a week in tips each. It was a fabulous place. There was a room to dance in, one to eat in, one to drink in, and another upstairs for gambling.
D. Musicians often talk of sums of money like that in those days. Taking everything into consideration, it seems a whole lot as compared with what they get today.
W. It was, and you didn't have to pay income tax or an agent. Agents and managers didn't mean anything then.
D. How did you spend the money?
W. On our night off, we'd hire a limousine and take a bunch of gals up on the North Shore. But that didn't last forever, because in 1917 I was inducted in the Army, and went to Europe, where I joined

Will Vodery's band. It was a big brass band, Pioneer Regiment 807. They had enough players of all the instruments except flute and piccolo, so I was told to take those. A French interpreter taught me how to play them, and that was useful knowledge.

Will Vodery was a remarkable man. He used to stand up in front of the band and call for some manuscript paper. With all the noise going on around, he'd write out all the parts then and there, and say, "Ten dollars for every wrong note!" That was Will Vodery! Later on, I was associated with him at the Cotton Club, when he was in charge of music there.

D. What did you do after you got back?

W. I went back to the Suntaug Inn, and then I got jobs with several different groups. I used to play at Freeburg's restaurant on Beach Street, and at the Avery Hotel. I had a fellow named Brownie who used to take his clarinet apart as he played. It was at the Avery that I met Johnny Hodges one day in 1920. He was about fifteen years old, and he came up the back steps and said, "Hey, can I play?" I said, "Sure, come on and play!" He had a C-melody sax, and he started playing, the same then as now—sweet, singing. He's a gifted man, another genius.

There was a nightclub on Washington Street near Dudley, and Walter Johnson had the orchestra there. That was where Duke first heard Johnny and told him to come on over to New York. Walter played piano, and his brother, Howard, played sax. All the Johnson family were great musicians. Bobby and George both played guitar. Walter had charge of all the music in Boston—all the big things. He had an office, and I used to be in it with him. We would contract bands for dances. After World War I, it wasn't so good. There was an avalanche of white musicians, and we had to struggle.

Things got really bad in 1922. I sent a team up to Lake George, and they came back with around $1800 for three months' work. I sent them up there, and I'm starving in Boston! So the next year, I went up there, but I had to borrow fifty dollars to get back home. I'd lost all my money gambling. Oh, those damn racing men! I'm not lucky, that's all. But it was a great experience.

I first met Louis Armstrong in Boston with Fletcher Henderson's band in 1922. I had a car then, and I'd get Louis and we'd go all around different places. He never forgot that, and afterwards he always referred to me as "My man, Tom." When I was in Chicago with a show called *Stoppin' the Traffic,* I met him again, and he said, "Come on by the Sunset Café." So I went there, and he said, "I want you to meet a new boy I got playin' piano." It was Earl Hines, and, believe me, he was playing his own style before he ever met Louis. He's a *natural* player. He gets ideas, hears something, and he's gone!

45

He's still great today. Down to Duke's White House party on April 29th, 1969, everybody was talking about Earl Hines. Billy Taylor was great, and Dave Brubeck was great, but that Earl Hines—that was *all!*

D. Well, when did you really leave Boston?

W. Wilbur Sweatman, the guy that played three clarinets at once, came to Boston, and he was looking for a piano player. I traveled all over New England with him, and ended up in New York. After I left Sweatman, I joined George Stevens and went up to the Washington Arms in New Rochelle, When the man fired George, we all quit, "What are you doing?" the man asked. "Well, you fired the boss," I said.

After that, it was tough luck for a long while. They didn't want Boston musicians in New York, and we couldn't even join the Clef Club.

D. It was restricted to local musicians, something like a union?

W. Yes, all New York musicians. But the Clef Club was a great thing. They had all the good jobs. I finally got in when the piano player with a tenor singer got sick. I'd had that sort of experience while I was in the Army. I used to play for Opal Cooper, who knew five hundred songs, words and music. We'd go all over the A.E.F. in France and play the officers' clubs. Margaret Wilson was over there then, and she said she never heard a black man sing *To a Wild Rose* the way Opal did.

Then I got a band together—Whaley's Serenaders. We used to play in Brooklyn and all over. I got in the nightclubs . . . with the gangsters. Big Green, the trombone player, was in that band, and Nelson Kincaid on alto sax. It was a good band, and we played the Lafayette Theatre, in the pit.

D. You had to have pretty good musicians for that. Did they all read?

W. Oh, yeah.

D. Big Green?

W. Sure. They all read. Big Green was a real trombone player.

D. Where did you first meet Duke?

W. In New York. I seemed always to be playing out at Suntaug Inn when he was in Boston meeting Rabbit [Hodges] and Carney. I had just come from Boston, and I was playing in this restaurant, and I thought I was pretty hot. Somebody said, "This is Duke Ellington," but I just went on playing. His name didn't mean anything to me then. Afterwards, they introduced me. Later on, I had the band down at Smalls' every Sunday afternoon, and somebody told me about Cootie Williams. I sent to his house and asked him to come on over and play.

46   He came, and he met Duke that afternoon.

Duke could already play in those days. He'd sit down and play, and do all right with all those piano players in New York, but he'd listen a whole lot, too. His great asset was listening. I could read music, but I couldn't play with guys like James P. Johnson, Willie "the Lion" Smith, Fats Waller, and Dan Carey. James P. would play thirty-two choruses in a row, and never one the same. Every Monday night was piano contest night at the Hole in the Wall on 129th Street.

Dan Carey was from Boston. Some other great ones from there were Pat Tory, who had little fingers, but could really play; George Rickson, a fine pianist who played all the shows in Boston, read music like mad and never looked at the keys; Slim Johnson, who was no relation to Walter; and LeRoy Tibbs, who played piano first, but went on to tenor.

D. When did you get into show business?

W. It seemed like everything fell apart in 1930, so I started rehearsing shows. The first was Will Morrissey's *Hot Rhythm.* It seemed as though the director wasn't able to read, so they asked me if I could direct. When I said, "Yes," I got the job, and I directed the show at the old Times Square Theatre for ten months. Then we went over on 50th Street to a theatre near Sixth Avenue for another ten weeks until the show folded up.

D. Who were some of the people in it?

W. Eddie Rector was master of ceremonies. Edith Wilson and Mae Barnes sang in it, and Pigmeat Markham was in four or five scenes. There was one scene in the show where a guy was walking that Last Mile—to the electric chair—and three fellows who had the part died during the run of the show. They capitalized on that.

After that, I went to Washington with Ralph Cooper, and we were going to play the Howard Theatre, but they closed up on us. So Ralph talked to Frank Schiffman, and he gave me the job of director of music at the Lafayette. Later that year we went to the Harlem Opera House, where I met Ella Fitzgerald. I used to tell her to come down there Thursday afternoon, when the band rehearsed, and I'd introduce her to the bandleader. Finally, Chick Webb and his wife got interested in Ella, and that's where she was actually discovered, *there.* Of course, she used to go around all the amateur hours and take all the prizes.

D. I take it you had acquired a lot of musical knowledge along the way to equip you for jobs of this kind.

W. I started to arrange at the Lafayette. The producer of the show said, "Can't you arrange music?" So I started, and, oh, I made so many mistakes, leaving off sharps and flats and all that! "Just play what I got down there," I'd tell the guys, "and I'll correct it later."

47   D. Did you ever go to any school for arranging?

W. No, I got it by listening to Don Redman, Joe Jordan, and all those guys. Joe Steele, who was at the New England Conservatory nine years, used to tell me a whole lot of things. He knew only music. He'd tell you *where* everything was, and *why* everything was. When he played *Rhapsody in Blue* at the Lafayette Theatre, George Gershwin jumped up on the stage and kissed him! Joe was a Boston boy who played with Chick Webb. We got along great. And I used to hang around with Fats Waller. He would look up from the piano and say, "You here?" And I'd say, "Yeah, just following you around!" I had a little money then. Oh, I had a good time with Fats! If he needed fifty dollars, he'd just sit down and write a number. He wasn't like Jelly Roll Morton, who always had a lot of music with him, and was always complaining that he wanted some money. But Jelly was a great individual, too. I used to laugh at him, always talking and saying, "These people don't know what it's all about!"

D. Where were we? At the Harlem Opera House?

W. Yeah. I went from there to the Apollo. I enjoyed conducting, but drummers were very important, especially where dancers were concerned. I think that Jo Jones was the greatest in the world. He would watch me conduct and *never* change tempo. After I got in the theatre, and got a reputation, everybody'd come to Tom Whaley for music. Jimmie Lunceford had been in the Apollo before he went into the Cotton Club. When the manager asked him if he knew an arranger, he said, "Yeah, get the guy down at the Apollo Theatre . . . Tom Whaley." So they had me arrange a number for Avon Long and Lena Horne—*As Long As I Live*—and then another called *Here Goes.* I thought I was charging a whole lot of money—$150—for each arrangement, but when that band went to work on them, the word soon got around that Tom Whaley had written them. Don Redman came by. "Did you arrange those?" he asked. "Sure," I said. And after that I got more work than I could handle.

In 1940, the chorus girls at the Apollo went on strike, and Schiffman did away with the chorus line, and I lost my job. So I went on my own at Smalls', at Connie's Inn, and all around. I was at the Hurricane, downtown, when Duke heard me. It was just like the theatre there. All the big bands would come in, and I'd go to Washington or Philadelphia to rehearse them in the show, which I wrote and arranged. After Duke left in 1941, he sent me a wire from Canton, Ohio, to come and join him. Joe Howard, the manager at the Hurricane, couldn't understand me leaving.

"Man, you're making $400 a week," he said. "What're you gonna do? Cab Calloway's coming in."

"You'll have to get somebody else," I told him. "I'm joining the greatest band in the world. I'm going with Duke."

I left right that next day.

D. At that time, he already had Billy Strayhorn as arranger and deputy pianist.

W. Yeah, so all I did was copy music, and I just became lazy and lax. I had met Billy when he first came to the Apollo with Duke. I used to get a hundred dollars for directing his show at the theatre, but this time he introduced Billy and said, "I have my own piano player." So I went out and got drunk. Now Strayhorn, not being used to the theatre, didn't stand back when the curtain came down, and the curtain hit him on the head. He went up to Duke's room and sat down, and Duke asked him, "What's the matter?" After he told Duke what happened, Duke sent for me and I got the job for the rest of the week, but Billy put it out that I told the Puerto Rican to let it drop on him!

D. Apart from that, I take it your relationship was harmonious.

W. Until 1950, when I wanted more money, and quit. I went down to South America for nine months with Norma Miller's dance group in *Moods in Rhythm*. I had a ten-piece band. When I got back, Duke called me, and I've been with him ever since.

D. How about that number by Count Basie called *Tom Whaley?*

W. Oh, I was just visiting with him on a record date one day, and

Tom Whaley
(standing) talks
to Earl Hines,
with Frank Driggs,
Whitney Balliett
and Stanley Dance
in background

Basie asked, "What're we going to call this number?" It was just a good jump number, and Buck Clayton, I think it was, said, "Call it *Tom Whaley.*"

D. So, most of the time it has been copying parts up until the Sacred Concerts?

W. Yeah.

D. Had you had much experience of choral work?

W. In the theatre, we used to take a number like *St. Louis Blues* and one like *Mammy o' Mine,* and put the two together—one group singing against the other. And I used to do things like *Eli, Eli* for choirs.

D. Did you find Duke's arranging methods unorthodox compared. . . ?

W. Compared to others, yes, because he goes against all rules of music. He says, if it sounds good, that's all that matters. And he is right. Years ago, when I was playing, I used to make some funny chords, and to me they sounded good. "What kind of chords you playing?" they'd ask. "I don't know," I'd say, "but keep on listening." They were all squares 'way back then. They didn't know anything about augmented fifths, etc.

D. Would you say Billy Strayhorn was more orthodox than Duke?

W. Yeah, Billy always had a very good idea—a picture. The way he pictured music, when you looked at the chord you could almost hear it, right in your mind. Sometimes, with Duke's, you have to stop —he has all those notes in there! The first time I was copying his music, I said, "Duke, you got an E natural up there against an E flat." He said, "That's all right. Put it down." After you hear it, it sounds great.

D. But on paper, you think it won't?

W. Just like Wild Bill Davis saying at the record date the other day, "Hey, you got an F sharp down there and an F up here!" I said, "That's right." I've gotten used to it. It took time. At first, some of the things he would do seemed so fantastic, but they always sounded great. When you get used to that sound, you know it's Ellington.

D. He must be able to hear it.

W. He knows it before he puts it down. He has a great idea of the tone he wants up there. Like the baritone: a lot of arrangers always put the baritone at the bottom, but Duke will put it in the first note, second note, or third note, according to how he hears that tone. Of course, he always writes up to the last minute. Strayhorn was the same. That's why I'm always copying parts in the record studio. I'm working under pressure, and there are a lot of distractions, as you know. They really ought to rehearse *before* record dates. I went to Miami once with Strayhorn, and we stayed up four days and three nights writing music for a different version of *Jump for Joy.* It ran three weeks.

D. With all the responsibility he has, and all the different things he gets involved in, I can never understand how Duke manages to accomplish so much as he does.

W. He's really gifted, and, to me, he's the greatest guy in music. He's also the greatest accompanist. Dizzy Gillespie gave him that honor when we were recording. Duke came in late, sat down, and turned the whole thing over.

D. You can hear the effect he has in the difference between the way the band sounds at the beginning of the program, playing by itself, and after he has come on stage to the piano.

W. We've said nothing about him as a composer. And what can you say, except that he's *great,* too? He wrote *Black, Brown, and Beige* 'way back in 1944, and when I was copying the parts I used to say, "What are you going to do with this?" He didn't say anything, but then, in 1963, we put it in that show in Chicago, *My People.* He's always twenty years ahead of his time.

D. Was that all organized when you got it?

W. Yes, he had it all lined out. He very seldom changes those big things. The same with *Harlem.* He worked on that, and followed it straight out. With a normal composition, you can juggle it around. When he comes in the record studio, he knows the order of it in the arrangement: A, B, C, D, E. Now, after the band plays it, he'll say, "We'll start at E and go back to D, and then go to A...." The suites like *Suite Thursday* and *Deep South Suite* are different again. They're done in parts, each separate from the other, although a motif may recur in them.

D. Who else is going to play works like *Black, Brown, and Beige,* to give them their true value?

W. Well, I think some big symphony will take Duke's music eventually and make a whole concert of it.

D. Do you think performance by others is inhibited by the fact that his music always sounds so much better when played by his own band?

W. Yes. A lot of bands just don't have the conception. Like I used to call Roger Segure when I got overworked at the theatre. He's a very good musician who arranged for Lunceford at one time. I'd have ideas, and he'd help me with them. "If you need any more material," he used to say, "you go to the book and open it at D-5, and you take that out and put it in the arrangement." That's how a lot of arrangers work, and that's why all the bands and all the arrangements sound the same. They're not original. Ellington is original.

51   [*1969*]

Shorty Baker, Ella Fitzgerald, Clark Terry

Willie Cook and Paul Gonsalves

Ellington and Billy Strayhorn

THE MUSICIANS

The interviews in this section are arranged chronologically in accordance with the entry of the musicians into the Ellington band. Some of them were to be a part of it for most of their adult lives, others for relatively brief periods, but their impact and influence were often quite unrelated to the length of their stay. Some inherited roles created by their predecessors, while others fashioned fresh roles for themselves and contributed new colors to Ellington's orchestral palette.

Considerable space is often devoted to their careers both before and after their association with Ellington, an association which almost invariably had a lasting effect on the character of their work. In showing the variety of backgrounds from which his musicians came, emphasis is indirectly placed on Ellington's genius in molding and maintaining—for more than four decades—such an immediately indentifiable ensemble.

The world of Duke Ellington can be viewed as a microcosm of the world of jazz. In fact, it is that and much more, but all facets of jazz are reflected in it, some affectionately, some humorously, some ironically. The "stride" tradition of the East Coast pianists, for example, is strong in his own playing and orchestral translations. The New Orleans idiom survived fruitfully in Barney Bigard's clarinet playing, in Bubber Miley's muted trumpet (inspired by King Oliver), and in the irresistible flow of Johnny Hodges's saxophone improvisations (a very personal development on Sidney Bechet's foundations). The band as a whole was one of the more significant forces in the creation of the Swing Era, and Benny Goodman's influence was reflected in Jimmy Hamilton's clarinet playing. It was no accident that the presence of such masterly exponents as Ben Webster and Paul Gonsalves coincided with the rise of the tenor saxophone as the most popular solo instrument in jazz. Among those who joined after World War II were men like Clark Terry and Willie Cook, whose familiarity with the language of bop was knowingly utilized by Ellington from time to time. Fashions in Latin American rhythms were duly acknowledged; and a longstanding appreciation of Wild Bill Davis' skills led eventually to the inclusion of the organ in the band.

Toby Hardwick [alto saxophone]

Otto Hardwick, later exclusively known as "Toby," was born in Washington, D.C., in 1904. His home was at 1395 "T" Street, and Duke Ellington lived at 1212 "T" Street N.W., one block away. They saw each other daily, at school, in the street, and playing baseball. Hardwick won a place in Ellington's circle of teen-age friends when, at fourteen, he was hired to play bass in Carroll's Columbia orchestra.

In the hearts of the neighborhood's adolescent elite, music had supplanted baseball as an enthralling passion. The True Reformers Hall in northwest Washington became the meeting ground for young aspiring musicians and their coterie of admirers. Ragtime and debate resounded nightly in the course of excited rehearsals, and in 1917 the seed of the Washingtonians came to life there in Room 10. Its vitality derived from a loose-knit group of lively talents that included, besides Ellington, Arthur Whetsol (trumpet), Elmer Snowden (banjo), William Escoffery (guitar), and the Miller brothers. Bill and Felix Miller came from one of those musical families in which everybody played one or more instruments.

At the time Hardwick made his initial appearance at the Hall, he was still too small to carry his bass, so he was accompanied by his father, who carried it for him. Hardwick Senior never minded this, an opportunity to check up on "his boys" being always welcome. Recognized as a disciplinarian, he maintained a keen interest in these teen-agers who constantly visited each other's homes. Jerry Rhea's parents, living in the same neighborhood, also shared this sense of involvement, and Ellington's many relatives were fascinated by his rapidly expanding circle. Rhea, who studied drums and occasionally sang with the group, was to remain close to Ellington through the years, and later serve as secretary and confidant.

Both Hardwick and Ellington retain fond memories of those early days. "Considering myself a veteran," Ellington recollected, "I took it on myself to break Toby in. I made him get a C-melody saxophone,

55

and got him a job. Later on I used to send him out on other jobs, and pretty soon he was known as one of the best in town."

"Just being together, playing together, was all that mattered then," Hardwick elaborated. "There wasn't any money involved, not to speak of."

But there was plenty of work, for Ellington boldly advertised himself in the yellow pages of the phone book, where his name was as prominently displayed as those of Meyer Davis and Louis Thomas. Before long he had as many calls as he could handle, often sending out several groups the same night.

Eventually William "Sonny" Greer appeared on the Washington scene, and the first three ingredients essential to the Ellington legend coalesced. Greer, from Long Branch, New Jersey, enjoyed a reputation as a flashy drummer, "practically out of New York." In the capital he was soon at work in the pit band of the Howard Theatre. Hastening there to observe him, Ellington, Hardwick, Whetsol, and Snowden conceded he was fly.

"But we decided to give him the works," Ellington reminisced. "Everybody used to stand on the street corners then, trying to look big-time. So along comes Sonny. I'm sure that I'm a killer with my new shepherd plaid suit, bought on time. I take the lead in the conversation. Sonny comes back with a line of jive that lays us low."

It wasn't long afterwards that Sonny quit the theatre to join Ellington, and the Washingtonian nucleus was formed. They considered themselves extra special, the three friends admit. Close to the threshold of the age of consent, they smoked big cigars, imbibed corn whiskey and gin, and fancied they looked like Stuart Holmes in the movies. Hardwick had a weakness for expensive suits, and bought himself a Pullman automobile nicknamed the Dupadilly.

Claude Hopkins, another famous Washington musician, also had a car and by then Ellington owned a Chandler. After work, going nowhere as fast as they could, Hardwick and the Miller brothers used to race the other two cars. But the Dupadilly had to be pushed to start. It had no crank handle and inevitably stalled on a hill. It stopped somewhere one day and they just got out and left it.

Hardwick returned to the second-hand car dealer, who rejoiced in the name of Dear-Me. "But there was only one Dupadilly," he observed. "Still, the fine times were only beginning. Sonny decided that he wanted to go to New York. I had to be the greatest yes-man he ever had. Because I was never satisfied—I always wanted to see what was on the other side of the hill. And Washington had no hill!"

From New York, bandleader Wilbur Sweatman contacted Greer about joining the stage band scheduled to play at the Lafayette Theatre. Greer stipulated there must be a job for Hardwick and

Ellington as well, but the latter at first hesitated to abandon what had become a lucrative business. With little more than the train fare in their wallets, Hardwick and Greer set out alone.

"We rehearsed for a while, and rehearsed some more—but nothing much really happened," Hardwick recalled, smiling ruefully. Sweatman's job petered out, and what was worse, Duke had come up, ready to start work. We had to get going on the rounds of the clubs, carrying our horns. Sometimes there'd be tips and that way we existed—after a fashion, everything divided three ways."

Ultimately, hungry for homecooking, the three returned home, not to return till the following year when Fats Waller persuaded Elmer Snowden that he had a good job lined up. He wanted Whetsol, Greer, and Hardwick as well. With Waller at the keyboard there was no place for Ellington, so as before, he remained behind for a time.

It was just as well, for on their arrival the group encountered the same story. The gig had vanished and Waller was already elsewhere. Without a pianist, they had no band. Ellington had to be persuaded to join them. Optimistic messages were dispatched, and eventually in ducal style Ellington arrived, his money blown on the journey up.

"Artie and I were the first there when he got in," Hardwick recalled, with a chuckle. "Duke was all smiles. 'Hi, fellows,' he said. 'Oh, we're so glad to see you,' we replied. 'Let's get on uptown. You've got cabfare, we hope!' "

The weeks multiplied while they auditioned again and again, but no work was to be had. There were individual offers, but hungry or not they determined to stick together. At last Bricktop came to their aid, Bricktop with whom Ellingtom had once worked at the Oriental in Washington and who was to become the darling of Paris. At 134th Street and Seventh Avenue there was a popular nightspot called Barron's, and Bricktop knew Barron Wilkins well. She talked him into letting his current band go and hiring the Washingtonians in their stead.

"We'd got our feet on the first rung of the ladder," observed Hardwick. "It seems they liked us. Our music was different, even then. We were only five, but we had arrangements on everything. It was sort of conversation music, soft yet gut-bucket. Besides Duke, Sonny, Artie, and myself, there was Snowden, and for a time he handled the business. After a while we made Duke take his place, and that's when Freddie Guy came in. Even then, we were already pulling for Duke. He had everyone on his side, he was that kind of guy."

After Barron's, they went to the Kentucky Club at Broadway and 49th Street. They were a great success and the engagement lasted for five wonderful years. Consistent airtime over station WHN helped make the band nationally known. Whetsol's return to medicine heralded the advent of Bubber Miley, the trumpet player who became a legend before his untimely death in 1932.

"Bubber growled *all* night long," Ellington said. "It was then we decided to forget the sweet music."

They had been at the Kentucky more than three years when impresario Irving Mills encountered them, and reacted swiftly. Soon they were readying material for their first session with an important record company. Until then their efforts had been confined to relatively obscure labels like Perfect, Blu-Disc, and Gennett. Now, for Vocalion, the band recorded its theme, *East St. Louis Toodle-oo,* a classic Miley-Ellington collaboration. Other titles like *Birmingham Breakdown, Immigration Blues,* and *The Creeper* featured Hardwick on alto saxophone. Then came the first widely distributed *Black and Tan Fantasy* on Brunswick, featuring Hardwick and Miley.

Mills fully anticipated the Washingtonians' success in the studios. He recognized the significance of the way in which Ellington melded their contrasting and individual styles into a distinctive, unmistakable whole. Witty and urbane, Ellington injected a touch of party manners into his most experimental music, while from behind the drums, Greer's humor and exuberance imparted a dynamic quality to every performance. Guy and Miley were temperamentally opposed, the former being consistently suave and detached, the latter unpredictable, uninhibited, and like Charlie Irvis, a primitive in the best sense of the word. By comparison Hardwick seemed somewhat low-keyed.

An elongated Goyaesque face and a balding head lent him an air of distinction. His expression was sophisticated, witty, and curiously warm. Friendly and relaxed, he exercised an unselfconscious charm.

"Toby played it sweet and straight," commented Ellington. "Lots of chicks wanted to mother him—so every now and then he'd submit! It meant he was in and out of the band rather unpredictably."

It was in Atlantic City, during one of his brief absences from the band, by way of a romantic legacy, that he became "Toby." It was a metamorphosis that suited, and "Toby" he remained. "I hope I've worn the name well," he said. "I was never a serious money-making man. I preferred just being Toby." Intuitive, sympathetic, quickwitted and adventurous, Toby never lacked for much, certainly not friends.

It was during one of his absences that Harry Carney was brought in from Boston to take his place in the saxophone section. Later Carney on baritone, and Hardwick as co-composer, were closely associated with one of the band's early song hits, *Sophisticated Lady.* Written in 1933, this coincided with Hardwick's return to the fold after a sojourn in Europe.

"In those early days Duke wasn't thinking about traveling," Hardwick recalled, smiling. "In 1929 you couldn't get him to cross the Hudson river! He didn't like water. He wouldn't even venture to Hoboken. But as for me, I wanted to see the world. I thought to myself: 'I have no chance at all of going to Europe with this guy.' The band was a hit at the Cotton Club and I guessed we'd be there for some time. So I decided: 'What the hell—give me my horn and I'll go anywhere.'

"The band laughed at me. I set out for the pier, and they asked, 'How are you going to Europe? You have no money. . . .' When they laughed, I was more than ever determined. I said: 'That makes no difference: I've got a horn.' And sure enough, when I got to Paris, I landed a job with Noble Sissle. We traveled all over, and later I went with Fats Waller, and ended up at Bricktop's. I had a ball. To the guys that stayed behind I sent a card. It was a plain one, and I wrote, 'If you want to see the pictures, you'd better come over yourselves.' "

One thing Hardwick discovered during his time abroad was the reputation that Ellington enjoyed in England and Europe. "I told Duke when I got back," he said. "It was a terrific field for him. It took a couple of years to soak in, but it did eventually, once Mills got wind of it. For myself, when I hit New York again, I had a great stroke of luck, a chance as a full-time front man for a full-time band. I was offered a first-rate engagement at the Hot Feet Club in Greenwich Village and I kept that band a little over three years. It was quite an outfit, we had a lot of write-ups."

In view of the band personnel, that was not surprising. Hardwick was one of the first leaders to employ and write arrangements for a full saxophone section. He had four reeds in the band, five counting himself. Chu Berry starred on tenor, Wayman Carver played flute, Garvin Bushell was the other alto and Theodore McCoy was heard on baritone. Fats Waller propelled the rhythm section. Musicians admired the band, and the club became so popular its owner made plans to open a second location in Chicago. Unfortunately he never gave enough thought to the gangsterdom which was at its peak in the Windy City. His ambitions cost him his life, and shortened Hardwick's career as a band leader.

But one eventful night, before its untimely demise, Hardwick's band took part in a memorable battle of music. A benefit at the Astor featured, besides his group, the Ellingtonians from the Cotton Club! This was in 1931 and Ellington had expanded to include Louis Metcalf (trumpet), in addition to Miley and Whetsol; and Barney Bigard (clarinet) and Johnny Hodges (alto), in addition to Carney. Joe "Tricky Sam" Nanton had replaced Charlie Irvis on trombone. But Hardwick derived confidence from Waller's presence and was proud of his reed section. He experienced a compelling drive to excel. Unforgettable music was made that night, and in later years, to Hardwick's lasting satisfaction, the Ellingtonians conceded the honors were his.

"It was an evening I'll never forget," he said. "Fate was more than kind."

Eventually, when the doors of the Hot Feet Club had closed for good, Fats Waller left, and a replacement was necessary. For a time James P. Johnson graced the band, but then when they were hired to play the Lafayette Theatre, the pianist seated at the keyboard was William "Count" Basie. "And to this day," Hardwick marveled, "everytime Count sees me, he calls me 'Boss Man.'"

Wearying in time of a boss man's burdens, Hardwick reverted to a sideman at the musicians' mecca known as Smalls' Paradise, and shortly thereafter Jerry Rhea sought him out. Always close to Ellington, Rhea had been instructed to survey and entice.

"When I rejoined the band," Hardwick mused, "it was just like I'd never left. Except this way, maybe. It wasn't *our* thing any longer. It had become Ellington's alone. This was inevitable, I guess. Ten years ago it was 'We do it this way,' and 'We wrote that.' Now, the we was *royal*. It seemed more inspiring, maybe more inspired, too, the other way, but I guess it had to come to this. You love the guy right on. You have to admire him for all he's accomplished. You've got to be happy for him, he's that kind of guy.

"But in those early days, how we enjoyed what we did. We were privileged to make suggestions. If he liked it, or if he didn't, he'd go along with it, anyway. Every man in the band had freedom of expression. It was *fun*. I don't think money had much to do with it. You made a living, that was it. But the work—actually the work was a pleasure. And then it was more or less like family, even with the people who paid us. We never liked making a change. We shared in everything, like in some of those numbers we wrote where two or three contributed a part. Of course, Duke wrote most of them, especially later on. You know, at first they sounded weird to us. We found out, before the fans did, that you've got to give Duke's compositions a chance to grow on you. That's how original they are. They had to grow on us first before we could put into them what they deserved, before the end result came out. He sure is brilliant.

"Another remarkable thing about him is his passion for people. He's warm-hearted, of course, but that's not quite what I mean. *He likes to manipulate*. It's a little quirk all his own. He thinks no one has the slightest idea about this. He likes to manipulate people around him, and gets the biggest kick when he wins. It's not like using someone, it's more like a game. Besides, what he does for you is beneficial. What he tries to get you to do—it's good for you, if you do it. But most times you don't even know what's going on.

"Probably where it started was with guys in the band. When you think of it, with some of the guys he's had to deal with, he's probably been forced into it. Pulling strings, sort of, for their own sakes, though maybe they couldn't say this for themselves, especially if they were getting bad advice somewhere else. He nearly always comes out on top. You can *not* back that guy into a corner. It can't be done. He's got an answer every time. What did he say when they reneged on the Pulitzer Prize award? 'They don't want me too famous too young.' Who could top that?

"The amazing thing about him is that the language, the slant, everything, it's all acquired. It didn't rub off from someone else, and it wasn't a legacy, either. He went inside himself to find it. He's an *only*, that's for sure. They threw away carbons.

"Another way he is different—he is a religious man, and always has been. He's very serious about this. I think it is something inherited from his mother. It's a part of him he didn't want other people to delve into too much. He always had his religious books, but sort of kept them hid, to himself. I've seen him come home at night, go into the bathroom and to the tub, and putting his Bible on one of those bathroom seats, keep reading until the water got cold. I believe it when he says he's read the Bible four times. Because this was way back in the '20s.

"Naturally he's serious about those Sacred Concerts. With them he's accomplishing one of his main goals in life. To my mind he still needs Ray Nance for that kind of thing. Ray's got plenty of soul, and a flair for presentation, too. That's why I nicknamed him 'Floorshow.' I nicknamed Tricky Sam, too. He could always do with one hand what someone else did with two. Anything to save himself trouble—he was tricky that way. Another one I named was Roy Eldridge. I called him Little Jazz. But my best tag was for Strayhorn.

"He hadn't been in the band very long then, and we were on the road traveling. I'd been reading Popeye—and you know how Billy was little and sweet, and everyone crazy about him. Well, on the train he went up the aisle, from one seat to another. He'd stop and talk to this one, then he'd go over and talk to the next. I told Sonny, I said: 'If that ain't Swee' Pea, *I hope somethin'*,' and Sonny fell out. We started calling him Swee' Pea from there on out.

"Strayhorn's death was the one thing I know of that *really* touched Duke. The *one* thing. You can tell by the number he played on that album, *And His Mother Called Him Bill*. His piano solo, *Lotus Blossom*. I read a whole lot just in that music. A whole lot. It's all there. There are things there that tell a lot about Ellington. Listen to that and you hear every emotion. A gang of tears. That hit him *hard*. Neither money nor business was an issue between them ever. Billy just wanted to be with Duke, that was all. It was love—a really beautiful thing.

"Another beautiful thing was that number of his. Was it *Blood Count?* That could break you wide open. The countdown for the day. It went from his sick bed to the studio for Johnny to play. He wrote his epitaph and then had Rabbit play it. . . .

"I miss the band," Hardwick admitted. "And I miss the guys. But I got *tired* of traveling."

In 1943, he departed for good, returning to Washington and a quieter life. Two years earlier Artie Whetsol had died, and in 1951 Sonny Greer turned his back on the road. The Washingtonians are represented now by Ellington alone.

"All things considered," Hardwick concluded, "I feel I've been truly blessed. Wherever we played I found friends. It wasn't money or a reputation I was after. If you scramble up that ladder, it can be lonely up there. Maybe the pals you leave behind are way off some place when needed—and don't hear your call.

"I have no regrets. I still feel like I'm part of Duke and the band."

[*1969*]

Sonny Greer   [*drums*]

"From the moment I was introduced to Duke, I loved him. It was just something about him. He didn't know it, but he had it then. I've never seen another man like him. When he walks into a strange room, the whole place lights up. That's how he likes people, and how he impresses them.

"I had been working in the dining room of the Plaza Hotel on the boardwalk in Asbury Park, in a trio with Fats Waller and a violinist called Shrimp Jones. The same hotel employed a string ensemble called the Conway Boys, and when I struck up a friendship with Sterling Conway he invited me to Washington for a weekend. So when the season ended, I went there for three days and stayed several years.

"I was a very good pool player at that time. Pool is like the violin —you've got to play an hour every day. There was a poolroom right near the Howard Theatre in Washington, which was then owned by A. J. Thomas and Louis Thomas. Except for the pianist, the drummer

62

and the leader, Marie Lucas, all the musicians in the pit band were · from San Juan, Puerto Rico. The drummer had a little alimony trouble, and rather than pay he ducked out to Canada. A half-hour before the show was due on, they came rushing into the poolroom, frantic. 'We've got to have a drummer,' they shouted. My financial position was such that I answered them, 'I'm the guy.' And that was how I came to play the Howard Theatre the first time.

"I struck up an acquaintance with Toby Hardwick. He played string bass then, no saxophone, and he and Duke were pals. When I was introduced, Duke wanted to know all about New York. I was an authority, because my two aunts lived there and I had spent a good part of my schooldays in the city. I painted a glowing picture, a fabulous picture. We sat around drinking corn and telling lies, and I won the lying contest.

"When I got through at the Howard Theatre, about eleven o'clock at night, I'd go right around the corner to the Dreamland Café and play there from midnight to about six in the morning. Claude Hopkins was on piano and Eddie White—Harry White's brother—on violin. There were about ten waitresses and they could all sing—blues or whatever you wanted. When I say blues, I mean the authentic material, and they sang so well it's a pity they were never recorded. Bootlegging was a big thing in Washington then and tips were flying. They brought in corn from Maryland and the bootleggers would often stack a deuce table with bills and tell the entertainers to help themselves. That's how the times were—come easy, go easy.

"Duke wasn't a professional then, but he would come in and play his *Carolina Shout*. He was a great admirer of James P. Johnson, and he had got his Q.R.S. piano rolls down fine. He really idolized James P. and he was the only man I ever knew who could play *Carolina Shout* equally well. But Uncle Ed, his father, didn't want him to go into the music field, because he had a degree in art illustration and was already in partnership with Ewell Conway in commercial illustration. But he knew which direction he wanted to go and, as we say, he followed the swallow.

"In those days, they would have piano contests as an attraction to get people to go to dances. Cliff Jackson was around and so was Claude Hopkins. Claude's father was a professor and his mother a librarian at Howard University, and he was born and raised on the campus. He was ahead of Cliff Jackson then in terms of finish and experience. Thanks to me, Duke had a cheering section of seven or eight with their noisemakers. So Duke would be all set to play his *Carolina Shout*, and I would be there to play the drums, and Toby the bass, so we couldn't lose. We won all kinds of things—suitcases

Toby Hardwick and Harry Carney

and I don't know what. We'd keep them overnight, sell them next day, and go have a ball again.

"After some adventures, we got to New York and opened as the Washingtonians at the Kentucky Club on 49th and Broadway in 1923. We were there five years and the club was so popular that it became a rendezvous for all the musicians. It was owned by Leo Bernstein and Frank Gary. We had six chorus girls in the show and they ended up as star dancers at the Cotton Club uptown, which at that time was known as Jack Johnson's De Luxe Club. The floorshow also included Johnny Hudgins, then the foremost colored comedian and an international star. His act was all pantomine. He never opened his mouth. Joe Smith, the trumpet player, worked with him, and Joe did the talking on trumpet, using his hand as a mute. The M.C. was Bert Lewis and in between the shows he would come out and do an act with Fats Waller as his accompanist.

"We went to work at eleven o'clock at night and nobody knew when closing hour was. We usually didn't get through till seven or eight in the morning, but it was beautiful. So many things happened. All kinds of people mixed there—show people, socialites, debutantes, musicians, and racketeers—and everybody had a lovely time. It was still Prohibition, of course, and nobody could get a drink of booze in the place unless I gave an okay. In the whole time we were there, we

Ellington and Sonny Greer

never had a raid or a pinch. We had an elaborate system and I had a good memory for faces. Any stranger was carefully screened.

"The club held only about 130 people, but after all the other clubs closed the musicians would come to ours, and often you would see forty or fifty name musicians in there at a time. There was just a small dance floor and there wasn't much dancing, but everybody could sit in. At three or four in the morning, you would see Bix Beiderbecke, Tommy Dorsey, Miff Mole, Paul Whiteman, and musicians like that. Whiteman had the band at the Palais Royal around the corner for a time. The bandstand was small, cramped even for the six of us, so when they sat in they played right from the floor, from a chair by their table. Bix and I were friends, and we would often go from one place to another, drinking Top and Bottom, but people who never knew him—and writers—have painted a picture of him that did him more than justice. They made him an invincible trumpet player, but he wasn't that good. You could never have put Bix up on a bandstand with Louis Armstrong, Joe Smith, and Bubber Miley when they were at their peak. The competition was pretty fast then, and he was never in life a legend.

"Because of the small stand, we couldn't use a bass player and we couldn't expand the band, but there were no small bands so well rehearsed as ours then. Most of them played stocks, which we never did. Duke wasn't writing so much, but he would take the popular tunes and twist them, and Toby was doubling on C-melody and baritone, so we would sound like a big band, but soft and beautiful.

"When Arthur Whetsol went back to Washington, we got Bubber Miley. We had heard him in Harlem at the club where Willie 'the Lion' Smith was playing. Bubber was a great man with a plunger, but Charlie Irvis had an old tomato can, smashed in at the bottom like a cone, to get the same effect, those low notes and the growl. That was what Charlie was famous for, and everybody in the music business knew him as 'Plug.'

"Word spread among the musicians about the fantastic sounds this trumpet player with us—Bubber Miley—was getting with a plunger. Red Nichols was playing a club not far from us and curiosity must have drawn him to hear Bubber perform. Lee Posner was writing a newspaper column then called 'Harlemania' and he asked Red what he thought about using a plunger with a trumpet. Red said he would rather drop dead than be caught using one of those so-and-so plungers!

"Sidney Bechet came in one night and pulled out his soprano. Right away, he, Bubber, and Charlie Irvis got to jamming against each other. It was wonderful. So then we hired him and he played with the Washingtonians, clarinet and soprano. He fitted our band like a glove.

"After Paul Whiteman, Ross Gorman had a band at the Palais Royal, and this was the first time we had seen a band all with gold instruments. Gorman had a terrific band then, and it looked so good with all those gold horns. One night, all the bands went up there for some kind of charity affair. Leo Bernstein, our boss, was a very aggressive guy from Chicago, and he insisted that we play before we went off to work. When we started playing, the house fell in. About the third tune we got into was one of those jam numbers we had then, and Bechet, Bubber, and Charlie came down front. Bechet had taken a table napkin and he held it in his mouth so that it hung down, and you couldn't see his fingers as he played his soprano. He cut everybody, Ross Gorman's band, everybody. When he had finished, the manager of the place came up to Gorman and said, 'Play waltzes. Don't play any more jazz.' That was our seven pieces.

"Bechet always played *Dear Old Southland* on stage, and he was Johnny Hodges' inspiration. He liked Johnny and Johnny studied him. But Bechet was always a rover who wanted to see over the other side of the hill. That got into Bubber the same way. Toby had it and he went to Europe with just carfare. That was when he played with Noble Sissle at Les Ambassadeurs. Arthur Whetsol went off to South America with Al Jolson. Claude Hopkins had it and he went to

Europe with Josephine Baker. They had such strong belief in their ability as musicians to stand on their own two feet in the middle of the Sahara and demand recognition. They were true champions, like Duke. And I've never seen him rattled under fire. After you've gained a certain amount of prestige, there are so many people on the outside like wolves trying to tear you down.

"When the Cotton Club opened uptown, they had a band called the Missourians, the band Cab Calloway took over later. Our band had become so famous at the Kentucky Club that they got us to follow them. That was one of the few times in my life that I wanted to leave the band. We were established and we were doing so well, but the pressure went on and we had to go up there. We had to enlarge the band, too, and that broke my heart, because everything had been so quiet and tasteful. We hadn't had written arrangements. We'd just talk things over and make suggestions on the interpretation. Even today, suggestions are in order with Ellington. The way he blended his band, our six or seven sounded like twelve pieces. We hadn't had a bass player, because of space, but now we stole a good one—'Bass' Edwards—out of Charlie Johnson's band. He was a big guy with blinker lights in the bell of his sousaphone, and he'd call for four or five choruses, just like a trumpet player, and play all of them different, with the red and green lights twinkling over his head.

"They put a coast-to-coast radio wire in the Cotton Club and we were lucky enough to have three top announcers of the day in Ted Husing, Norman Brockenshire, and David Ross, from six o'clock to seven every night. Many arguments arose in Harlem because the wives wouldn't cook dinner until the program was over. That was the beginning of Duke's national popularity, being heard coast to coast.

"When we got into the Cotton Club, presentation became very important. I was a designer for the Leedy Manufacturing Company of Elkhart, Indiana, and the president of the company had a fabulous set of drums made for me, with timpani, chimes, vibraphone, everything. Musicians used to come to the Cotton Club just to see it. The value of it was three thousand dollars, a lot of money at that time, but it became an obsession with the racketeers, and they would pressure bands to have drums like mine, and would often advance money for them. Leroy Maxey, who was with Cab Calloway, and Jimmie Crawford with Lunceford, both had equipment something like mine. I put timpani heads on my bass drum, so that it was always in tune with the bass, And I had Duke's name and my monogram on the front of it. I was the first in the world to do that. Of course, I used all this extra equipment for concerts, theatres, and week-stands, not on one-nighters and dances.

"In 1929, we were doubling from the Cotton Club to the Ziegfeld Theatre for *Show Girl*, one of the last shows Ziegfeld put on. They had a substitute band at the Cotton Club until we got there— Jimmy Ferguson fronted it, or Baron Lee as they called him. We played on the stage in *Show Girl* and closed the first half with *An American in Paris*. The full company would be on stage and there were twenty-two musicians in the pit. It was a terrible hassle with us 'way up there among the gorgeous settings. At first, we were always a little in front or a little behind. In the end, I used to let the pit drummer carry the rhythm while I played it cool, playing make-believe. We opened the second half with *Liza*. They couldn't get anyone to do this number right. Ruby Keeler sang it for a time. They tried Nick Lucas, and opening night Al Jolson—Ruby Keller's husband—came out and sang it, but eventually it ended up with just us playing it. I never really liked the tune, but it's okay for jamming. I remember when the kids got tired at rehearsals, Ziegfeld would call out, 'Duke, cheer 'em up a little bit!' And we'd start playing some of our original tunes. When we played *Liza* for them, I'd sing a couple of choruses, and he liked that.

"I did all the singing in Duke's band for five or six years. When Ivie Anderson and the three horns were down front for *Mood Indigo*, the high falsetto voice in the background was mine. I did it at the Palladium in London in 1933 and I was doing that sort of thing long before Kay Davis came into the band, but I never aspired to sing on the records. In the early days, it was essential to entertain as well as play.

"The last show at the Cotton Club went on at two and the club closed at three-thirty or four. Then everybody would go next door to Happy Roane's or to the breakfast dance at Smalls' Paradise, where the floorshow went on at six o'clock in the morning, like they do in Atlantic City now. It was the complete show with twenty-five or thirty people, including the singing waiters and their twirling trays. Show people from all over New York, white and colored, went there Sunday mornings. It's hard to imagine now, musicians coming out from the breakfast dance at eight or nine in the morning with their tuxedos on, and showgirls with evening dresses on. Or Charlie Johnson's band there, at six or seven in the morning, with maybe twenty-five musicians from the bands all over town, white and colored, playing at one time, all the top names in the music business. When the big touring bands came into New York for a short time, they always made the scene even if it was only for half an hour. Drummers like Chick Webb, Kaiser Marshall, Sid Catlett, Stan King, Chauncey Morehouse, and yours truly, not to mention Charlie's own George Stafford—the Powerhouse, we called him—all had the good fortune to play in back of those musicians. The average musician hated to go home in those days. He was always seeking some place where someone was playing something he ought to hear. Ten o'clock in the morning, someone would come by and say, 'Man, they're jamming at so-and-so's,' and over he'd go. The most authentic jam sessions were at Mexico's. He specialized in that. Monday would be trumpet night, Tuesday saxophone night, Wednesday trombone night, Thursday clarinet night, Friday piano night, and so on. That carried over to the Hoofer's Club, where you could sit at the social table and play cards or have food as well. It was a big place, but Mexico's was small and you could depend on piano cutting contests there. Jimmy Johnson, Willie Smith, and Luckey Roberts were the giants, and they were tricky. They would always wash you away if you were from the second division.

"We'd met Johnny Hodges up in Boston, and Harry Carney came down with us to Salem, because Mal Hallett's and our band were Charlie Shribman's regulars. He had New England tied up, and he booked all through it in beautiful ballrooms. We'd stay up there from Decoration Day to Labor Day. Practically any band in America that ever made any kind of reputation played for Charlie Shribman. He was one of the first people, outside of Irving Mills, to see the potential in our band.

"Irving Mills began managing us when we were in the Kentucky Club. It was imperative that we have a man like that, a front man, because I don't think we could have done it alone without his guidance. When anything important pertaining to Ellington came up, he was there in person. He didn't send someone else out. When he made the second European trip with us, he was so sick he had to have a doctor in attendance twenty-four hours a day, but he made it every step of the way. He was a businessman, sure, but he always saw to it we had the best in transportation. The band didn't know what a bus looked like in the early days. We had private Pullman cars, with 'Duke Ellington' on the side, and a private baggage car, through every state of the union, and we were the only band in the country, white or colored, that had that. On one-nighters, we lived out of the train, and everybody had a lower berth. We parked the cars in a station, and there was no running around looking for rooms, north, south, east, or west. That was the Mills regime. When it ended, we came to the covered wagon—the bus.

"You could be so comfortable in that parlor car. If Duke wanted to get up and write music, all he had to do was put his robe over his pajamas. You could rest all day if you wanted to, and that meant you arrived at the next engagement in good shape. Duke liked to rest, but this way of traveling also gave him such isolation. He wasn't bothered with people worrying him about a hundred different things all day

69

long. When we played a long engagement, we gave up the cars, but closing night the Pullmans would be back in the station.

"The band that came closest in terms of competition, in my opinion, was Jimmie Lunceford's. He had class, talent, and variety, and his band was full of terrific stars. Count Basie's and Chick Webb's were top bands, but they never had the variety of material and presentation. Jimmie Lunceford was a good man; he believed in discipline, and he never caroused. Duke, on the other hand, would always get down and fraternize with his men, and he had a reason for doing that. He'd go out with them or sit down and play cards with them. He'd never let them lose confidence in themselves. He'd sit up and ball with them, and he used to be able to drink them under the table. He doesn't do that now, but that's how you mature.

"Duke Ellington earned his success. He worked at it. The band was getting bigger and climbing all through the '30s, and that was when he began to express some of his dreams by putting different guys into special showcases. Each guy in the band was an individual artist. No two of them ever played alike, and that applies even today. As a team, they're unbeatable. The backgrounds Duke wrote for individual talents not only showed them off to the best advantage, but also made them feel comfortable. The art of presentation is ingrained in him, and when musicians moved out on their own, or into another band, they soon found out it wasn't the same.

"When we started to go abroad, that was something else. I always remember the concert we played at the Trocadero in London in 1933. It was a huge place, packed and jammed, and half the people were musicians. We had played a show at the Palladium, but we played *us* there. It was wide open, and we looked sharp, too, in those white suits and orange ties. That was years before other people began giving jazz concerts. They used to say Duke was twenty-five years ahead of his time, and you can see how true it was now. He's still ahead. The other guys never caught him."

[*1965*]

Harry Carney [*baritone saxophone and clarinets*]

"I began playing piano at the age of six—taking piano lessons, that is! It seemed as though every kid in the neighborhood could play piano by ear, and here I was going every Saturday, religiously, taking lessons, and practicing, but if you took the music away from me I couldn't play a thing. That went on until I was eleven or twelve, during which time I played student recitals—nothing but the classics. I couldn't get away from the classics to save my life, and I was pretty disgusted with myself. My brother was two years younger, but he seemed to have more of a natural talent for piano. He had no training whatsoever, but he would sit down and really start playing. I was the person who was amazed—when my brother sat down to play piano! Then there was a schoolmate of mine at that time, Leonard Withers, who was wonderful on piano, too. He had long fingers that would stretch a tenth and give him a good rocking rhythm in the bass, something I couldn't do through the construction of my fingers. He and my brother would be playing jazz, the popular tunes of the day, but not me. I remember *Dardanella* in particular.

"I belonged to a juvenile society and during the year we would have several functions. One of the members was Buster Tolliver, a fine musician. (He's still on the scene, writing for shows. He used to do the writing for a lot of Billy Rose's extravaganzas.) At our dances, he would play piano during the first half and clarinet after the intermission. He always seemed to be surrounded by the girls when he got through playing clarinet, and by now I had reached an age when I was conscious of the girls, so I thought maybe the clarinet would be the means of attracting them to me. So Buster advised me about how to acquire a clarinet.

"I joined a Knights of Pythias band in Boston when I was thirteen. They had an instructor who taught all the instruments in the band, and he taught me for the very nominal rate of fifty cents a lesson, the band furnishing the instrument. After alarming the whole neighborhood with my practicing, somebody thought I was a good clarinet player and started offering me jobs.

"My first influences were Buster Bailey with Fletcher Henderson, and Don Murray with Jean Goldkette. As a brash kid, I always wanted to play faster than anyone on clarinet, and both Buster and Don Murray were great technicians. Too bad I didn't stick with them! Perhaps I'd be a clarinetist today. Buster has always sounded to me like a perfect man for the symphony, and on those up-tempo numbers with Fletcher Henderson he always showed what a well-schooled musician he was. There was a lot of study behind his playing. I heard some things he did with Alec Wilder and woodwinds on records some time ago, and they convinced me that he'd be very able as a symphony clarinetist. The way he cares for his instrument, always cleaning it after a set, also shows good training. Back in the old days, the wood of the instrument didn't have treatment like it gets today, and consequently if you weren't careful you were likely to wind up with a crack in the clarinet. That was why we were so careful to use a swab and oil in the old days. Moisture gets into the wood, and changes in temperature, between the room and the street, particularly in colder weather, were dangerous. I didn't take up bass clarinet until many years later, about 1944. I never heard Buster Bailey play it. He usually has just the regular B-flat clarinet, but I'll have to go down and talk to him about it, and get some much-needed ideas.

"Well, after about a year of clarinet, I learned that saxophone was much easier. Clarinet *is* more difficult, but the kids are doing so much on saxophone nowadays that often I wonder. Alto was what I was interested in and I had to convince my mother that I should have one. Neither my father nor my mother played an instrument. Dad liked the operas, always went to them during the season, and he used to like to sing around the house. He was pretty familiar with the spirituals, too. But it was my mother who had to be convinced about the alto, and fortunately she went along with me, and we secured it. Now I felt the influence of Sidney Bechet and Johnny Hodges. Johnny and I used to live a few doors apart and we'd listen to all the records together. Some people began to think I could really play saxophone because I played it so loudly, and after-school jobs started to come in. I worked several spots in Boston with small groups, but in the meantime I heard so many bands from New York City that I knew I must get there to talk with musicians, and maybe get a chance to blow with some of them.

"This time I had to convince my mother that I was entitled to a vacation in New York, and I went there with Charlie Holmes. (Charlie used to sound like Johnny, because that was the accepted alto style in those days and everyone was trying to borrow ideas from Johnny and get his sound.) My first job was playing in the relief group at the Savoy ballroom on one of those big nights when they had a masquerade ball. The dance would start early and run all night, so they had three bands, and I was in the third. My good friend, Johnny Hodges, was in the Chick Webb band at the time, and it was through Johnny I met the contractor for the relief band, who in turn had a job coming up at a place called the Bamboo Inn. I got the contractor to call my mother and explain to her that everything would be all right. It wasn't long before she arrived on the scene, by surprise, to see what her dear, tender son was doing! She allowed me to stay a little longer.

"This was, I think, in April, 1927. Duke was working at the Kentucky Club and on his night off he would come to the Bamboo Inn. The food was good, I was told, but I couldn't afford it, of course. We thought we had a very good band and I worked there three months until the place burned down. Shortly after that, I bumped into Duke one afternoon on Seventh Avenue and he asked what I was doing. I told him I was just jobbing around and he asked me if I would like to go with him on a trip up to Boston. Of course, Boston was my hometown and I'd been away three months—three months away from homecooking and listening to my mother give me the devil—and I was a bit homesick. To return with Ellington, already famous, was something to look forward to, so I didn't hesitate to say 'yes.' That's how I joined the band, and we played up there during the summer for the Shribman brothers, Charlie and Sy, who gave and lent so much to up-and-coming bands at that time.

"After we finished the three months up there, mostly one-nighters, I was supposed to have returned to school, but Duke has always been a fluent talker and he out-talked my mother and got permission for me to stay with the band. When we talk about it now, my mother will tell me that if I had joined the Army I would have been retired by now! But there were no papers signed when I joined Duke. He was to be a kind of guardian to me when I left Boston for the Big City at the age of seventeen. He was pretty well known by then, but it seemed a big deal to my parents and they thought I would end up being too taken by the fast city of New York—too taken for my age, that is. But it didn't turn out like that. Duke is a great fellow, and a great friend of mine, and it has not only been an education being with him, but also a great pleasure. At times, I've been ashamed to take the money!

"Duke had just augmented from six to eight pieces. Rudy Jackson was playing clarinet and tenor and I was playing clarinet and alto, and both of us were striving for the 'hot' clarinet chair. Lots of times during the evening you would hear nothing but clarinets from the reed section, so I decided to try baritone to give more variety. I was on good terms with an instrument company and they allowed me to try a baritone out. On the job that night, Duke and everyone seemed to think it was quite good. My greatest kick with the instrument, which then seemed so much bigger than me, was that I was able to fill it and make some noise with it. I enjoyed the tone of it and I started to give it some serious study, and I've been carrying it around ever since.

"I'd heard Coleman Hawkins often by then. Every time Fletcher Henderson came to Boston, I'd always be down front, under Hawkins, listening. To my mind, he could do no wrong. I think he did play some baritone then, but it was his tenor that inspired me. I admired his tone and facility on the instrument, and I said, 'Gee, if I could make the baritone sound like that, I'd really have something.' So I was always trying to play like Hawk on the baritone.

73 "After coming back to New York with the Ellington band, I used

to go into record stores and listen to records made by the small bands. In those days, on recordings, the main thing was who could play the most intricate break. Breaks were very popular, and that was where the improvisation was. Often, the introductions and endings to records were really long, four-bar breaks. Or there'd be a two-bar break and the band would hit a chord. I think the first time I heard Adrian Rollini was on a record of *Ida* by Red Nichols. He was my next influence after Hawk, because now I tried to give the baritone something of the bass saxophone sound. I tried to make the upper register sound like Coleman Hawkins and the lower register like Adrian Rollini. And I always strove for a good tone. That had been drummed into my head when I was taking clarinet lessons. Later, when I took alto lessons, it was always hammered home that if I only played one note, I should play it with a good tone. I've always adhered to that and I'm very glad my teachers made me see the importance of good tone.

"Bubber Miley contributed a lot in those early days. He had a wonderful sense of humor, but you had to know him to detect whether he was being serious or not. He always gave the impression of being very serious, but the surprising thing was the way he would crack up when something funny was said. He was always serious, though, about his playing before other musicians. He wanted them to know he was a great trumpet player, and he was a man who liked to battle. He and Tricky Sam got great pleasure from playing something together in harmony that came off well. They were always blowing for each other and getting ideas together for what they were going to play. It was wonderful watching the two of them working and hearing the sounds they got from those plungers. What they created has stayed with us as a major part of Ellington music. But there were quite a few other growling trumpet players, of course. In the Charlie Johnson band, besides Sidney DeParis, Jabbo Smith used to do a wonderful job growling, as well as fanning with a derby. Bobby Stark, with Chick Webb, was good at it, too, and so was Frankie Newton when he was with Lloyd and Cecil Scott. Frankie was a good all-round trumpet player, for that matter. And Ward Pinkett could growl. At that time, it was part of the trumpet's role to carry around the mute and the plunger. It got so that there were growling specialists who really studied growling technique. I mustn't forget to mention Cootie Williams. Of all the growl trumpets, he was the one with the power.

"And there were other trends. Everyone was very conscious of Paul Whiteman in the late '20s. He made a lady out of jazz and everybody wanted to have those lush and plush introductions that bordered on the symphonic side. On Sunday nights at the Cotton

Club, what we called the big-time musicians then, those who worked for Whiteman, Isham Jones, and Ben Pollack, and made the small-group jazz records—they used to come up. If they sat in front of us, we'd become very self-conscious, because we knew they were great players. We'd heard so much about Bix, and we'd heard him on records, so we looked at him with awe, although he sat in with the band.

"As Duke's band grew and new members injected their personalities, he was inspired to write. He was always a great compiler, and one of the guys' ideas would suggest something else to him. The Cotton Club was our first big job after I joined, and the band became suddenly inspired because we were asked to do so many remote broadcasts. We were all young and proud and we thought we were doing a great job.

"Immediately after our early broadcasts, about six or seven in the evening, we'd run on down to the corner of 131st and Seventh, where all the musicians used to hang out, and get their reactions. In the beginning, a lot of them made us feel like crying, they were so critical, but finally the band began to go great guns, and then it was a pleasure to go down to the corner, not only after broadcasts, but after we got through working, too. Sometimes we'd stay up all night listening to the praise, but when we did a bad broadcast, that would be the night we'd get some sleep.

"Fortunately or unfortunately, there's nearly always been a better clarinet in the band, and I've left the clarinet up to him. After Barney Bigard joined, I continued to do a few solos. I admired Barney's great facility, imagination, and big tone. He remembered so many things the New Orleans clarinets used to do that there was always something for me to be listening and paying attention to. As the baritone became my specialty, my clarinet playing sounded bad to me in comparison with his. Today we have Jimmy Hamilton and Russell Procope, both of them fine clarinet players, with different styles. The style of Jimmy Hamilton is the kind of clarinet I'd like to be able to play. He's a real clarinet player, very facile, with a beautiful tone, and another one who could do a very good job in symphony. Procope has taken over a lot of Barney's things.

"The Albert system generally seems to result in a bigger tone than the Boehm. The Boehm has so much auxiliary fingering that it's possible you can do more with it, but there's a new, improved Albert system which also has auxiliary fingering, and which both Procope and Barney use. I used Albert to begin with, but changed to Boehm because of Buster Bailey. There was a time after Barney joined the band when I was so impressed by his fullness of sound that I went back to Albert, but I found I had been playing Boehm too long to leave it. Fazola used Albert, but I think Albert Nicholas is a Boehm man. He tries for and gets that New Orleans bigness out of it. Jimmie Noone was an Albert man. Goodman and Artie Shaw were Boehm, of course.

"When we left the Cotton Club, we went on a tour of one-nighters across the country, arriving in Los Angeles to make the picture with Amos 'n' Andy, in which we played *Three Little Words*, *Ring Dem Bells*, and *Old Man Blues*. This was the era of Irving Mills and he was pretty sharp. He'd go along with anything that stood a chance on records. In fact, he even used to sing with our band. Around this time, some of the things on records became pretty big, which resulted in a new style for the band. When Duke first started writing for the baritone, I wanted to impress everyone with the idea that the baritone was necessary, and I very much wanted to remain a part of that sax section. There was so much competition in our reed section that I had to work hard. I liked the band and was always afraid of being fired! That was one school I enjoyed and didn't want to be expelled from.

"The Missourians had been using a baritone sax when we followed them into the Cotton Club. Even in bands with two altos and two tenors, there was always someone who could double on baritone. Sax sections were also using clarinets and sopranos, usually in trios. The baritone was usually a double until five-piece reed sections became the normal thing, and mostly it was an alto player who doubled. The sound of sax sections was very light at the beginning of the '30s. The lead was usually a big-toned alto, and the other saxes more or less stayed under him. He would have good phrasing and expression—the big sound. I think the George 'Fathead' Thomas style of alto playing had a lot to do with the McKinney's sound, but when Don Redman joined that band his was a strong influence. Otto Hardwick played lead for Duke until I joined. He came back when we went into the Cotton Club, and I went from first alto to third alto.

"Lunceford used to feature his sax section more as a section than Duke did. Willie Smith was largely responsible for the sound of the Lunceford reeds and on records they had more presence than ours, but I don't believe they had the power of Ellington's. We only played against them once, in Philadelphia, as I recall. It was a very interesting battle. There had been much controversy about the respective merits of the two bands, but on this occasion I'm happy to say the Ellington band came off the better. Lunceford featured growling trumpets, a varied program of music, and he was very entertaining. He played quite a few of Duke's numbers, and he would come up with versions of some of Duke's record hits, like *Rose Room*. They did some marvelous things on records and I think I was always among the first to buy their new releases. Jock Carruthers was a very good man on baritone, and then there were Willie Smith on alto and Joe Thomas on tenor.

"We always said in the battling days that Chick Webb's was the greatest battling band, and when Charlie Buchanan was at the Savoy he always saw to it that every new band hitting town battled with Chick Webb. Chick was a very competitive musician and he liked to battle. He would always prepare for a battle with a lot of new arrangements and rehearsals.

"But my band was Fletcher Henderson's. I can remember times when we battled with it in its prime and came away dejected. We battled with Smack several times at the Savoy, but one night in Detroit I'll never forget. They played numbers in which Coleman Hawkins was heavily featured, and Hawkins cut the whole Ellington band by himself. Then there was the Charlie Johnson band that used to play down in Smalls' Paradise. There was a wealth of good musicians in that band—Benny Carter, Jimmie Harrison, Jabbo Smith, and a wonderful drummer, George Stafford. There were really some bands around in those days.

"The first time we had five saxes was on the record date when we made *Truckin'*, a dance that was then very popular. Ben Webster did a solo on that number that became a classic. It was a good sound, an additional voice, and his tone and approach were so good on both ballads and up-tempo things that he was a sensation. Ben's interpretations were inspiring to Duke, and he brought new life to a section that had been together a long time. Ben was inspired and he inspired us, so that we worked together and tried to improve the section. We used to rehearse all alone, just the sax section.

"When you look back, you can see that from the late '20s onwards, every time there was an addition to the band, the new instrumentalist seemed to give Duke new ideas and something to draw from and add in his writing. In the '30s there were Ivie Anderson and Lawrence Brown. Those in the band who thought they were playing well tried a little harder and did better. Jimmy Blanton and Ben Webster were additional sparks and the tone structure of the band changed a bit. Everyone seemed to think the band was at its best then, but it was still playing well when we were at the Hurricane and the Zanzibar in '44 and '46. Later, guys like Willie Smith, Louis Bellson, and Clark Terry gave Duke something else to think about.

"Another big lift to us was when we first went to England in 1933, to play the London Palladium. That, we thought, was just about the greatest engagement a band could have. To start off with, we were greeted by so many people who knew so much about the band that we were amazed. We couldn't understand how people in

Europe, who heard us only through the medium of records, could know so much about us. They'd ask us who took which solo on this or that tune, and we had to sharpen up so that we could answer halfway intelligently. Another thing was that they knew exactly what they wanted to hear—a great and very pleasant surprise to us.

"Since those days, the baritone has come into its own. There were many fine players who were often confined to section roles. Besides Lunceford's Carruthers, there was Jack Washington with Basie. Omer Simeon played in the Earl Hines band that I enjoyed so much at the Grand Terrace around 1940. It was very thrilling and exciting. There was Haywood Henry with Erskine Hawkins, and Haywood's my man. I used to listen to Ozzie Nelson's band on the radio all the time, for a very good baritone player who took the hot solos—Charlie Biwak. I mustn't forget that fine musician, Ernie Caceres, or Nick Brignola, whom I heard down at the Bohemia in '58. I just got through listening to Gerry Mulligan a night or so ago, and he really thrilled me. I like Pepper Adams very much, and I can remember his mother bringing him to hear us whenever we played Rochester, New York, and he'd stand down front there all night long. I got a big kick out of hearing him do so well. I never heard him, but I was told Coleman Hawkins played fabulous baritone, and I imagine he would do a wonderful job. I've been told he plays great piano, but

Ellington and Harry Carney

I've never heard that either. Charlie Shavers and Ben Webster are both said to play wonderful piano, too. For that matter, I don't know why Paul Gonsalves is so shy about playing guitar, because he is marvelous. I was always after Johnny Hodges to continue to play soprano, but for some reason he just put the horn down. He really is *the* soprano player. When he says it's a hard instrument it's because there's a certain way he wants to play it, and he won't be satisfied with less."

"After riding on the bus for so long, and having to stop and go when someone gave the word, I decided if I had a car I might have a little more freedom. I was tired of being cooped up in a bus with nothing to do but read, and the vibration of the bus made reading a strain on my eyes. Stage lighting doesn't do your eyes any good, either; and the lights in movies used to be even worse. I've always been car crazy, so in 1949 I got a car.

"At first, it was my intention to make short hops in and around New York, and in the Eastern area. Then I found I was enjoying it so much, and Duke was riding with me almost every day. That was how it started, until I found I was jumping all over the country. I drove out to Vegas last year. I left New York Sunday night and we were opening Wednesday night. Everybody was saying it couldn't be

Barney Bigard

The original "Mood Indigo" trio: Joe Nanton, Artie Whetsol and Barney Bigard

done, but I made it. Of course, if the weather was bad or if there was a big snow, I'd leave the car here rather than risk being unable to make a night.

"On most hops, I manage to get into a hotel around noon. We leave after the job and we like to go two hundred miles at least without stopping. Duke always says, 'Let's get some miles under our belt before we stop.' He calls himself 'The World's Greatest Navigator,' and he does have a wonderful knowledge of route and road numbers. He remembers them. Our greatest problem is arriving in a town for some private affair that isn't advertised. We pull into a gas station and ask, 'Where's the Duke Ellington band playing?' As a rule, nobody knows. A lot of times we've had to call the newspapers; others, we've just had to keep on inquiring from policemen and gas stations.

"When we get into the Mid-West, the average hop is about four hundred miles. Sometimes we may go two hundred and fifty, at other times five or six hundred. Duke sleeps occasionally, but not as a rule. He's a very good man to have along. He sits in the front and he does a lot of thinking. He'll pull out a piece of paper and make notes. We do very little talking, but if he thinks I'm getting weary he'll make conversation so that I don't fall asleep.

"The thing we enjoy most, after leaving a job, is breakfast and the thought of it. We may both be hungry, but still it's necessary to put this first two hundred miles under our belt. When we go in for breakfast, we look forward to a good meal. It gives me energy. We know most of the good eating spots that are open that time of morning. The challenge is always when we hit bad weather. If we make it through, we feel we've accomplished something.

"When we check into a hotel, I go to bed until about 6:30. Most of the jobs run from 9 to 1 A.M. The time we're on the stand is only a small part of it. When we play a concert that lasts only two hours, and we're staying in the town, I hate to finish a job and go straight to bed. I usually stay out to two or three in the morning. It's curious how when we play more than a week in one place a kind of boredom sets in. That's one thing about traveling: it always gives you something to look forward to, even if it's no more than going to another town to see the people there you know.

"We were in Vegas for twelve weeks and we worked until four in the morning. There's just one thing you must do there if you have, shall we say, the urge to speculate. You go around to the places where the musicians and entertainers congregate, and talk, and maybe try a few dollars, and watch other people gambling, and before you know it it's daybreak and the signal for us to go to bed.

"Most of us would sleep until maybe three in the afternoon, but there's plenty to do in Vegas. There are wonderful golf courses, a beautiful lake, mountains, and scenery. I used to play golf with Jimmy Mundy, and I liked the game so much I guess I overdid it, and I'd be tired when I was going to work. Another thing that was a kick: on our night off (Monday) I'd drive to Los Angeles. It was about three hundred miles. I'd leave after we got through at the Riviera and get to L.A. about nine in the morning. I'd visit with friends and do a little shopping. Often, I'd take my baritone to the repair shop. Because of the dryness of the air in Vegas, I had quite a bit of trouble with the pads shrinking. It's a desert area, after all, and extremely hot and dry, but every place is air conditioned and quite unlike those we played in in the early days. Then, during the summer, when there was no air conditioning, they had to throw open the windows because it was so hot and smoky, and people and kids would stand around in the street outside listening.

"At the Riviera, like most of the places out there, entertainment is not expensive, but to get to it you have to pass through the gambling rooms, and there's no other way in or out. In the room we played, there was no cover charge and no minimum. It would hold, I guess, about three hundred people. There were two bars and a lot of people would come in, buy drinks, and just stand at the bar. We were a kind of bait to draw people into the casino. Anyone who doesn't gamble can go out there and have better entertainment, more of it, and more reasonably, than in any other city of the U.S. You get all kinds of people out there. Girls go out as office workers just to see the city, but most of the business comes from Los Angeles and Texas, and from people in the East who want to gamble. The city has spread out a lot since we first went there. There's a big shopping center downtown, and from there you drive out a little way to what is known as the Strip, where all the fabulous hotels, nightclubs, and casinos are located, the casinos being in the hotels. It's healthy. You rarely find anyone with a cold out there. Except the financial kind, that is."

[*1961*]

Barney Bigard [*clarinet*]

Born in New Orleans on March 3rd, 1906, Barney Bigard had an uncle (Emile) who played violin, a brother (Alec) who played drums, and a cousin (Natty Dominique) who played cornet, yet before embarking on a professional career as a musician he had become proficient in a couple of trades—cigar-rolling and photoengraving. Eventually, the excitement of the music he heard at picnics and dances, and on parades, proved too strong, and he began to put to use the tuition he had previously received from Lorenzo Tio, Jr.

"Lorenzo and his uncle taught me almost all the rudiments of clarinet," Bigard recalled. "The whole family played clarinets—the great-grandfather, the grandfather, an uncle, and a nephew. They were straightforward people and very nice. If a guy came to take lessons from them, and they didn't see any possibilities in him, they'd tell him right off, 'Don't waste your time and money. Try something else.'

"The clarinet is a hard instrument. It's supposed to be the daddy of the wind instruments, just like the fiddle is king of the strings. I started with the Albert system and still play it. You get a bigger sound on account of the bore. The fingering is a little farther apart than on the Boehm system. Boehm is easier for sax players, and that's why it was built. But I can do a lot with my horn that they can't do on Boehm, and as long as I can execute, I see no reason to change. The woody tone that Duke likes was a New Orleans specialty, and it owed a lot to the Tios and Alphonse Picou, the guy who played *High Society*. They were the famous clarinetists in those days."

Bigard used to substitute for an older man named Big Eye Nelson, but one day, when he heard his clarinet playing disparaged by other musicians, he decided to change instruments, and shortly afterwards made his debut at Tom Anderson's Cabaret on the then relatively uncommon tenor saxophone. The group was led by Albert Nicholas, a young man who was also to become famous as a clarinetist, and Bigard was soon recognized, in his own description, as "the slappingest and poppingest sax man in all New Orleans."

In December, 1924, Joe "King" Oliver called both Nicholas and Bigard to join him at the Plantation Club in Chicago, where his band enjoyed a long run. When Nicholas and the other clarinetist, Darnell Howard, decided to go to China, Oliver remembered that Bigard had once played clarinet.

"At first, I had been crazy about sax, because I used to slap-tongue a lot," Bigard remembered with a chuckle. "I had the offer to go to China first, but I didn't want to go, and Nick told the guy he would play tenor. I had been playing soprano sax as well as tenor for about three years, because the way they wrote then you had to change from tenor to play clarinet, and I could play the clarinet part on soprano.

" 'Say, didn't you play clarinet before?' Oliver asked me one day.

" 'Yes, but I was so sad I thought I'd use soprano instead. All I could do on clarinet was read. I couldn't improvise.'

" 'If I buy you a clarinet, will you study it?' Oliver said.

"What could I lose? He got me the clarinet, and I started playing around with it, and I discovered a little trick to playing it: if you're in A flat, in the upper register, with your finger down below, you could be in E flat. Then I began to listen to Jimmie Noone, Sidney Bechet, and all the good guys around there. I'd steal something from them, but so it wouldn't be too noticeable, I'd add something of my own. I liked to put little extras in there, and to play with a feeling, and I have always tried to play as good as I possibly can. I used to get the records and fool around. I learned a lot, and I began to improvise, and it all came out from there. I started to like the clarinet so much that I didn't want to play sax anymore.

"King Oliver was past his best then. He had pyorrhea so bad that when he put his mouthpiece to his lips he didn't have any control. It bent his teeth back in. The majority of the nights he couldn't play, but *some* nights he could play like mad. When he felt good, he played like the old King, but I had come in at the tail end of the Oliver era. Even so, when he played the Savoy, he nearly ran Chick Webb out, and Chick had the house band. Joe could have had that job, but he wanted more money. They wanted him to stay, but he went to Baltimore and got stranded.

"I remember the time in Chicago when Johnny Dunn came by to cut Louis Armstrong. Joe had brought Louis from New Orleans, and Johnny, who had got a big reputation in the Mamie Smith days, had heard a lot about him. Louis was playing second, and he and Joe fitted so well that they would play the most perfect duets you would ever hear. Where there was a break for the trumpet player, Joe would play it about eight bars ahead, so Louis would have it figured out before he got to it. All the musicians, even the white boys, used to come around to hear them. They couldn't understand how Louis did what he did. This night, Johnny Dunn came in with a gal and wanted to show off. So he got on the stand, but all he could do was ta-ta-ta-ta-ta (very fast). A lot of people applauded, so Joe told Louis, 'Go get him!' That's when Louis came out. He played so much trumpet that when they looked for Johnny they couldn't find him. He was gone! Everybody was laughing. It broke up the house.

"Another guy I remember seeing when I first went to Chicago was Freddie Keppard. That was a man. He could hit a note so soft— he had a beautiful tone—and then bring it out and shake up the whole building. His reputation was really deserved. When he was playing with Jimmie Noone at Paddy Harmon's Dreamland ballroom, he'd have a fifth of gin and a pitcher of water on the side. He'd drink all that up before the job was over, and then go to an after-hours place and do the same thing again.

83

"I left Oliver because he wasn't getting any work. I hung around New York, and I use to jam at a place called Mexico's. Wellman Braud, a bassist from my hometown, knew I was around and came there. He told me Duke was going in the Cotton Club and wanted another clarinet player. I had progressed quite a bit by then, and, although I only used to read the parts on tenor, I had a lot of ideas on clarinet.

"I joined the band at the Cotton Club. Duke had to augment to ten pieces, and that's how I got in. First of all, he had only three saxes —Toby [Hardwick], Harry [Carney], and myself. Then he got Johnny Hodges in there. Before Tizol came in, he had another guy from Washington—Harry White—on trombone.

"In the early years with Duke, he'd hand me the part before recording dates, and we'd rehearse it. When I had to make a break on clarinet, I'd practice that at home, but when we got to the studio I'd sometimes find I couldn't play it. So I said, 'Phooey on that—I'm just going to do something there.' Luckily, it came out all right, so I decided not to go to all that trouble in front. One thing led to another like that, and I just kept going. The more you do, the easier it becomes, and you don't worry so much. But those mikes will scare you! You think, 'Am I playing too loud?' or 'Am I playing too soft?'

"I remember the time Juan Tizol had to make a break, and he made the darnedest break you ever heard in your life, but he stopped and said, 'That's no good.' Duke said, 'What did you do that for? That's the greatest thing you've ever done!' Tizol was funny. He was not really an improviser, but right from the beginning he was a terrific musician. He used to come and sit in the sax section and play, and all that sort of business."

Bigard's name appears as a collaborator on many Ellington compositions besides *Mood Indigo*. *Saturday Night Function*, *Ducky Wucky*, *Clarinet Lament*, *Clouds in My heart*, *Lament for a Lost Love*, *I'm Checkin' Out*, *Goom-bye*, *Honey Hush*, *Barney Goin' Easy*, and *Mardi Gras Madness* are some of them.

"At first, just after I joined Duke," he explained, "I used to think everything was wrong, because he wrote so weird. It took me some time to get used to hearing all these things. He would make the chords all the wrong way, giving to someone else the part he should have given the clarinet player. When he wrote a tune, he'd write the theme, and then leave it open where he wanted you to take a solo. He'd just write, 'eight-bar solo,' and you'd have to figure out something to play that would fit. It was good, and it gave me a lot of experience. And Duke was smart. He still is! When I played a solo, or Johnny Hodges played a solo, he'd be listening, and if you made a passage that he liked, he'd write it down and build a tune on it.

"You know the record, *Daybreak Express?* Well, when we were in the South, we'd travel by train in two Pullmans and a baggage car. Duke would lie there resting, and listening to the trains. Those southern engineers could pull a whistle like nobody's business. He would hear how the train clattered over the crossings, and he'd get up and listen to the engine. He'd listen as it pulled out of a station, huffing and puffing, and he'd start building from there. Then, for when it was really rolling, he'd put something that Bechet played into the song. He had the whistles down perfectly, too. He's quite a man!

"All composers borrow from one another. That's nothing new, so long as they don't go too far. Over eight bars of anybody else's song, and there's likely to be trouble. You take *Moonglow.* That was taken from *Lazy Rhapsody*, and I believe Mills arranged a big settlement with Duke over that.

"But we all gave ideas in the early days. I contributed part of the melody on *Clarinet Lament*, and then Duke helped out, adding what I couldn't think of right. 'How do you like this?' he would say, or, 'How do you like that?' And that was fair enough."

Bigard was with Ellington fourteen years. His closest friends seem to have been Wellman Braud and Johnny Hodges, and he was responsible for getting the latter in the band. According to Ellington, the alternative at that time was Buster Bailey, the reigning clarinet virtuoso, with whom Bigard could foresee undesirable competition for the clarinet solos. "Get that little ol' young boy from Boston!" was Bigard's worldly wise advice. Hodges, in turn, had to fight to get Cootie Williams in the band.

"They had been good buddies in Chick Webb's band," Bigard continued, "and when Arthur Whetsol left, Duke needed another first-chair trumpet. So Johnny talked to him and finally got Cootie in. Johnny played soprano and not clarinet then. He could really play soprano, too. He was a student of Bechet's, just like this Bob Wilber that I heard out here at Disneyland with the World's Greatest Jazz Band. Truthfully, if you're going to play Dixieland, you don't need any arrangements. It should be played from the head, the way it used to be. Wilbur DeParis had a good band, but he played too much from the music, and that takes something away from it.

"I remember when, late at night, maybe an hour before closing time, Duke would say, 'Just play anything,' and everybody would ad lib. *Ol' Man River* was just getting popular, and Bubber Miley wanted to play that. He started out, and his tone was so bad—'cause it was just straight tone—that he wanted another chorus. So he took the plunger and started growling that thing. It was a different *Ol' Man River* altogether, and Duke had to make an arrangement of it.

"Bubber used to get his ideas from those Holy Roller churches, where they sing, and everybody's clapping hands, and passing out. Joe Oliver was the king on that plunger mute, and Bubber got his idea for using it from him, although he had a style of his own different from Oliver's. Joe Smith's was another, and sweeter.

"King Oliver just used the plunger. He never did use the mute with it as Duke's guys did later. This Paddy Harmon who had the ballroom in Chicago came where we were playing one night and saw Oliver using his plunger. So he designed the little silver mute with the thing in the middle for the guys to work with their fingers and wa-wa. He designed that for Oliver, and I think he made quite a bit of money from it. And although he didn't have to, he gave part of that money to Joe.

"When I joined Duke, I'd never heard Tricky Sam [Nanton] play. The first night, he was sitting there holding his horn down, and everybody else was taking solos. 'Duke, the man wants to play *something*,' Toby Hardwick said. 'Turn him loose. Let him go!' So Duke told Tricky, 'You take it!' and he grabbed his plunger. He could use that thing, too. It talked to you. I was sitting there, looking up at him, and every time he'd say 'wa-wa,' I was saying 'wa-wa' with my mouth, following him all the way through. I used to get a bang out of him. Nobody has ever taken his place. The nearest guy I ever heard was Tyree Glenn, but his tone is too good, too pretty.

"Bubber and Tricky used to hang out together. At that time, Duke's band was respected because it was so neat. We all had nice outfits, and even Bubber and Toby wouldn't drink to excess so that the customers would notice it. When the job was over, Bubber and Tricky would get sloppy drunk on the way home. In those days, we used to wear dickies, and they'd get theirs all dirty, so they bought a great big eraser to clean the stains off their dickies. When they got too dirty, they'd go and steal one of Henry Wessel's. He was an exotic dancer in the show, and he was always immaculate every night.

"We used to have trouble with Toby Hardwick. Some nights he'd show up, and some nights he wouldn't. It baffled me. He and Bubber were mainstays of the band, and when one or the other of them was out, it was always when important people were coming to the club to hear the band. So I got tired of it, and I said, 'Toby, I want to go out with you after we finish one night. I want to see what you do.' So this one time I went out with him. He'd go to a bar and have a drink. Then he'd say, 'Come on, I'll show you a dame.' He was making the rounds of all the women he knew who were up. We had more and more drinks, and by ten or eleven next morning I was stoned. The kids in the band were worried that night, wondering where I was. Finally, I came straggling in, but I'd found out what Toby was doing all the time. Bubber used to do it, too, and Mexico's was one of the favorite places where they used to hang out. Some of the Cotton Club girls would be down there.

"Toby wasn't an improvising musician, but he played some beautiful things. He was a melody boy. He used to have all the first parts, because Johnny Hodges couldn't read so well at that time. Johnny could blow like hell though. He was a natural musician. My two favorites on alto were he and Benny Carter."

Mention of Hardwick brought back memories of many pranks in which he was involved. Bigard continued:

"When Duke got to the Cotton Club, there was a prima donna there named Ada Ward. The band we followed had been going with the showgirls and this prima donna. They were sorry to see the other band go, and they made up their minds to make it miserable for us when we went in there. So during rehearsals, they'd made it hard for us. Duke had hired a fiddle player for some numbers, and after we'd played a fanfare, he played an obbligato behind this prima donna. On opening night, Toby took his bow and rubbed soap all over it, so when he started to play there was not a sound coming out of the fiddle as the girl warbled away. She came off the stage crying, and the owner of the place told her, 'I told you not to fool with them boys.' From then on, she was nice as pie.

"Toby played another prank on Freddy Jenkins. Like a lot of trumpet players, Freddy had a habit of licking his mouthpiece when he first took it out. Toby got some Limburger cheese and cayenne pepper and dipped his mouthpiece in it. When Freddy took up his horn to play, he nearly hit the ceiling.

"Another night, somebody put a toothpick under one of my pads, so when I went to solo—nothing! And I made one big mistake. Wellman Braud, bless his soul, used to try to play tuba, and I used to sit right in front of him. They took a bucket of water and put it in his tuba one night. When he switched from bass to tuba—all over my head, water! That broke up the place!

"Tizol was another mischievous one. We were playing in Philadelphia, and the stage was so small that the backdrop was just about a foot from the wall. They had klieg lights at that time, and we were boiling up on the stage. Tizol had bought some stinkbombs, and he broke one off when Artie Whetsol, Tricky, and I were out front playing *Mood Indigo*. The fumes started coming from the back. 'C'mon, man,' I said to Whetsol, under my breath, 'you must be crazy.' Tricky got mad, and then it got to the front row of the people and they started laughing. Duke was laughing, too, and I just walked off the stage. 'You should be ashamed of yourself,' I said as I passed Johnny Hodges, and he got mad.

"That was Tizol. We found out he got it from a little shop around the corner, and Johnny and I went there and got itching powder. When he went out to eat between shows, Johnny and I put this itching powder around the shoulders and armpits of his uniform. He came back for the show and put this jacket on, and when the lights hit him he was in trouble. He was really mad, and called everybody every kind of name. He played *his* jokes, but he didn't like this one."

The gangster era has always been the source of many humorous (in retrospect) anecdotes within the jazz profession. A couple that Bigard remembered were quite typical.

"A famous gangster, a dangerous man, was just out after a stretch in prison," he said. "He came to the Cotton Club and requested *Singin' in the Rain.* Somehow, Duke overlooked it, so then Herman Stark, the manager, came and explained to him who the man was. Do you know we played *Singin' in the Rain* for just about an hour after that?

"When we were in Chicago, there was a lot of talk about gangsters were going to kidnap Duke and Bojangles Robinson. So Owney Madden called Al Capone from New York. When the kidnaping party arrived, three of Al's men stepped out from behind pillars with drawn guns.

" 'Where you fellows going?'

" 'To see our friend.'

" 'What friend?'

" 'The Duke.'

" 'Since when has he been a friend of yours? Get the hell out of here!'

"That was the end of the threats."

Although Bigard's style is immediately recognizable as belonging to the New Orleans tradition, it is extremely individual. His supple phrasing and beautiful tone, particularly in the lower register, are at the service of a strong personality. Among his favorite performances with Ellington are *Clarinet Lament, Barney Goin' Easy,* and *Across the Tracks Blues.* In view of their stylistic differences, his choice of Artie Shaw as his favorite clarinetist is rather surprising.

"What Shaw did to begin with," he explained, "was to make the clarinet sound unusually beautiful in the upper register. He wasn't a low-register guy, but he was more creative than Benny Goodman. Benny did all popular tunes and standards, but Artie made up his own and played them so well. The guy could execute like mad. Benny could also execute, and had much more drive than Artie, but I like Artie for the things that are almost impossible to do on the clarinet.

"I thought Buster Bailey was one of the fastest clarinetists there ever was. He had his own style, and I could always tell his playing.

88

He was a good musician with good execution, but he didn't have a jazz drive, or the soul in there like Goodman and some other guys. In other words, it didn't have the *oomph* to it. Where Buster was great was in a studio or a show. That's the same way I figure with Jimmy Hamilton. He's a terrific clarinetist, but he doesn't have that soul to go with what he's doing. He should have been in classical music. He's got that studio tone to begin with, and he plays straight and fluent, but it's not jazz.

"Omer Simeon was a fine musician, an unsung hero, and a great clarinet player. I tried to get him in Duke's band, but his wife dominated him and decided she wanted to live in Chicago. He went back there and was with Earl Hines and, later, Jimmie Lunceford. When we went on the road, he and his wife came to a dance we played in Chicago. 'Now kick me,' she said. 'I need to be kicked for not letting him go in that band.'

"Duke was very fortunate. We never had hard times during the Depression. Where the other bands were struggling to get a job, we were working every night. One thing about Duke: when we came on the air, everybody knew it was Duke's band, as they still do today. It was funny, though, how everybody in it had his own individual style. And Duke was smart about that, too. Say he was going to build a number around me. He always studied a person's style, to make it comfortable for him to play. He knew the guy's limitations and his exceptional qualities. Most of the other bands had outside arrangers, and the leader would say, 'Make me an arrangement on *Stardust*,' or some such number. The arranger would write it the way he wanted it, and he would probably write a part the soloist would not be comfortable with. But Duke studied all this—the capacity of what each man could do.

"The band that came closest to Duke's as competition was Lunceford's. It was a very good band. We had a contest one time in Philadelphia I'll never forget. Lunceford and Duke were in their heyday, and Lunceford's guys had been running up and down Seventh Avenue telling everybody, 'We got 'em now! We gonna cut 'em!'

"Lunceford went on first that night, and they played all Duke's numbers that they could, and, oh, boy, were they happy! Willie Smith played my *Rose Room*. 'What're you doing, Willie?' I asked him. We were both laughing. So Duke is a funny character. He's going to play all slow tunes with no bounce to them, until Cootie Williams got angry. 'For crying out loud, Duke, play something!' he said. 'We got to get with this thing!' So Duke finally opened up—*St. Louis Blues, Tiger Rag*, and that was it! Lunceford and his guys were standing over by the window, and Sy Oliver, the arranger, came over and said, 'I didn't think much of you guys before, but I take everything back. Have mercy on us!'

"Basie's band has a style of its own, and he had the best rhythm section I ever heard. Lunceford had a good rhythm section, too, and the only thing I didn't like was that trumpet player who used to try to blow those high notes. Willie Smith was a very good leader on the saxophone. Marshall Royal, who's with Basie now, reminds me of him. He's another good first man."

Bigard remembers his years with Ellington with such satisfaction that it is a little surprising he ever left. Asked why he did, he replied: "Well, you remember I told you how we traveled in our own Pullman cars. When World War II started, we couldn't get them any more. We often couldn't get a seat when we got on a train, and a lot of times you had to sit in the vestibule on your horn, or something like that. 'The devil with it,' I said. 'I'm going to get away from this.' So I came out to California and worked for Billy Berg for a while. Then I played the studios, where I doubled on tenor. You've got to play a couple of instruments at least there. Some guys play three or four. I made good money without a lot of hassles, but it was sterile work. After that, I worked two years with Freddie Slack, bless his soul! *Every* month we had a picture to do, and then Saturdays, when we didn't work the studios, we'd go and play a dance."

In 1946, Bigard joined Louis Armstrong's All-Stars, and was thereby returned to the New Orleans context in which he had begun his musical career.

"I made the longest one-nighter in my life with Louis," he recalled, "from Sydney, Australia, to Calgary, Canada. Not only did we cross the dateline, but the difference in weather was something! They were wearing parkas up there. A lot of people think traveling is fun, but after we'd finished playing a concert, there'd be people waiting for autographs, and then we'd try to get something to eat. We might have to get up at four or five next morning to catch a plane to another city. When you're doing this constantly, you get so you don't know where you're at. When you fly, it nearly always involves about five hours besides the flying time. You could at least lie around and sleep in the hotel until it was time to leave when you traveled by bus."

Since 1960, Bigard has lived and worked mostly in California, practicing every day for forty-five minutes, and often playing at weekends with small groups. At the decade's end, he seemed content in his comfortable home, but he wanted to record again.

"I'd like to make some numbers with strings, piano, and a soft drum," he said. "I've got three or four tunes ready right now. There are plenty of good guitar players out here I could use. One number

90

I've always wanted to record is *Where or When?*, and I never did make *Mood Indigo* with strings. I'd like Benny Carter to do the writing. He's quite a musician, and plays good clarinet, too."

[*1969*]

Johnny Hodges [*alto saxophone*]

Back to back or side by side, Duke Ellington and Johnny Hodges form a duo which, in terms of sustained jazz artistry, has never been rivaled.

"Johnny Hodges," Ellington said, "has complete independence of expression. He says what he wants to say on the horn, and that is *it*. He says it in *his* language, which is specific, and you could say that his is pure artistry. He's the only man I know who can pick up a cold horn and play in tune without tuning up. And I've heard plenty of cats who can't play in tune if they tune up all day."

His qualities have been similarly emphasized by other associates. "Rab's a pure jazzman," said Russell Procope, who plays alto saxophone alongside him and is another veteran of the big bands. "Above all," observed Clark Terry, "he's always been true to himself." The late John Coltrane, who once worked for Hodges, said years later, "He still kills me!" Paul Gonsalves, another section mate, was more explicit: "He is, in my opinion, the top alto of jazz. He has done so much, and he has remained himself all along. I wouldn't expect a pioneer like him to change just to be fashionable, but the fact is his style has that basic, earthy quality which really endures. As one of the mainstays of the Ellington band, he contributes greatly in the section as well as in his solos. He has a wonderful sense of rhythm, an exceptional feeling for the blues, and a rich, romantic way with numbers like *Passion Flower*, a way that is all his own. Besides the earthiness of his playing, there is also a professional sophistication, but when he really feels like blowing he stirs us all." Another perceptive comment came from an unlikely source, Lawrence Welk. "He plays from the heart rather than from the notes," he said. "Besides everything else, he plays the prettiest saxophone of anyone I know."

Hodges was opening up the box of orchestrations that lay on the piano.

"Too much music," he muttered. "The best record sessions are those where you go for yourself. The one I made out on the Coast with Booty [Wood], Lawrence [Brown], and Ben Webster—we had no music."

But this date was to turn out well, too. It was the first for a Verve album to be called *Hodges by Hodges*, and it was made up of new numbers he had recently composed.

"I get a whole lot of ideas when we're recording," he said. "I don't know why it is. If I had plenty of time to sit down and try, I couldn't think of them."

They were making another take of *The Hare*, a rocking blues— "the kind Norman [Granz] likes." There were six horns besides Hodges—Ray Nance, Shorty Baker, Lawrence Brown, Booty Wood, Jimmy Hamilton, and Harold Ashby—and pretty well everyone was getting to solo. He had suddenly decided that he would like a riff behind his own second chorus, and he was twisting between chairs, microphones, and musicians to whisper in the appropriate ears. He arrived back in position a split second before his solo was due to begin, but the first notes came out as serenely poised as ever. Feet spread wide apart, left toe and right heel marking the time, he was immediately swinging with his smooth phraseology, and then building to a climax through accentuations and intensity of tone.

The next night they made *Wiggle Awhile*, *Twinkle*, *Hygiene*, and *The Peaches Are Better Down the Road*.

"Where do you get titles like that last one?"

"Well, it's like *Things Ain't What They Used to Be*," he answered dryly, "the kind of saying I hear people use. Like if you ask waiters in these clubs how they're feeling, and they have real tired feet, they'll say, 'The peaches are better down the road.'"

Maybe the continuing *naturalness* of his music derives from the fact that fame and years of traveling haven't separated Hodges from his roots. That was most apparent in Boston, his hometown, a few weeks later. He was as eloquent on the subject of a new school, the apothecaries' stores, and ancient tombstones as he normally is in New York about his favorite baseball team. Around three o'clock one morning, he encountered in a pharmacy some of his old boyhood pals ("we used to run through the alleys together"), and they began to bait Tom Whaley, his and their senior by several years. Whaley's musical career also began in Boston, and he could remember Hodges playing with him at the Avery Hotel, but Hodges would take no part in the argument that ensued. Enjoying every second of it, he was lolling back against the counter, apparently much more concerned with the nickel's worth of peanuts in his hand.

On stage or stand, Hodges customarily wears a cold, immobile

countenance. It is at curious variance both with his music and the quick, warming, boyish smile that momentarily surprises in conversation. Sardonic comments, issued from the side of his mouth, are obviously not for the audience. Sometimes the microphone picks one up, addressed, say, to an overzealous colleague in the back row:

"I've been playing this for thirty years, man, and I don't need that kind of help."

His big sound can dominate the saxophone section, and as its physical center he will turn briefly to left or right to correct the phrasing or better the blend. Unseen out front, he will occasionally "conduct" new members of the trombone section with one hand behind his chair. When it is his turn for solos, he advances on the microphone with seeming reluctance, sometimes casting reproachful glances in the direction of the pianist.

"Nobody knows," Shorty Baker once said, "what Johnny Hodges feels inside when he walks out to the mike. He may look as though he's on his last walk to the gallows, but he appreciates the applause and he thanks the audience with a million dollars' worth of melody!"

Repetitition is a penalty of lasting success. Certain numbers that have become closely associated with him are requested over and over again.

"I used to like *On the Sunny Side of the Street* a whole lot," he confessed, "but after you play it night after night, you get away from it. You find yourself playing the same chorus, and you can't change it. *Warm Valley* is one of my favorite records. I like playing that kind of number—if it has the right backgrounds. *Daydream*, too. When I'm playing that, it's supposed to be very, very soft, and you're supposed to close your eyes and dream a while."

"What other alto players do you especially admire?"

"Oh, Willie Smith. I always did like Willie Smith. And Benny Carter."

"How about trumpet players?"

"Ray Nance, Shorty Baker ... Cootie Williams, he was a powerful man."

"Offhand, now, whom else do you like?"

"I've always liked Hawk [Coleman Hawkins]. Louis Bellson was the end. Then there's Lawrence Brown. And Earl Hines. I enjoy recording with him. Oscar Peterson plays so much you can't get started. He'd play the first two choruses ahead of me, and I'd be so wrapped up listening I'd forget to come in. Erroll Garner knocks me out. I like Eddie Heywood. Duke, of course, and as an accompanist he's *it!* I was listening to *Stompy Jones* this morning, on that *Side by Side* album, and he just got carried away in the last four or five choruses. They look on him now as an arranger and composer, but he's never had enough credit as a pianist. When he wants to, he can really play. He gets a big kick out of playing, but you can never tell how *much* he's going to play.

"Then I always did admire Ben Webster, years back, when he was playing with Blanche Calloway. We went to Boston and played some club, and at that particular time we had four saxes, but Duke had written some song with five saxes and just wanted to see how it sounded. It sounded so good to him he put Ben on, started with five saxes, and we made all those records like *Cottontail*, *All Too Soon*, and *Settin' and a-Rockin'*."

"Younger guys?"

"Paul Gonsalves—he's very beautiful on slow numbers, but I think he's been judged too much on driving things. There's Harold Ashby, and Booty Wood, and Cannonball [Adderley]. I haven't heard that Ornette Coleman yet."

"How about . . .?"

"Young man, I've got to go."

[*1960*]

"Will my bodyguard be ready at seven?"

It was six years later, and Johnny Hodges was preparing for his daily march from the Hotel Dennis to the ballroom at the end of the Steel Pier in Atlantic City, where Duke Ellington's band was playing a week. It may not have been a mile, but it seemed like it this hot, humid evening, because holidaymakers jammed the boardwalk. Although he had been blowing with Wild Bill Davis until nearly daybreak, he looked surprisingly fit as he sauntered along.

"I don't sleep long at a time," he explained. "I gave up cigarettes six years ago, and I haven't had a drink since April 26th, when the doctor said it would be best for me to quit. Now . . . you see that shape?"

A girl was moving down the boardwalk ahead with a provocative, undulating walk. Hodges was silent, but observant.

It was barely eight o'clock when he reached the dressing room behind the ballroom stage. The band didn't hit until eight-thirty, and as he leisurely changed he began to reminisce:

"We were in Antibes this summer, the town where Bechet was married, where they had the parade and everything. They have a square named after him there, and a bust in the park. It's about three feet tall, I'd say, and mounted on a pedestal. They took my picture looking at it, and it brought back some memories. It's kind of odd that it's where it is, but he was very well known and liked in France for years. There isn't anything similar in this country that I know of, but there ought to be.

94

"I met him in Boston, years and years ago, when I was thirteen years old, and he was playing in burlesque, in Jimmy Cooper's *Black and White Show*. I had a lot of nerve when I went backstage to see him, with my little curved soprano wrapped up under my arm, but my sister knew him, and I made myself known.

" 'What's that under your arm?' he asked me.

" 'A soprano.'

" 'Can you play it?'

" 'Sure,' I said, although I had only had it about two days.

" 'Well, play something,' he said.

"So I played *My Honey's Lovin' Arms*.

" 'That's nice,' he said, encouraging me.

"I think sopranos were played more in those days, but I just liked mine because it looked so pretty. Later, I changed to alto, for so many people told me where it fitted in the family of saxophones, although at that time a lot of musicians were playing C-melody, and some bass saxophone, besides the others. I took to alto, but later I ran into Bechet again. I had taken a liking to his playing, and to Louis Armstrong's which I heard on the Clarence Williams Blue Five records, and I just put both of them together, and used a little of whatever I thought of new. I didn't have any tuition and I didn't buy any books. A friend, Abe Strong, came back and showed me the scale just after I bought the horn, and I took it up from there by myself, for my own enjoyment, and had a lot of fun. So far as reading went, I took a lesson here and there, and then experience taught me a lot, sitting beside guys like Otto Hardwick and Barney Bigard. They were very helpful to me.

"Before I got the saxophone, I had played drums, but not professionally. I also played piano, house-hop piano. I used to play house parties for eight dollars a night, and I remember once, when he was in town with a show, that Count Basie sat down and relieved me. Everybody in my family plays a little piano for enjoyment, from my mother right on down to my son and daughter.

"After we had moved from Cambridge to Hammond Street in Boston, there were several other young musicians nearby. Howard Johnson used to live around the corner from me on Shumant Avenue. His was a very musical family. He played saxophone, his brother Bobby played banjo, his mother, his sister, his other brother, and his uncle—they all played piano. Charlie Holmes lived on Tremont Street, and I think he took up saxophone in the high school band. Harry Carney lived just a couple of blocks away on Cunard Street.

"I went back to soprano again when I joined Sidney Bechet [always pronounced *Bashay*—S.D.] at his club, the Club Bechet, on
145th Street and Seventh Avenue in New York. He had another

Ellington and Johnny Hodges

Johnny Hodges

soprano, a straight one, which he gave to me, and he would teach me different things in the duet form. Then I learned all the introductions and solos, and if he was late I would take over until he got there. This was in 1923 or 1924, before I joined either Chick Webb or Duke. Duke used to come to Boston every summer, and he would ask me then to join him.

"Neither the straight nor the curved soprano is easy to play, and both are just as hard to keep in tune, but there is an advantage on the curved one. You can cheat more on it. There are a lot of ways of cheating, though many saxophone players might not approve of them. I think you can get the same tone on the curved one as on the straight, but you've got to practice every day. You can't just pick it up and play one chorus tonight, and then play it again two nights later. You have to be in control of it. There's so much lipping to be done. You have to lip up to get it in tune, and there are a lot of tricks to it. Then you have to practice on the low notes, so it won't sound so foggy—like a foghorn—and speed up the vibrato to make it sound more like an alto.

"I gave it up when Cootie Williams left the band in 1940. The last thing we played was *That's the Blues, Old Man*. There was no definite reason why I gave it up then, but I started having a lot of alto solos to play, and I figured they were responsibility enough. Duke

96

Cootie Williams

had been writing a whole lot of arrangements with soprano on top, and the responsibility of playing lead, and then jumping up and playing solos, too, was a heavy one. So I just laid it away. I know the soprano is popular again, and some day I hope to get mine out. I'd like to get it together, and then make a record.

"Bechet was the first I ever heard do the growl. Growling wasn't anything to do with covering up. I think it was the way they wanted to play. Bechet used to call it 'Goola.' He had a dog by that name, and he used to take it with him, and it would always be somewhere around. 'I'm going to call Goola,' he'd say. That was his way of calling the dog.

"I always did like the growl. As long as I can remember Duke, there's been growling, right back to Bubber Miley. It's a part of jazz. Where Bubber got it from is before my time, but he was about the first growl trumpet I ever heard. Johnny Dunn used to play in a bucket, the kind you'd send kids out with to get you a bucket of beer. That was what he used to hang on his horn, but he wasn't growling so far as I can remember. Bubber was the first I knew to use the mute *and* the plunger. He had a lot of imagination, and he could do more with one note than anyone I ever heard, outside of Tricky Sam [Nanton], and those two were like twins.

"No one has ever come completely up to Tricky in that kind of trombone, but Booty Wood came very close. When Duke got him on it, at first he didn't want to play it, because he figured he couldn't make it, but I told him, 'Just keep on trying. You can't do it in a day.' And he got better all the time."

Before Antibes, the Ellington band had been to Dakar, Senegal, for the first World Festival of Negro Arts. Hodges seemed to have taken Africa in his stride.

"There was the city, of course, and the people," he said. "The drummers were Sam Woodyard's stick, but I've been listening to drummers for years, and I heard a lot when my daughter was dancing in the African Village at the World's Fair. I used to go out there regularly. The Watusis had that terrific rhythm. They'd put those big drums on top of their heads, a hand at one end, and then take the sticks with the other and rattle them. I don't think Sam Woodyard ever heard them, but he'd been doing that rhythm for years. He just fell right in there. Every night he did it, but I don't think more than two or three guys in the band knew what it was.

"It was a funny thing, but when you were out at the Fair and you got within two or three blocks, it was as though those drums would draw you. I was talking to a clarinet player who worked out there with Olatunji, and he was telling me that after you put those drums on top of your head, you could imagine you could hear a whole arrangement with violins, harps, flutes, piccolos, and everything— through the drums and the beat. I guess it's something like when a bass player puts his head down on the strings.

"Hey, it's time for us to blow!"

The night before, there had been a live recording session for RCA Victor at Grace's Little Belmont, a club on North Kentucky Avenue. The room was small, but producer Brad McCuen and engineer Ed Begley had managed to get all the recording equipment into a window alcove. Wild Bill Davis (organ), Dickey Thompson (guitar), Bob Brown (tenor saxophone and flute), and Bobby Durham (drums) normally had minimal working space in the middle of the oval bar, but now Hodges and Lawrence Brown were added to their number and accommodated by a slight extension of the stand into one of the bar gangways.

Although it was very hot, the atmosphere was happy and full of excited anticipation. Across the street, the doors of the Club Harlem were wide open, and the loud sounds of the alternating Willis Jackson and Jimmy Tyler bands were wafted in between numbers. There were numerous jazzmen working the Atlantic City clubs that week, and the Ellington musicians, Duke and Mercer among them, came by to size up the situation. Buster Cooper and Chuck Connors, of the trombone section, were there all the time. "We have to support our leader," Cooper said with a grin, nodding in Lawrence Brown's direction. Paul Gonsalves arrived from another club, where he had been jamming. He listened appreciatively to Hodges. "He's got a heart, believe me," he said, "and he'd give you the shirt off his back, if he knew you needed it."

Lawrence Brown was causing a lot of excitement, too, playing with unusual fire and energy. The word got around among young, local musicians, who soon came in to listen.

"They don't often get a chance to hear trombone playing like that down here," Hodges said, as he sipped a Coke at the bar during intermission. "They nearly all play saxophone, because that's what they hear most of with the organ groups, and they go around like gunfighters trying to cut each other down. You can tell by the way they look that Lawrence got to 'em."

Then everything was shaking on the stand again. Russell Procope was celebrating his birthday, and he, his wife, Cue Hodges, and Buster Cooper were dancing, like a chorus line, in the aisle. Hodges looked down on them with the amused, youthful smile that is so seldom seen on stage. He leaned over, too, to express approval of Bobby Durham's part in the action. "It's a long time since I felt a beat like that," he said. Emmett Berry, the trumpet player, who had come over from across the street, concurred: "He was laying it like Walter Johnson used to do."

The tempo changed as the group went into a standard Hodges had thought of while he walked by the sea from the pier to Little Belmont. "Let's do it again," he called to Brad McCuen. They did it three times, and then it wasn't the famous standard any longer.

"You see what I mean?" Lawrence Brown asked when he came off. "He's been doing that all his life. He gets an idea, thinks up a countermelody, and you end up with a whole new song. Yet nobody seems to recognize him as the composer he is."

Hodges was happy with what had happened. "I think that will be enough for tonight," he said.

Later, having stopped for a nightcap on his way back to the hotel, he looked up from his tea and lemon, and asked, "You remember when Duke went to England with Ray Nance and Kay Davis, in 1948, after his operation? Well, while we were laying off, Russell Procope and I came to Atlantic City with our wives for a little vacation. One night, we decided to go to the Belmont to hear Wild Bill. He invited us to a jam session, so we took our horns and we jammed and jammed, until seven or eight in the morning. Our jamming drew most of the people over from the Club Harlem, and a couple of clubowners from New York heard us. One of them had the Apollo Bar on 125th Street, and when we got back he approached me about getting a little band together. So Billy Strayhorn, Tyree Glenn, Jimmy Hamilton, Sonny Greer, Al Hibbler, and I went in there, and we got very lucky, and started putting 125th Street on the map again. Later on, we added Junior Raglin on bass, and we stayed there for seven weeks, until Duke came back. He got right off the boat and came to the Apollo Bar to find out what was going on, and whether we were going to continue with this little band. But we were loyal, and we broke the band up, and came back.

"That was one result of going to jam at Little Belmont. Another came years later when I started making the Verve series of records with Wild Bill Davis that began with *Blue Hodge* and was followed by *Mess of Blues*, *Blue Rabbit*, *Joe's Blues*, *Wings and Things*, *Blue Pyramid*, and, on Victor, *Con-Soul and Sax*. Bill is very easy to work with. Then I got into something else with Earl Hines when we made *Stride Right* together. We did his *Blues in Thirds* for that album, and he told us Bechet was 'evil' when they had made it a long time before. But they sure made a good one. I first met Earl a long time ago in Chicago, and then I used to go by the Grand Terrace where he was playing. Later, when we were at the Blue Note, he'd come by whenever he was in town."

A few days afterwards, Hodges was into something else again, this time in Rudy Van Gelder's Englewood studio. The band consisted of Snooky Young, Ernie Royal, trumpets; Tony Studd, trombone; Frank Wess, Jerome Richardson, Jimmy Hamilton, Don Ashworth, reeds and woodwinds; Hank Jones, piano; Kenny Burrell, guitar; Bob Cranshaw, bass; and Grady Tate, drums. Jimmy Jones, who had written the arrangements, acted as conductor.

"I tried to give Johnny a new framework," he said, and it was certainly unlike any in which the alto saxophonist had previously been recorded. The musicians quickly grasped the significance of their parts and were soon creating an agreeably smooth ensemble sound, but Jones detected imperfections and began to wrestle with them. Hodges, as soloist, stepped out of the frame and away from the debate.

"That's why," he said, taking off his summer hat, "I still have all my hair!"

When the problems had been ironed out, and a clean take of *Blue Notes* made, he came over to where Tom Whaley was sitting. Whaley is close to Hodges, and his seniority permits him to act as the voice of dissent.

"You ought to record with some gutbucket musicians," he said. This was somewhat unexpected, to say the least, because he never hesitates to declaim against any instance of sloppy playing that may occur on Ellington recording dates.

"There's a difference between 'inside' and 'outside' musicians," Hodges admitted. "Studio musicians play more exact."

They acquitted themselves extremely well on a pretty ballad original he had entitled *Say It Again*, Royal skillfully answering the alto's phrases with plunger-muted trumpet. Whaley, meanwhile, was paying careful attention to Jimmy Jones's writing.

"You know," he said suddenly, "I think I'll go and take one of these modern courses in arranging. There's always something new to learn."

At a following session, the guitarist was Eric Gale, who was perhaps then more famous in the field of rock 'n' roll than of jazz. "He adds a great pulse to what is essentially an updated blues context," said producer Creed Taylor, and this was evident enough on the takes of *L.B. Blues*, a typical Hodges creation. The composer, however, wasn't satisfied with the first performance.

"It's too stiff," he said. "Hold the tempo and bend."

Next they did *I Can't Believe That You're in Love with Me*, another reminder of how Hodges was leisurely working his way through all the most beautiful ballad standards of the jazz repertoire. As featured soloist, he was supremely relaxed, and afterwards there were contented smiles all around. Then it was time for *Broad Walk*, with Royal again using the plunger effectively in a big, shouting climax. The theme had a vaguely Latin flavor.

"Now where did you get that title from?" Whaley asked.

Hodges smiled. "Remember the boardwalk in Atlantic City, young man?"

[*1966*]

Johnny Hodges died on May 11th, 1970, of a heart attack. His health had not been good for some years. He had had warnings, and had been hospitalized on three occasions, yet his will had carried him courageously through recent strenuous tours of Europe, the Far East and Australasia. Whatever he suffered, he kept very much to himself, and right up until his last public performance—at the Royal York Hotel in Toronto—he was playing as well as ever, a gratifying fact in view of the high standards he customarily demanded of himself.

Harry Carney, his near neighbor as a boy on Hammond Street in Boston, and for so long his companion in the reed section, looked back on their years together with affection, admiration and grief. "He was basically a shy person," he said, "and people often misinterpreted his shyness. Even after he got to play a lot of horn, he wouldn't want to go out to the microphone, but would prefer to take his solo

101

sitting down." Carney also revealed the true origin of his nickname. "He used to be crazy about lettuce and tomato sandwiches, and we said he was always chewing them like a rabbit, so he became 'Rabbit' to us."

Duke Ellington also remembered those early years. "He was very unaffected," he said. "Although everybody was crazy about him, he just didn't make anthing of it."

Recognition of Hodges as one of the greatest individual talents in jazz history was worldwide, but so now was the sad realization that the Ellington band had lost its most attractive soloist.

"Because of this great loss," Ellington said, "our band will never sound the same. I am glad and thankful that I had the privilege of presenting Johnny Hodges for forty years, night after night. I imagine I have been much envied. May God bless this beautiful giant in his own identity. God bless Johnny Hodges."

[*1970*]

Cootie Williams [*trumpet*]

"In the beginning, you didn't think about the money," Cootie Williams said, referring to his years with Duke Ellington. "The idea was to have the ability to do something, to suggest something good for the band to play. That was the general feeling. Everyone would pitch in to give. It was exciting and we were young. 'Do it like this, Duke,' we'd say. 'We want it this way, and that.' Everyone made suggestions, it was a family thing."

Occasionally, he conceded, one of the musicians might get peeved. But mostly they had the band's interests at heart, and money had not yet entered into it. That came later, as they became more sophisticated.

"Most musicians today," Williams commented, "have got payday on their minds. And they think, *What is this going to bring me?* So this is something missing right now, where creative things are concerned. Contributions from a number of minds."

Although Williams' eventful career in jazz has had several unusually dramatic peaks, it has been characterized throughout by his steadfast dedication to music. He demands a great deal of himself and of others. He was the youngest of four boys and inherited the musical talents of his mother, a pianist and church organist in Mobile, Alabama. When he was five years old, he began to study music and to play drums. He was allowed to join the school band at seven because he could read. His first instrument was trombone, but he could not cope with the positions since his reach was too short. He was transferred to tuba, and the trumpet was something he managed to pick up on his own.

"They were having band rehearsal," he recalled. "During intermission I got hold of someone's horn and began playing *Twelfth Street Rag* on it. How come I could do that, teacher wanted to know? 'That's your instrument,' he told me then, and from there on it was."

Williams was eight when his mother died in giving birth to twins, of whom only one lived. An aunt came to raise the four boys and his father insisted they persist with their music studies. "I was the only one, though," Williams explained, "who stayed with it, and when I got older, my father handed me to a teacher by the name of Charles Lipskin. He had a cleaning and pressing shop, but he also used to play with the Excelsior band. He was a fine trumpet player. I worked for him, and he would teach me when I wasn't delivering clothes. But I stayed angry with him all the time, because he wouldn't let me play jazz." He grinned.

Since this arrangement lasted eight years, it afforded him an excellent foundation. Although from the start he sneaked off to play jazz, he never got official permission until he had mastered the fundamentals. "And in those days, if you had a teacher, you didn't dare fool," he recalled. "If you hadn't learned your lesson, well, he had a right to plonk you on your head. This didn't bother me, though. I was madly in love with my horn; Dad used to have to take it away to keep me from blowing too much."

One of Williams' earliest experiences was a summer spent with a circus band headed by Lester Young's father, built round the family. They all played saxophone, the mother and sister as well as Lester. The band would come on to a stage out front and ballyhoo. After playing for a while, they would go inside and do the show, using trumpet, trombone, and rhythm as well as saxophones, accompanying singers besides doing their own act.

Williams remembered how excited he had become when his father took him to the carnival. "I *sure* would like to play with them," he'd insisted. His father went back to talk to Mr. Young, and small though he was, his son was given a chance to blow. "They took me," Williams smiled, remembering. "I was only fourteen and my brother had to go, too, my father said. I got fifty cents a day and ate with the family. It lasted a summer and was great."

By the time he was sixteen, he'd played with a number of bands around Mobile, since New Orleans was close enough to allow the better known orchestras to come in for occasional one-nighters. Williams got to hear musicians who impressed him, like trumpeters Sam Morgan and Kid Punch, and clarinetist Edmund Hall who was with the Pensacola Jazz Band. In turn Hall was sufficiently impressed to get Williams a job alongside him when he switched over to Eagle Eye Shields, a pianist with a job in Jacksonville, Florida.

"My father, who ran a gambling house in Mobile, had a partner who lived in Jacksonville," said Williams, explaining how he had been permitted to leave home, "and not until he said I could live with him, could I take the job. Hall and I stayed about a year, and then he and I and Richard Fulbright on bass left and went with Alonzo Ross. He used to play Miami Beach and sometimes broadcast. That was how the owner of the Rosemount Ballroom in Brooklyn heard us." Remembering how the band made it up North, Williams laughed. "We came up by boat, from Savannah, Georgia. I guess no one else ever arrived in New York that way!"

He could not remember how long it took to get there, but what seemed ridiculous even then was that the job was only of two weeks' duration. He made a droll face. "When the time was up—I had to tell them goodbye! Down South I used to listen to Louis Armstrong on the radio playing with Fletcher Henderson from the Roseland. 'Boy,' I used to say to myself, 'if I could only get to New York and hear *him*.'"

"I was lucky, too," Williams went on, "because in time I got to see a lot of Louis. I had the good fortune to stay at bass player Wellman Braud's house and he and Louis were longtime friends from New Orleans. In New York, he would stay with Braud, too, and when the bank played the Savoy, I'd walk backwards and forwards to work with him. I was in my glory. That was 1929 and by then I was with Duke, so I'm getting ahead of myself."

Brought back to the subject of his first week in New York, Williams laughed. "I wasn't nervous," he explained, "because of that right upbringing. I was better at reading then than I am today! It helped me when I went with Fletcher Henderson, too. Fletcher's band played in all hard keys, which you don't do now. Fletcher was very conscious of sound, and he'd think about the brilliancy of certain things being geared to certain keys. He played no favorites. It seemed like ABC then, and I remember Coleman Hawkins saying, 'Ain't that kid somethin'?'"

Williams recalled that Richard Fulbright worried about being stranded up North, and returned with Alonzo Ross. There was the question of money, too. Ross fronted a cooperative band and after he'd drawn double, the rest was divided among the sidemen. Still in his teens, Williams was making $150 a week down South, and sending the money home. The money did not count with him, however, compared to making it in the big city, where the real musicians were. "I began getting myself ready," he recalled, smiling. He'd heard about the Band Box at 132nd Street off Second Avenue, by the Lafayette, where they featured cutting contests. Finding out which was trumpet night, he went over from Brooklyn to blow. "It seems the word got around fast," he confessed, "and the first buddy I made was Chick Webb. I had to move in with him, although I was out of a job."

Their relationship was exceptional. Williams' obsession with music was at least matched by Webb's. Theirs was a pact which called for neither to work unless the other was alongside. The first job Williams played with the drummer's band was at the Savoy, and among others he remembers Don Kirkpatrick on piano, Elmer Williams, tenor sax, a trombonist called "Slats," and Webb's closest friend, John Trueheart, on guitar. They sounded great, the trumpet player recalled, but work was scarce and they were often laid off. It was during an interim period that Fletcher Henderson sent for Williams. He was needed to replace Russell "Pop" Smith. Packed with sidemen like Benny Carter, Coleman Hawkins, and Hilton Jefferson (saxophones), Rex Stewart and Bobby Stark (trumpets), Big Green (trombone), John Kirby (bass), Clarence Holiday (guitar), and Walter Johnson (drums), the Henderson band enjoyed a unique reputation. Henderson stipulated he needed a replacement for a week only and, typically, Williams was less daunted by the company he was to keep than by the necessity to part from Webb.

"Chick insisted, though, that I go," the trumpet player recalled with admiration. "So with them I went, trying to play it cool. The day we got back there was a matinee at the Roseland Ballroom. I didn't show—I thought that was our arrangement. Was that band mad! They had no first trumpet. Uptown, Chick took the call and said, 'Go down and help the man out . . .' Big Green didn't see it like that, and he about scared me to death. 'I'm going to kill you, baby, when you get off the stand,' he threatened." Williams grinned. "That band took its music *real* seriously."

The going remained tough for Chick Webb and he wouldn't allow the trumpet player to stick to their bargain, especially since after he'd been with Henderson a while, Ellington asked him to take Bubber Miley's chair. A choice had to be made. "Fletcher had the greatest band around," stated Williams unequivocally. "But Duke's was coming up. 'You better show enough sense,' I told myself, 'to move in the right direction.' A funny thing was that Duke never asked me to play like Bubber. Night after night I sat up there and nobody said a word. When Tricky Sam played, I laughed because it was funny. Funny-sounding, to me. But it dawned on me, finally. I thought, 'This man hired me to take Bubber's place. And he played with the plunger—like Tricky Sam.' "

Williams began to listen to Joe "Tricky Sam" Nanton seriously. That was the way, he explained, that he learned to use the plunger. In addition, he found Tricky Sam a wonderful companion and they were often together. "For me it wasn't hard, learning to use the plunger," Williams went on. "I'd never in my life thought to play like that, so it seemed funny at first. After I'd been doing it a while, though, it became *me*. Or I became it—although I always played open as well."

At the Cotton Club in the late thirties, his open horn was a recognizable feature of the magnificent Ellington brass section. Here was a tone built up over the years, aided by studies with Bill Costello in Manhattan. He was so strong that his lead remained audible even when the brass played all out. "Those were my two ways of being," he clarified. "Both expressed the truth. My plunger style was not like Bubber's. His soul wasn't my soul—and vice versa. The difference wasn't in technique, it was in range and color, I think. He only liked to play the one way."

Artie Whetsol and Freddie Jenkins were in the trumpet section when Williams first joined Ellington. Artie played first on all the sweet numbers; it was when when power was required that the lead switched to Williams. Ellington wrote for individuals even in those days, and even so far as a section was concerned. "Even outside the lead, if he had a note he wanted dominant," the trumpet player specified, "he would give it to me. If it were tender, Whetsol would be the one.

"It seems that Duke," Williams mused, "opens the way for you. He's done that for us all, I guess. I developed myself as well, though. Because I was determined on doing a lot of things. I was serious about the music always and got mad at the rest if they fooled around!" Growing progressively more thoughtful, he continued. "Even today I feel the same, but I've learned to control myself. I tell myself now that it doesn't matter much. If you've high blood pressure, like I have, you must gain control. A lot of times people see me sitting up there on the stand by myself, and probably think I'm acting real mean. Not everyone knows I've a health problem to face. I've learned to cut everything off, close my ears to the noise, drinking, and everything else. You can take medicine for blood pressure, but keeping calm is the thing."

Working with Ellington taught Williams a great deal. There was no one, he felt, with whom he ever worked from whom he could not learn something. He would watch every move made and gain something from it. When he fronted his own band, this stood him in good stead. When that time came, the most important understanding he'd acquired concerned certain types of musicians, musicians like Charlie Parker or Bud Powell, who both worked for him. "One night maybe," he said, "they'd give me a lot of trouble. Maybe the next night, too. But the one after, they'd play so fine and great it would all even out. That's when I came to see why Duke handles different guys the way that he does. . . ."

If any musician he hired was really talented, Williams explained, he would string along with him. A mediocre musician he could not put up with. "I shouldn't say this, perhaps," he confessed, "but if a musician doesn't have talent, I'm his bitter enemy while we're working. After I get off the stand, if we meet on other terms, we're all right. But when we go to work—I don't like him."

Whether many musicians felt like that or not, he did not know, Williams said. "In Duke's band, even in the old days, there were some guys who didn't care. Sometimes for weeks they wouldn't play, just sit there not really blowing. And Duke wouldn't say anything. I'd be the one to scream and holler and do his work for him."

It amused Williams to reminisce about some of the things that happened in that band. For months, sometimes, Johnny Hodges and Barney Bigard sat side by side and never spoke. Then some odd thing might occur and they would be the best of pals. The musicians had worked so long together, it was like a family affair. In this unique Ellington world Cootie Williams acquired an extra role he did not wholly approve. Certain vocals were entrusted to his charge. "I'm no singer," he explained. "Being critical myself, I can imagine how my delivery must have struck those who were . . . . Just the same, Duke was the boss." (Williams' vocals on records include, with Ellington: *Hot Feet*, *Ring Dem Bells*, *Sweet Chariot*, *Lazy Rhapsody*, *Baby, When You Ain't There*, and *Dinah*; with his own bands: *She's Gone*, *Dry So Long*, *Gotta Do Some War Work*, *Let's Do the Whole Thing*, *On the Sunny Side of the Street*, *That Old Feeling*, *You Got to Laugh*, *The Saints*, and *Sweet Lorraine*.)

Another thing that provoked his disapproval was remaking old songs. "It doesn't improve you," he said. "I always look forward to something new. Before I came back with Duke this time, I told him, 'I don't want to play *Black and Tan* and those things I did forty years ago. My mind is different now.' The public," he added ruefully, "doesn't understand that when you've played a thing for six months, it may be finished for you."

Neither did the public understand when, after nearly twelve years with Ellington, Williams was lured away by Benny Goodman, or so it seemed to the world. Raymond Scott penned a number entitled *When Cootie Left the Duke*. Everywhere Ellington fans were angered by Goodman, and Williams himself received letters that reviled him. The facts underlying this switch were not known at the time, but the truth was that Ellington helped Williams make the deal. "I didn't just jump up and leave—I wouldn't do that," the trumpet player stated. "Duke knew about it, and helped set everything up. He got me more money, and I told him I'd be back in one year's time."

It occurred to very few people that the Goodman band held something which appealed to Ellington's trumpet star. And Williams never explained. "If Duke didn't want it to be known like it was, it wasn't my place to tell," he said simply. "But that Goodman band— I loved it. It had a beat, and there was something there that I wanted to play with. When it comes to music, I forget about the world— everything else leaves me."

Goodman has always had Williams' admiration. "He is a great musician. He has talent, and I love him for it. Another thing, he's the same with everybody. He's just Goodman, not one way with this man and another way with someone else. The same with everyone. I think I was happier in music the first year I was with him than I ever was."

Playing with the sextet provided the greatest kicks. Sometimes Count Basie sat in at the piano, and there might be Charlie Christian on guitar, Davey Tough on drums, and Georgie Auld on saxophone. "Each man," Williams said, "could take care of himself. The thing would just move, that's what I enjoyed. There was never a let-down. Soon as one guy stopped playing, here came another, right in on top. With Benny no one could sit back—and *he* couldn't sit back, either."

Going with Goodman fitted in with Williams' ambitions to play with the greatest bands of his time. His thinking did not include the idea of going out on his own. He had told Ellington he would be away a year, and when it concluded, he phoned him to say he thought it was time to come back.

"I'll tell you," Duke had replied. "You're a wonderful guy. You've got a big name now. You can go out on your own and make money. Do it. . . ."

Surprisingly enough, Williams never considered fronting his own band the greatest of all his experiences. His point of view was always uniquely personal and inevitably based on his concept of music. That he evolved, as a leader, into a money-making proposition, never meant that he became a businessman. The foremost interest he took in his group was concerned with the talents he discovered and developed, and his perception and knack for uncovering latent capabilities are not as much a part of his reputation as they deserve to be. Charlie Parker worked for him in 1944 and Bud Powell joined him at sixteen, his first big band job. Williams also discovered Pearl Bailey and put his heart into helping develop her full potential.

He discovered the altoist and blues singer, Eddie "Cleanhead" Vinson, in Texas. "I went out there," he recounted, "to find Arnett Cobb. He was working in a roadhouse outside San Antone, selling insurance by day, which meant his wife didn't want him to leave. I was at the place where they were playing, and during intermission —they split up the band, half would play while the other rested—I was sitting in the kitchen with some of the boys. Then all at once, I heard Eddie Vinson: he was kidding around. The band never featured him as a singer, but he got up and started hollering the blues for fun. Going right out of that kitchen and down front, I said, 'That's what I want.'

" 'Are you *sure* you want me in the band?' Eddie asked, when I told him. I answered, 'Yeah.' But when he got to New York, he said, 'Man, I can't make it here. I want to go back home. I can't stand it here.' I had to take him up to my house, feed him, keep him, take him around. When he got off the train at Penn Station, he had a silver alto in his hand, no case or nothing, no paper round it. We were going to rehearsal, so I had to carry him past Manny's music store and get him a new saxophone, with a case. The boys would have kidded him, and then I knew he'd have gone back home. I got him this brand new saxophone, but the boys kidded him, anyway, because he had a bald head.

" 'Man, I can't make it,' he said, because he was scared. 'You all *right*,' I told him, 'everything is all right with you. Come on, let's have dinner. . . .' For the first week he was here, I had everything to do to keep him. Soon as he got to sing, though, the boys broke up, and that was *it*. He sang *Cherry Red Blues*, and after that he felt all right.

"Bud Powell was something else," said Williams, emphatically, "He was sixteen when I found him right here in New York. He was a genius. But he got into trouble while he was with me and got hurt. This was the first time he went into the sanitorium. We went to play a job in Philly and he was a little late. And high when he got there. So he didn't come back with us that night when we finished work. The next day the F.B.I. called and told me they had him in jail. I gave them his mother's phone number. She found they'd beaten him so badly 'round the head that she had to go get him. She couldn't bring him back on the train and had to hire a car. His head was so damaged he ended in Bellevue; his sickness started right there." Williams was silent.

In a moment he resumed his reminiscences of the musicians he had hired. Eddie "Lockjaw" Davis was another he had uncovered playing in New York. He could not explain why no one else had found these musicians who were there for all to hear. "I guess I was that preoccupied with music," Williams commented. "At one time or another I had George Treadwell, Money Johnson, and Louis Bacon [trumpets] in my band. And Gus Johnson on drums, and later Ed Thigpen, Jr. . . . it was his first major job." Don Kirkpatrick made the arrangements for Vinson, and because there were three singers, he had several others. "Pearl, Bacon, and Vinson were all different," he said. "I couldn't buy Pearl's arrangements from the same guy who would do them for Bacon.

"I was real interested in Pearl," he went on, "and had a contract with her. If you've got somebody with talent, you can do a lot with them. I can detect different things in a person, what gifts they may have. But I had to *fight* with Pearl. She didn't want to do this, or maybe that. If you find someone talented, they're all the same, you've got to fight with them to get it out. Often it's the artist who himself doesn't know what he does best. Pearl, for instance. Maybe what she did best, she didn't want to do. She preferred doing something else instead. You can't see your own best points," he emphasized, "or detect them fairly. It takes someone else to do that, and someone else to bring them out. If it's someone you have confidence in, whose judgment you trust, you have the battle won."

Williams maintained this was the ideal that should exist between artist and personal manager. It must be possible for the artist to place his confidence in his manager, so that even if he thinks he's wrong, he will, in any case, be guided by him. This, he thought, was the only way an out-and-out musician could be a commercial success. Because he isn't naturally equipped to think in business terms, he can't think that way consistently. He could queer things if he allowed his own judgment to interfere.

"Possibly this is what happened with Duke," he added, after deliberation. "He has lost a fortune in business because his mind couldn't go in two directions at once. And there's no one he has that much confidence in to allow a free hand."

The fact that comparatively few band numbers were built around Williams was accounted for by his belief, built up during long years as a sideman, that every band member with the urge and ability to blow should be given a chance. He could feel for musicians who were silent night after night. The nature of Williams' career has been shaped by the integrity and generosity of his musical tenets. Once he fronted his own group, he was never tempted to change his thinking. When he called the shots, every talented musician got a chance to blow.

"I loved good trumpet players in my band," he said. "They kept me up, made me watch my Ps and Qs. I would hate to get lazy."

Such high standards may not have been considered good commercial tactics, yet Cootie Williams' orchestra was exceptionally successful for a number of years. Around the time of World War II, the band hit its peak, and from coast to coast was in constant demand, with several hit records testifying to its excellence. The theme, *Round Midnight*, was written, not only by Thelonius Monk who was briefly on piano, but also by Williams. The strain he contributed is not often featured by Monk, but is heard on the trumpet player's recorded version.

Eventually, Williams explained, big bands came to find the going too tough. With others he was forced to conclude it would be stupid to keep on till all the money was gone. Influenced by the manager of the Savoy Ballroom, Charles Buchanan, in 1955, Williams agreed to front a six-piece house band for the "home of happy feet." "Feature yourself, Cootie, and nobody else," Buchanan advised. Williams shrugged, smiling, "I took that no more seriously than I had before," he said, "but the fact there were fewer of us, naturally I got to blow more." The band became closely identified with his style and maintained a steady popularity which persisted for seven years until the Savoy was demolished.

"I guess it would still be going strong," he claimed, "if the site hadn't been bought earlier for a housing development. For a ballroom to make it today," he added, "there would have to be space for three floors, because it's a seasonal thing. You have to accommodate a lot of clubs during the winter months."

It was probably Louis Jordan, mused Williams, who first turned the tide against big bands. When the promoters saw his little outfit drawing as many and more than predecessors who used three times as many men, it was the beginning of the end. He sighed, regretfully. After the demise of the Savoy, he became musical director for Belle Barth, a singer of risqué ballads. He was at the Round Table during her engagement, and she asked him to accompany her with his band. She was an unpredictable artist, but he anticipated her intentions so well that it resulted in an offer too royal to resist, at least temporarily.

"She wasn't a very good musician," he noted, smiling. "She would jump the meter, and wherever we were playing I would get headaches from the musicians. During rehearsal I would tell them, '*Please*, watch me at all times. This is the way we ordinarily do it. If she don't get high.' She might sing eight bars, jump two in the channel, come back right in here, and end up somewhere else. The musicians would tear out their hair. I got no chance to blow, either."

This was the spring of 1962 and Benny Goodman, just back from Russia, persuaded Williams and Teddy Wilson to rejoin him. It was an amusing stint, he recalled. "Sometimes Goodman would let you play," he explained, "and other times he wouldn't. He has his ways, as everyone knows. At Freedomland one night there was no bass player—he'd forgotten he'd fired him the evening before. Benny, though, is a great musician," he laughed, "but I'd already been talking with Harry Carney. 'Tell Duke,' I'd said, 'that I'm ready to come back.' "

Working as a single was another kind of activity which Williams disliked, but which his office promoted. "They are thinking of the money, not the music part," he complained. "Sometimes you would land up somewhere and find the musicians, well—horrible, really. Just poor musicians. I had to learn to do what I'd never done before, shut everything off in order to blow. This was good experience, of course. You had to blow as though you couldn't hear. Other times, then, I'd run across modern musicians. They would be able to play all right, but it would be awkward for them to move in my vein."

Necessity demonstrated to Williams the advantages of being able to lock things out. "Remember," he commented, "a lot of musicians sound bad when they're drinking. They are at their best when they're sober. I've heard fine big musicians sound like amateurs when they're high. Because drinking affects coordination—a drummer can't play up-tempos at all, and horns get sloppy all over. No, I've never seen anyone under the influence who could really play." Then he added, with a look of dismay, "They may *think* they're playing . . ."

Why, he wanted to know, do talented musicians mess up like that? Why hurt something you love? "One time," he related, "I told somebody, 'You're an artist—when you're not drinking. Why do you drink and destroy something that means so much to you?' He answered, 'I like to have fun.' So I put it to him straight, 'Why don't you have fun when you get through?' "

Williams was teetotal when he was with Duke. He never drank with Goodman, either. But when he fronted his own band, he began to drink Scotch. Maybe, he specified, it was because of tensions or excitement. "I don't know," he said, thoughtfully, "maybe I just wanted to try. I found I loved the taste of Scotch, and I'd take a fifth to work and drink all of it. Scotch was something I never gave away," he grinned. "I might go to a bar after work, besides, and then drive myself home. I never got knocked out, but for a while I didn't realize what was happening to me. I wasn't producing what I thought I could. Things you wanted to do, by the time you'd be ready, they'd have gone right past. I wasn't in control. That's why I stopped. With the Ellington band I drank Coca Cola *only*—I still do!"

Returning to Ellington held no qualms for Williams. He was relieved to be leaving a lot of drags behind. He'd learned that musicians are just people who, like a good part of the rest of the world, don't want to worry too much about someone else's responsibilities. "Like, musicians don't always show up on time," the trumpet player said, "or maybe they're high, when they do." On his last job, at The Embers, there was just rhythm and himself. "Each night the piano player came in five or ten minutes late. And I got tired," he sighed, "of having the boss on my neck." Even a job as simple as that was a drag. "Going back to Duke," he volunteered, "made a happy man out of me. I was lucky to find everything more or less the same. And I don't get excited now the way I once did. I'm getting more like Duke. Although no man in the world is like him." He added, smiling, "It certainly is good to be back."

This sentiment is shared by audiences all over the world who unfailingly greet his trumpet artistry with storms of applause. The qualities of soul revealed by his tone, the power and brilliance of his open horn, his almost vocal plunger statements, are all an indispensable part of Ellington's orchestral magic, and they substantiate the enviable reputation enjoyed by Cootie Williams.

[1967]

Juan Tizol [valve trombone]

Juan Tizol was born in San Juan, Puerto Rico, on January 22nd, 1900. He studied with his uncle, Manuel Tizol, and as a young man he played in municipal concerts, a career in jazz being then unimaginable.

"My uncle was one of the best musicians the island ever produced," he declared. "He played quite a few instruments, but especially string bass for the opera. Then he became conductor for the symphony and the big municipal band. He believed in teaching solfeggio, so I got that first. Then I got the trombone in school. It was valve trombone, because at that time we were using valve trombones, valve basses, and a lot of instruments like that in Puerto Rico. The only musicians who used slide trombones were in the army band.

"In 1920, I came to Washington, D.C., in a band that played in the pit at the Howard Theatre. We were legitimate musicians—no jazz. They would have a jazz band in one of the boxes in the theatre. We'd play an overture, and then they'd play a jazz tune.

"That was where I first met Duke Ellington. He would come there sometimes and play piano with four or five pieces. It wasn't called Duke Ellington's Orchestra or anything then. He just picked up men in Washington as he needed them. Anyway, I met him, and he heard me.

113

"From there I went to New York, and I was working in New Jersey with the piano player, Cliff Jackson, when I was asked to go to one of those broadcasts Duke used to make from the Cotton Club with that big announcer, Ted Husing. Duke asked me to bring my trombone there and broadcast with him, to try it out. Afterwards, he said, 'Well, one of these days soon I'm going to send for you.' And he did that in 1929.

"When he sent for me, the only other trombone was Tricky Sam [Nanton]. There was a big contrast in the way we played, of course, but the advantage to Duke was that I could also play fast work with the saxophone section, or with the trumpets. I played the second, third, or fourth part—just the notes. Nobody else did that at the time. Who was thinking about *me* playing trombone in a jazz band? When he knew what I could do, he used to write little parts specially for me. Later, I started writing myself, and I wrote Spanish melodies, and I played my own self.

"I wrote a lot of tunes—*Admiration, Moonlight Fiesta, Pyramid, Lost in Meditation, Conga Brava, Caravan*—but I never did go much for arranging. I left that to Duke, because he understood his band. And at that particular time, he didn't let anyone else arrange for the band. Even if it was a stock tune, he'd rather go ahead and make four choruses of accompaniment, one ensemble chorus, and that's all. He believed in writing his own stuff, which nobody could do just like he did. At that time, I copied the parts, and I did some in pencil. I did some in the book they're using now. I see parts in there that I copied years and years ago—still in pencil. I used to be pretty fast in doing that. The transposing I had learned to do in my country helped me a lot. Duke wrote all in concert, and when I played a trumpet part, I had to transpose it, just like the altos and tenors.

"We got Lawrence Brown when we came here to California—he was with Louis Armstrong at Sebastian's Cotton Club—and that gave us a trombone trio. *Slippery Horn* was a nice thing Duke tried it out on. We were three different styles: I had my style, Tricky Sam had his style, and Lawrence Brown had his style. But that was how it was through the whole band. Every man could get up and do a solo and be altogether different—every man in the band.

"I stayed with Duke fifteen years. I left because I wanted to come to California. I had sent my wife out here to take care of things and look out for places until I could get through. I was playing with Duke at the Zanzibar, on 49th and Broadway in New York, when Harry James called me on the telephone at the club, and asked me if I could join him. 'My Lord,' I said, 'I just signed with Woody Herman!' I would rather be with Harry because he was a California man, and my wife was already out here. So I talked it over with him, and I talked it over with Woody Herman, and Woody said, 'Well, if that's the case, you go with him, and we'll tear up the contract.'

"So I went with Harry James and stayed seven years out here. Then I went back with Duke Ellington for three more years. And in between I used to go with Louis Bellson and Pearly Bailey on their show.

"Well, it seemed I was just getting sick of the road, and missing my wife. I could only be home once a year. So I had to leave. I used to beg Duke, 'Let me go home, let me go home. . . .' I used to ask him to let me come home for six weeks, when we were out this way, and then I'd rejoin the band. This went on until I couldn't stand it any longer, and I said, 'I've got to leave you, that's all!' Oh, yes, I was getting older, but it wasn't that. It was the road. It was too long, and I couldn't take it. Now they're traveling on planes, but that's as bad, and I don't travel on planes."

When his good friend, the late Willie Smith, came out of the Navy, Tizol was responsible for getting him a place in the James band. In 1951, with Louis Bellson, they joined Ellington together. Looking back on that time shortly before his death, Smith had this to say:

"Duke and Tizol are lifelong friends. They're almost like brothers. Tizol and I are, too. He is the most punctilious man in the world. He gets everywhere a half-hour early, rarin' to go. So when I got into bad habits in that band, he was really disgusted."

Tizol smiled when told of this, and continued: "Punctuality has been my habit always. I want to be there on time, so that in case there's any kick, I'll be the one who'll kick, not the leader. I believed all the time in being ready—a half-hour or an hour in the dressing room, blowing a little bit on my horn, so I would be ready to go to work. I got myself a reputation for it, but I suffered quite a bit in the band, because I couldn't take all the foolishness. I tried to get along with everybody, and I didn't have any special buddies. I was born right and raised right. I'd take a drink here and there, but it was never a case of where I'd *got* to have it all the time. I never drank like that, and never smoked marijuana, nor took dope—nothing like that. I stopped smoking in January [1969], and I could use a cigarette right now, but I won't touch it. It's hard, especially after dinner.

"I am retired now, and I don't play at all. I did the Frank Sinatra show for over a year when he was on television. I was with Nat Cole for a year or two. See that piano in the corner? He gave me that before he died. I worked for Nelson Riddle, too, recording with all the stars, and I liked that kind of work very much."

Despite a reputation for punctuality, conscientious musicianship, and moderation, Tizol is also remembered in the Ellington band, surprisingly, as a practical joker. An infamous incident with a stink-bomb onstage in Philadelphia was not soon forgiven.

"I used to kid around and play jokes in the band," he admitted. "Once I put itching powder on Duke's arm just before the curtain went up. 'Duke, what time is it?' I asked, and while pretending to look at his watch, I was rubbing this powder on his arm. When the curtain went up, he was doing all kind of funny things with his arm, because he didn't know what was wrong. But they stopped me for good one day when we were at the Mills office on Broadway. They were giving us a party, for Christmas or something like that, and we all had little presents. Somebody put one of those firecrackers under my chair. When it blew up, I thought I would go through the roof. That stopped me completely.

"One of the funniest things that happened to me was in 1939 when we went to Europe and played two concerts in Paris, in that bomb-proof theatre [the Palais de Chaillot]. The place was sold out for I don't know how many weeks ahead of time. People were there in full dress and evening gowns. The critics were there, and friends, and enemies. Everybody was there to find out about this Duke Ellington band.

"Usually, *Caravan* was the second number in the program. I got so excited, and I passed word, 'Duke, don't play *Caravan*—wait until later on!' I was shaking like a leaf, so he promised he would wait until later on. 'Don't worry,' he said, 'don't worry about anything. It'll be all right. Don't worry about it.' That's when I learned about Duke Ellington: don't trust in what he says on things like that.

"I was beginning to relax a little, and all of a sudden he's announcing the second tune, *Caravan*, and my name. I called him all kind of names. I was supposed to go to the mike, but I couldn't walk to it. All I could do was just get up from my chair on the bandstand and play. My stomach was going 'ga*loo*, ga*loo*, ga*loo*,' and one chorus of *Caravan* seemed to last two hours. It was an awful thing. The people were so quiet. There was no noise except when they turned the pages of their program—you could hear that! Acoustics were terrific in there. Playing with the trombone wide open, I thought, 'My Lord, I wonder how it's going to sound?' If I missed a note, it was going to sound all over the place.

"My cousin was in the balcony, and he told me afterwards he thought I was kind of nervous. So I got prepared the second night. I went to a bar and got me one of the little gills of brandy, and drank it all to get myself together. I told Duke, 'You can play whatever you want tonight. I'm ready to go out there!' So he called *Caravan*, and I went out to the mike. When I came back to my chair, I gave him an army salute.

"I had some wonderful times with that orchestra—wonderful, wonderful times. Years ago, Duke used to have me rehearse the band when he couldn't be there to do it. I was doing the copying, and knew what was going on. At the opening of the show, he wasn't supposed to be on the stage. He'd only come out as the curtain went up, so I'd do the opening. When we were at the Cotton Club, Cab Calloway would follow us in there, and I had to rehearse the whole show for him, because his band was going to play the same show, exactly, as we had done.

"Duke's a wonderful man. He's been wonderful to me. Right now, all I'd have to do is say, 'Duke, can I make it?,' and he'd say, 'Just come in here as soon as you can.' "

[*1969*]

Lawrence Brown   [*trombone*]

When Lawrence Brown joined the Duke Ellington orchestra for the first time in 1932, the impact of his musical personality was soon apparent in such classic performances as *The Sheik of Araby, Ducky Wucky,* and *Slippery Horn.* The last was primarily a feature for the trombone section, but Ellington has affirmed that the title itself was inspired by Brown's presence and playing.

The trombone trio in which he became such a vital element was unique in every way, consisting as it did of three distinctive voices. Juan Tizol, on valve trombone, was entrusted with exotic melodic statements, for jazz solos were not his *forte.* To Brown, nevertheless, he was "the pivot, the solid rock of the section," whereas Joe "Tricky Sam" Nanton was the plunger specialist *par excellence.* "Tricky had a perfect feeling for it and he could play the proper thing to fit the plunger. His parents were from the West Indies, although he was born in New York, and I always felt that he had picked out some of those West Indian phrases and rhythms to play on his horn." Alongside these two, Brown added a smoothly mobile style, one that he had developed out of his great affection for the cello. Yet it was not his romantic way with a ballad that originally impressed musicians. It was his *speed,* as on *The Sheik of Araby.* Nor was this the first demonstration of it on record, but, because it was in the Ellington context, it was the first to command wide attention.

"I had made a record like that with Paul Howard in 1929, a take-off on *Tiger Rag* by Charlie Lawrence called *Charlie's Idea,*"

Brown remembered. "Victor had given us a contract and that was the first time I ever recorded, but I was playing that fast stuff 'way back then."

The years between have brought many changes, but one of the most unexpected is that today all the traditional Ellington trombone roles are united in Brown. The melodic theme statements fall to him; the romantic variations and "that fast stuff" are delivered in the style he originated; and, despite the fact that "they affect tone adversely, tending to make it sharp or flat," he is also responsible for the plunger solos. "I did it at first as a favor," he explained, "but I guess it developed into a saving, as when you've got one man who can do two things. So long as Ellington has his music, something has to revert to the first, basic type, and the plunger is the connection between the beginning and the band now."

Lawrence Brown was born in Lawrence, Kansas, in 1907. His father was a minister, and in 1914 the family moved to Oakland, California. After some years there, and a year in San Francisco, they went to Pasadena, where Brown remained until he was nineteen.

"Music was always something of a gift, something I had a feeling for," he recalled. "My mother used to play organ in the church, and my father always thought he could sing, there being two or three

Lawrence Brown

Juan Tizol

really goood singers in his family. I had two brothers and the older was a very good pianist of the concert type. The younger one and I both took piano and then studied violin together. The violin was too hard—it's the hardest of all the string family—and I shopped around a little bit, because the school system permitted us to play almost any instrument we chose. So I played tuba and even, in its infancy, the saxophone.

"The leader of the choir in our church was a trombone player, and he used to leave his horn in church all week. We lived next door and used to keep the place cleaned up. Now, I made a deduction of my own about this time: all the musical instrumemts were being played, but you didn't see many trombone players. This helped me decide on trombone. And I'd been taught that the trombone was the violin of the brass instruments, but I also liked the cello—for its nice voice—and I thought I would try to pattern my style on the cello.

"It was my own idea, and I wasn't following anyone else. 'Why can't you play melody on the trombone just as sweet as on the cello?' I asked myself. Everybody was playing so loudly and raucously on trombone. I wanted a big, broad tone, not the raspy tone of tailgate, and if you think of the cello you can see how it influenced me."

In those days, the public schools had excellent orchestras, and the teachers—usually symphony players—were very particular that

Lawrence Brown, Juan Tizol, Joe Nanton

their pupils be taught correctly. Pasadena High also tutored advanced students at the junior college level, and among the schoolmates Brown remembered was singer Donald Novis. "They put on operettas and everything," he added, "so there was a whole lot of musical experience to be gained right there in school."

A Pasadena men's club selected Brown as a soloist on its radio show, and it was while he was at the radio station that he was heard by Aimee McPherson, which led to his appearance before a Mother's Day crowd of six thousand in her Los Angeles "temple." By that time, he had progressed with his theory of cello-type playing to the point where its originality was easily recognizable.

"After I began playing professionally," Brown said, "the musician I liked was Miff Mole. His work was very artistic and technical. To get the smoothness I wanted, I tried to round the tone too much, instead of keeping it thin. Mine, to my regret, has become too smooth. It doesn't record well, because it isn't sharp enough. I think Tommy Dorsey was the best tone man I ever heard. He could keep his tone so thin, keen, and cutting. I don't have that. I have the 'ooo' but not the 'eee,' and in all of the recording you get that baritone horn sound. The climax I reach in *Don't Get Around Much Anymore* is a matter of interpretation. You play along smooth and all of a sudden you get what I call 'dirty,' act loud, and drive."

Brown had to face parental disapproval. His older brother, Merrill, excelled as a pianist, but he also studied organ and became so good that he was offered a job in a Sacramento movie theatre. To this, his father said, "No!," and in such a way that he dropped music altogether and went into the post office, where he remained until his recent retirement. Lawrence reacted differently to a similar attitude.

"I had slipped around and played a lot of dances in Pasadena, although my father didn't like it, which was one reason I went professional when I was nineteen. 'Either behave yourself and quit disgracing me, or get out!' he told me. It was the life he was against more than the music. 'You'll wind up in prison in a year or two,' he used to say later, but I never did. He kept his eye on me for a long time, and resented me, but when I was a success he accepted me again.

"I never smoked, drank, or gambled, but I didn't keep myself away from those who did. The bar is still the main place where I meet my friends. I have a Coke and buy them a whiskey. When marijuana became popular in the West around 1932, I used to see them having a ball, but it never attracted me. I remember going to one party with a quart of milk. They drank their liquor and smoked their weed, and I drank my milk."

A career as a professional musician did, however, entail the end of one ambition.

"When I was in school," Brown explained, "I studied with a view of being a doctor and went though the preliminaries of medical training. I liked the idea of medicine. I like anything where success depends on your individuality. In those days, too, you didn't have so much specialization. You were a doctor and did everything. We got so·far as going to the hospital to study different ailments, but I just decided I could never operate. It wasn't the actual operation, but the worry about the result. I felt if I operated on anyone, and lost them I would never get over it. Now, I think, they're taught to look at each case as a problem, which they either solve or they don't, and the person involved becomes secondary."

Within two weeks of leaving home, Brown was working in the 401 Ballroom in Los Angeles as a member of of a seven-piece band led by one of his Oakland schoolfellows, Charlie Echols.

"The 401 was a dime-a-dance place," the trombonist continued. "You played one chorus and they tore up a ticket. After that, I worked a short time in a similar place called Danceland, and there I got the invitation to join the Quality Serenaders at Sebastian's Cotton Club."

The Serenaders were two saxes, trumpet, trombone, piano, banjo, bass, and drums. When the Cotton Club changed bands, as it frequently did, Brown got a job at the Club Alabam on Central Avenue. This was owned and managed by a former musician, Curtis Mosby, who eventually opened a second Club Alabam in San Francisco, "right on the edge of Chinatown." The band and the show—"chorus girls, acts, and everything"—would do a month in Los Angeles and then go on up to San Francisco. After a period of this kind of activity, Brown returned to the Quality Serenaders, who were now expanded to ten pieces, directed by pianist Charlie Lawrence, and nominally led by Paul Howard. For a time, this was the best band in the West, but eventually it began to deteriorate.

"Then," Brown said, "Sebastian got the idea of handing out contracts instead of having some of the men run him out. Lionel Hampton and I were the two he contracted to the club. and we stayed regardless of who came. When Louis Armstrong first came, he fronted Vernon Nelson's band. Later, we were in Les Hite's, and there were others in between.

"I was doing a lot of solos, going from table to table answering requests, and I had a gimmick that was very popular. I always emphasized softness then, and I could put the bell of the horn right among the customers at their table and play so soft, with no mute, that they would be happy listening. I can't do that anymore. It was really the same principle as sub-tone on the saxophone and I don't think anyone ever developed it completely. It would be good in recording on sensitive mikes—if you could keep the wind out. You know how it is with a saxophone sometimes. You'd have to back up and use enough pressure to cover up the wind.

"By the time Louis Armstrong came out, I was pretty well known locally. He was so terrific out there then, and he was really the only player that influenced me. He'd stand up all night and play, and sometimes broadcast for as long as three hours. We had little arrangements and we'd take different choruses. If he got tired, he'd just say, 'Take one,' or 'Take another,' or 'Take two.' He was the kind of musician you could sit there all night and listen to, and be amazed at the technique, the poise—and just everything! People used to come from 'way up around Seattle to hear him. Every trumpet player at that time tried to play *one* of his choruses.

"I think the two greatest influences in the music of this century were Louis Armstrong and Paul Whiteman: Armstrong for his melodic style, for bringing the musician to the front of the band, playing and singing, as an individual; Whiteman for making a complete change in the band style and effecting the transition from the symphony to the dance band. If you see that picture he made in 1930, 'The King of Jazz,' you can see all the components that are still in use today—the choirs, the little groups, and the big bands playing a kind of symphonic jazz. I mean this in terms of popular music generally, not just in those of straight jazz, but before him there was nothing quite like that, no joining of popular music, jazz, and symphony.

"Louis Armstrong had a manager I didn't like. I always was an independent-minded man and he made the mistake of calling a rehearsal on Easter Sunday. I always went home to see my parents Sundays, and this rehearsal wasn't important, because it was chiefly to take pictures for him to put in the press Monday.

" 'I'm sorry,' I said, 'but I don't work Sunday, and I have this contract here.'

" 'If you don't want to make it, we'll get one of those studio men!'

" 'You do just that,' I said.

"He made me mad right quick and that was the first fight I had with a manager. Until then, I hadn't run into much of what we have now with managers, agents, bookers, leaders, and everything. All that was just coming in. Anyway, although I still had my contract, this meant that I had more or less refused to play with Louis Armstrong."

It happened that Duke Ellington was in town, playing the Orpheum, and that his manager, Irving Mills, came out to the Cotton Club a couple of nights later. The club was a huge place, the most popular nightclub west of Chicago, and usually there was a packed house well sprinkled with stars and starlets. Brown came out on the floor during each show and was featured playing *Trees*. Donald Novis was in the audience this particular night, and Sebastian persuaded him to sing the same number with a chorus as an addition to the trombone interpretation. Mills heard all this, sent for Brown, and asked him if he would like to join the Ellington band. Because of the trouble with Armstrong's manager, this suited him, although he wasn't enthusiastic about the new prospect, insisting that he would be back within a year. He went to see Ellington, however.

"I don't know you and I've never heard anything about you," were the leader's first words to him, "but Mr. Mills says to get you. So come on in the band."

"Okay," Brown answered, and soon afterwards he found himself on the train with the band in which he was to play for the next nineteen years.

"I really meant to stay only a year," he remarked with a wry grin, "because I had just bought a great big automobile—a sixteen-cylinder Cadillac convertible. I used to be an automobile fanatic, changing cars every year, and always getting a bigger one. Anyway, I put this one up on blocks. Now it seemed that as soon as I went with Ellington, the bottom began to drop out of the nightclub business in L.A. This was 1932 and the Depression, and at the end of a year I said to myself, 'This looks like the best deal to stay in right now.' So I stayed, although I still didn't like the traveling.

"There were soon things written for me like *Ducky Wucky*, but we also kept *Trees* for the theatres. It was a big number at that time, quite different from most of what was going on in the music field, and no one before had ever come out with a trombone playing a concerto, a whole, complete number built around the trombone. I did that for several years. Then Tommy Dorsey started playing that way, five or six years after I'd been with Ellington, and I don't know where he developed that beautiful tone, because he didn't sound like that before. I really don't know how he did it. Trombones didn't work like that.

"Every time Ellington played a concert tour, there would be a new showcase for the trombone. One year, I decided to write my own—*The Golden Cress*—and it was twice as long as on the record. I also wrote *On a Turquoise Cloud*.

"When I left in 1951, it was because I was tired of the sameness of the big band. It's the worst thing in the world if you get in a big band and have to play the same old mess night after night, show after show, especially if you're doing theatres. Pretty soon, you know, you just can't play anything. Things were at their peak when I quit so far as my money was concerned, but the flexibility of the small band, the opportunity to spread out, make it interesting to the musician. And

123

Johnny Hodges had a terrific little band. We had Emmett Berry on trumpet first, I think, and he's a good trumpet player. Then we had Shorty Baker, and Shorty had worked with us before so it was like getting with your brother. Then there was Hank Jones on piano, and he was terrific, and everything smoothed out then, although we were lacking one of the old bunch. Al Sears had gone into publishing after he had that big hit with *Castle Rock*.

For about a year after the Hodges band broke up, Brown freelanced successfully in New York, playing in various shows and recording. Then he secured a staff job at CBS.

"Warren Covington resigned," he said. "That's the only way you get one of those studio staff jobs, when somebody gets out. I had been over to see the contractor, and you have to spread your name around, of course. Maybe they can use you when somebody's on vacation. Anyway, I took Warren Covington's place. How did I like that? That's the best job in the business! No headaches. Everything was beautiful. You could record, do anything you wanted, so long as it didn't conflict with the studio schedule. But then came the cancellation of all the transcontinental radio programs, and everything started going into tape, and they didn't need the same set-up or number of men. Three of four others came out the same time I did.

"The field is crowded in the first place. And then there's a peculiar thing about studio musicians: they all sound alike. They're great musicians, and any one can sit in another's chair, and it doesn't change a thing at all. My thing is too individual, and I usually played second parts. There are more seconds than firsts around, anyway."

After working clubs for a while, Brown received a call from Duke Ellington and joined him again in Las Vegas, in 1960.

As he intimated earlier, Lawreence Brown is an independent-minded man, and he doesn't hesitate to express his distaste for many aspects of the music world in which he works.

"When I was attracted to music in the beginning," he explained, "there were no commercial challenges and I played as I felt. Then I got deeper into it and found out it was a business, and rotten business—and, well, I resented that! I've always had an eye for what should be and what shouldn't be. I don't go along like some of the fellows who'd rather play their horn than eat. I quit the Armstrong band on a matter of principle, and I've tried to be like that all the way. The business, as it is, is nothing but a series of situations like that, so you get disgusted, and music has come to mean nothing but a job to me."

124   Yet it is a job he does well, conscientiously, despite all circum-

stances, as was shown in his assumption of an additional role in the Ellington orchestra.

"I don't like using the plunger," he declared, "but I imitate the tops—Tricky. That buzzing breaks your lip down and you have to wait a little while to get back to normal. Another problem is that there's no way to get anything to fit in there unless you change the tuning. The back pressure from the plunger and the mute takes the horn out, so you have to try to tune it with your hand. At least, I try to tune it there, because I don't feel like changing positions to fit the tone. It's all right when you've got someone who can do it in the third chair, where the parts are neither high nor important, but the first chair is important and usually the first man won't touch it. It can really mess your lip up so that you won't be able to play straight at all."

Asked about "modern" developments on the trombone, he expressed himself with similar candor:

"In each case something has been sacrificed to get something else. Where's the tone? If you're going fast, executing all those gymnastics, you give up tone. I feel it would be better to get a little of each of these things, and to hold on to others, rather than to go all out in one direction. We have to recognize that being popular is nowadays more important than producing something of value. Take the most popular of these singing groups—they sound like hell! Somebody thought of something different, and the publicity department decided it was a great way to make a million dollars. The music business has never been so commercial."

As Lawrence Brown comes gravely down from his chair, through the Ellington saxes, and up to the mike to participate in the *Mood Indigo* trio, to solo on *Irresponsible,* or even to answer to a request for that old favorite, *Rose of the Rio Grande,* he is the epitome of the professional musician who maintains his standards despite the dictates of fashion and commerce.

[*1965*]

Ben Webster   [*tenor saxophone*]

Stride piano, the left hand fast and precise, filled the receiver.
"Hello!"
"Ben?"
"Yeah. Wait till I turn my wakin'-up music off."

125

James P. Johnson was abruptly diminished.

"You downstairs? Come on up."

One of Ben Webster's afternoon musicales was in progress. A tape on which the Lion, the Lamb, James P., Fats Waller, and Art Tatum strove mightily together—his wakin'-up music—was still on the Wollensak, but an album by Tatum was now placed on the phonograph. A facet of that pianist's genius was about to be demonstrated to Ernie Shepard and Sam Woodyard, who occupied nearby rooms and had come in to discuss the previous night's activities.

Webster had sat in for a set with the Ellington band at its Basin Street East opening, and he was happy about the experience. Chuck Connors' arrival having been delayed, he had taken Connors' seat in the trombone section and been duly introduced by Ellington as an expert on claves in the "cha-cha-cha." When he came down front later, Ellington had suggested *Cottontail,* but Webster, demurring, asked for a warming-up number, and they went into *Tea for Two. I Got It Bad* came next, with a courtly bow in the direction of Johnny Hodges, and then *Cottontail,* which ended with a chase between Webster and Paul Gonsalves. It had been a kick.

"If Duke likes you," Webster observed, "you're home free."

There were "brews" (Schlitz) on the windowsill outside, cold and ready to drink, and Ballantine's Scotch on the dressing table, but the main business was music and reminiscence. A tape of a 1940 performance at the Crystal Ballroom, Fargo, North Dakota, was produced.

"It was so cold there that night, we played in our overcoats, and some of the guys kept their gloves on!"

The band played with an exciting kind of abandon—the abandon, perhaps, of desperation.

"Sometimes," Webster added, "when you've traveled all day in the bus, and had no sleep, and are dead tired—that's when you get the best playing out of a band. It just happens. And sometimes the opposite."

The material was inspiring. After *The Mooche* came *Ko-ko, Pussy Willow* . . .

"I learned a lot from Rab, but you know what his only advice to me was when I came in the band? 'Learn your parts!' "

The continuing program included *Chatterbox, Harlem Airshaft, Jack the Bear, Rumpus in Richmond, Sidewalks of New York, The Flaming Sword, Never No Lament* . . .

"That's why Duke leaves his mark on you, forever."

Then there were *Clarinet Lament, Slap Happy, Sepia Panorama, Rockin' in Rhythm,* and *Cottontail.* . . .

"Sonny Greer, and he's *swinging!*"

Conga Brava, Stardust, Rose of the Rio Grande, and *Boy Meets*

Horn preceded the finale, an uproarious version of *St. Louis Blues*, on which Tricky Sam Nanton took over from Webster and carried through to the coda.

"We were drinking buddies," Webster said, and laughed, "but you heard how he tore right in on me there?"

Then it was time for some "lies," for the tale of the impetuous milkman and his fearful threat, of the leaking rocket at Cape Kennedy, and of the watermelon salesman who had lived it up, only yesterday, with a truckload of peaches. After that, the conversation came back to piano, steered by the host, and the striding hands of yesterday stretched out again on tape and vinyl. Often they belonged to Fats Waller.

"All that fun, but never a wrong note," Webster remarked with admiration. "If only he could have lived until TV!"

Contemporaries were considered and Ralph Sutton commended as "a wonderful cat." Earl Hines, too: "Earl swings his ass off!" Then a memory of the Beetle intervened, the diffident-seeming Beetle who took part in the piano battles uptown and seldom played anything faster than an easy, rocking, medium tempo, but who triumphed nevertheless. Another memory returned, of the Lamb, Donald Lambert, who came to the battlefield once or twice a year, astounded everyone, and then retired to New Jersey again. From that point, it required very little egging on to get Webster to tell of his own first experience of the Harlem piano school.

"I shall never forget the time when I met Count Basie," he began. "It was while he was in Kansas City with Gonzel White, and he used to stop the show. I always did like Basie and I always did want to play the piano. He bore with me for a long time and he told me that in the event I ever got to New York I was to be sure to find The Lion, Willie Smith. He had already told me that the bosses were James P. Johnson and The Lion, and that then came Duke, Fats, and Willie Gant. I don't remember all the names, but there was a gang of great piano players in those days.

"Clyde Hart and I managed to get with Blanche Calloway. Clyde was a friend of mine, a piano player, and Edgar Battle sent for us in Kansas City. We played the Pearl Theatre in Philly, on 22nd and Ridge, I think it was, and Clyde and I got on the train the first day we had off and came to New York.

"Basie had briefed me. 'Go to the Rhythm Club,' he said, 'and that's where you'll find the Lion. He knows all the piano players and all the good musicians. They all hang out there and The Lion will introduce you right.' Naturally, I wanted to hear people like Benny Carter, Johnny Hodges, and Coleman Hawkins, too. Basie had also told us how to approach the Lion, so that he would bear with us. Basie said he liked a little taste every now and then, that he loved cigars, and that maybe he would play a little for us.

"So we walked up to the Rhythm Club on 132nd Street and Seventh Avenue and we met The Lion. There was cigar store right on the corner and in those days they had those great, big El Productos, three for a half.

" 'Mr. Lion,' we said, 'would you care to have some cigars?'

"The Lion rounded on us and said:

" 'Say, you kids are pretty nice kids. Yes, I'll have a cigar or two.'

"So we walked with him to the corner and asked him how many could he smoke.

" 'Oh, maybe two.'

"So we bought him half a dozen, and then he smiled and said:

" 'You kids are *really* nice kids!'

" 'Then we asked him:

" 'Would you care for a little drink, Mr. Lion?'

" 'Yeah,' he said.

"Then we told him we would like to hear him play, and at that time there was a place right across from the Rhythm Club, and he took us over there, and he got in the mood, with his cigar and a little taste in between.

"It was one of the greatest experiences of my life to hear a man play like this. Though I had heard James P. Johnson around 1925 in Kansas City, that was a little early, and I think I could understand more of what I was listening to when I got to The Lion.

"He played for us for three or four hours, and we kept buying him a little taste, and he kept saying we were nice kids. I had a beautiful day and I never will forget it."

After his mother and then his grandmother died in the same year, Ben Webster had no important ties in California. "There's nothing happening on the West Coast, anyway," he claims, and now he regards himself as more or less permanently based in New York, which is certainly a blessing to his many fans and friends in the East. He hasn't yet moved his entire collection of tapes and records, but those he has with him are well varied and include, for instance, Stravinsky's *Firebird Suite* and Kodály's *Sonata for Unaccompanied Cello, Opus 8.*

He has brought back to the ingrowing New York scene the good humor and expansive generosity of spirit that have been dwindling for some time among its hard-pressed musicians. Webster is big physically—broad-shouldered and straight-backed—and he is bigger than the rat race. One is very soon aware that music occupies his mind far more than money, and music as, above all, a means to enjoyment. Ellington's wasn't the only band he sat in with during January. Gerry Mulligan's Concert Jazz Band found it had an impulsive new pianist one night in Birdland, and at the Metropole on another occasion Webster took Marty Napoleon's place at the keyboard for a set, much to the pleasure of an old friend, Shorty Baker, who was playing trumpet in the group.

The appearances with his own quartet at the Shalimar, Birdland, and the Half Note have proved very popular and there are lessons to be learned from the success of his kind of music. His material, consisting mostly of the better standards and famous Ellington numbers, is quite strong on melodic content. Just as he did twenty years ago, with men like Marlowe Morris, Sidney Catlett, and Johnny Guarneri, he likes to open and close a performance with a statement of the theme. Good melody, well phrased, communicates as strongly in the jazz idiom as in any other, and there are distinct advantages from the audience viewpoint to having the melody established in the mind when following the variations. Ben recognizes this and the importance of good tempos. Despite the fame of *Cottontail,* he is at his best at slow and medium tempos, where the emotional warmth and very rhythmic phrasing produce what one recent listener at the Half Note aptly described as an "irresistible *surge.*"

Stylistically, he illustrates the evolutionary process always at work within the music. The jazz audience was probably first widely aware of him on the explosive records of 1932, which indicated the musical ferment in Kansas City, made by Bennie Moten with Basie, Lips Page, Eddie Durham, and Eddie Barefield—*Moten Swing, Lafayette,* etc. In his subsequent recordings, there was uninterrupted development, but up until the time he joined Ellington, listeners generally recognized the influence of Coleman Hawkins rather than the personality of Ben Webster. Yet as Hugues Panassié perceptively noted, "the grace of his melodic line makes one think of Benny Carter." In fact, it is Carter whom Webster names first among saxophonists, then Hawk, then Johnny Hodges ("the most feeling"), and then Hilton Jefferson ("the prettiest").

Established stylistically by 1940, Webster himself became an important influence. Prominent among those to acknowledge it was "Lockjaw" Davis, at one time known as "Little Ben." When Paul Gonsalves eventually took the tenor chair with Ellington, his ability to play Webster's solos in Webster's style profoundly surprised the leader, but in the fourteen years that followed, Gonsalves' musical personality itself developed on strongly individual lines, a fact evident when he and his early mentor played *Cottontail.* It was even more evident in a jam session at Count Basie's Bar in Harlem during

February, when Webster, Gonsalves, and Harold Ashby were together on the stand. Ashby is a close friend who proudly proclaims
the Webster influence, but all three were individually and instantly
identifiable by tone and phrasing. Ashby had played in the *My People*
orchestra in Chicago and in Jimmy Hamilton's chair with the regular
Ellington group while Hamilton was vacationing.

"He's improved so much he scares me," Webster said, wonder-
ingly, and using his most admiring epithet.

Gonsalves, too, he esteems highly. One of the records often
played on his phonograph is of *I've Just Seen Her*, from Ellington's
All American album, a Gonsalves performance that never fails to
impress all saxophone players. At one of Webster's musicales, Gonsalves reminisced about the first time he heard Tatum. He had gone
to a club with Webster, Basie, and Harry Edison, but the master
didn't feel like playing that night. So Webster had sat down at the
piano and played a while, then Sweets, and finally Basie. With that,
Tatum decided to play, and he chose *Get Happy* at a very fast tempo.
What astonished Gonsalves and the other three musicians was the
way Tatum's left hand took care of business while the right reached
around for a drink. Perhaps this anecdote passed through Webster's
mind at the jam session at Count Basie's. He called *Get Happy*. They
took off, lightning fast, and Gonsalves went into a furious and fantasti-
cally devised solo.

"Paul's getting so hot," Webster exclaimed with mock alarm, "I
don't think I should have called *this* tune!"

Another afternoon visitor was Budd Johnson, and it was Johnson
who first showed Webster the scale on saxophone and how to play
Singin' the Blues. Webster had been taught violin, but had not liked
the instrument, on which, he says, he always seemed to have a fast
vibrato. There were two pianos in the house, his mother's and his
cousin's ("I ruined my cousin's piano playing blues!"), and when he
should have been practicing violin he was usually busy on one or
other of them. He always wanted to play piano, and Pete Johnson,
who lived just across the street, taught him how to play the blues. "If
you lay the violin down a week, you're in trouble," he says, "but you
can lay a horn down a year and be okay." So when he switched to
piano, it was the end of the violin phase. He was playing piano in a
silent movie house in Amarillo, Texas, when Gene Coy's band came
to town and he met Budd and Keg Johnson. The saxophone fascinated him and in 1929, hearing that the Young family band needed
another saxophone player, he went to see Lester Young's father.

"I can't read," he said.

Mr. Young was amused.

"I haven't got a horn," he added.

Mr. Young was even more amused, but he provided Webster with an alto and taught him to read. "Lester's father mostly played trumpet, but he could play anything and, what's more, he was a master teacher." Lester Young played tenor and Webster insisted he was playing wonderfully even then. Lee Young and his sister Irma were also members of the band and played saxophones at that time, too. The group went to Albuquerque for some months and it was there that Webster, a strong swimmer, helped save the lives of both Lester and Lee. Lester got into difficulties in the Rio Grande and was carried away, tumbling over and over in the water, until Webster and guitarist Ted Brinson rescued him. On another occasion, Lee stepped off the bank into a deep sandhole and Webster managed to haul him out. "Lee dived right in again," Webster remembered, "but Lester didn't want to think about swimming for a long time after that."

Some months later, after Budd and Keg Johnson had left it, he got a call to join Gene Coy's band ("about nine or ten pieces") in which Harold Coleman was playing tenor. That was really the beginning of the professional career as a saxophonist that brought him, experienced and mature, into New York, 1964.

"I think I'm playing better than ever now," he said. Then he said again, "I think."

[1964]

Ray Nance   [*cornet and violin*]

"If you're going to do what you want to do," Ray Nance said, "you've usually got to sacrifice something. I like to play, and there's no type of music I'd rather play than Duke Ellington's, but playing it involves travel, and, if you're married, everytime you look around you're saying goodbye. Although it's part of the business, I don't like being away from my wife and home anymore than anyone else.

"The hardest thing is adjusting your mind to that road life. It's harder mentally than physically, because you really only work about four hours a day. One advantage I always had was that being small I could curl up in a bus seat better than most, but you ride and ride, and then you check into a hotel. And one of the big problems is sitting in a hotel room all day, waiting to go to work. I wouldn't have done what I did for twenty-three years with any other band than Duke Ellington's, but I've seen a lot of the world and had plenty of kicks."

131

Paul Gonsalves, Harold Ashby, Ben Webster

When Nance quit in 1963, it was primarily for the same reason that he had left the Earl Hines and Horace Henderson bands earlier. He settled down in New York, played club dates and two seasons at the World's Fair, rejoined Ellington for a highly successful European tour in 1965, and recorded from time to time with his old companions. His decision to leave was widely regretted, but it helped focus attention, as never before, on his great contributions to the Ellington story.

He entered it in 1940, when Cootie Williams left to join Benny Goodman. History repeated itself, for Tricky Sam Nanton was there to act as mentor when Williams took the place of the original specialist in growl trumpet, Bubber Miley. And Nanton was still there when Nance took Williams' chair.

"I joined at a good time," he recalled. "Jimmy Blanton and Ben Webster were in the band, and so was Tricky, the master. He and I had a lot in common. On the West Coast, especially around Seattle, everything was wide open then. People had plenty of money, and there was gambling and everything like that. Tricky and I used to make those joints together. I always remember him with his zipper bag full of mutes, medicines, and whiskey. He was an original every way. We'd be sitting at Frank Sebastian's Cotton Club, where Duke naturally didn't want people drinking on the stand, and Tricky would

Ray Nance

have a bottle in his inside coat pocket with a straw in it. Nobody out front would know, but he'd be sipping every now and then, and getting stoned all night long."

Rex Stewart was still with Ellington, too, and he could play growl horn "beautifully," but he had his own conception and his own parts to play. So Nance tried to "continue the sound of the band," and whenever he had a growl part that Cootie had played, he imitated it as best he could.

"It wasn't easy," he admitted, "because I'd never done it before. Apart from the pressure, you're blowing with one hand and manipulating the mute with the other. It isn't just a matter of blowing with the mute in there either: you've got to concentrate to produce a certain kind of sound. And you've got to *want* to do it. I like it because I think it has great descriptive quality. There's no way you can get the 'jungle' sound except with the growl."

His role as part of the trumpet section was the most important in his eyes, but all his talents were quickly utilized, and he soon found himself featured not only on trumpet and violin, but also as a singer and dancer.

When Ray Nance was six, his mother began to teach him piano. 133 This went on for three years until she became interested in violin, which a friend of hers, Charlotte Page, was studying at the Chicago College of Music. She persuaded Miss Page to give her son lessons, and after five years he was so proficient that his teacher suggested he be taken where she had been taught. His mother duly enrolled him, and through Miss Page's influence he was placed under Max Fischel, a Russian Jew who was renowned as the best teacher in the college.

"At first," Nance recalled, "it had been just a matter of doing what my mother said, but after a time I got to like it. I studied with Fischel for seven years, right through high school. When I graduated from Wendell Phillips at eighteen, I was playing in the school band and seriously considering becoming a professional musician. Meantime, I had picked up trumpet. I practically taught myself, with the help of a great bandmaster, Major N. Clark Smith. I wanted to hear myself on a louder instrument in a way I couldn't do with the violin in the orchestra. I guess it was a bit of an unusual double. Mostly, guys double on violin and piano, or violin and guitar, or violin and saxophone.

"By the time I graduated, I was also a drum major in the band, the shortest drum major anyone ever saw! It was funny, because Hector Crozier, the fellow before me, was a big, strapping guy about six foot three, and here I come five foot four! I don't know how I got the job, but you've got to put on a show, doing fancy steps and twirling a baton."

Always deprecatory about his own gifts and ability, Nance was at pains to point out that, despite his considerable training, he wasn't the best violinist in the school symphony orchestra. The best, and the two lead violinists, were a girl called Matilda Ritchie and a boy who was to make a great name for himself as a bassist—Milt Hinton.

After graduating, Nance went south the following fall to the Methodist College in Jackson, Tennessee. One of the prime reasons for his going was to start an orchestra there, but in one semester he got into so much trouble that he didn't go back. At Halloween, he was blamed for a firecracker thrown into the Dean of Boys' room, and soon afterwards, when someone kicked over a bucket beside his bed, a large part of the contents went through the dormitory floorboards on to the luckless Dean, who was asleep below.

Back in Chicago, now about twenty, he formed a six-piece band of his own which soon became the toast of the South Side. Its members had gone through high school together and they were like a little club. At least two of them had had no intention of playing professionally, but the others persuaded them, Jesse Simpkins even making the switch from piano to bass. Spencer Odon, who later arranged for the Southernaires and the vocal group on the Arthur Godfrey show, was

134

the pianist. Oliver Coleman, who was teaching in Chicago before his death in 1965, was on drums. Leroy Harris, later with Earl Hines, played alto and clarinet.

"Claude Adams, one of my closest friends, played guitar and violin," Nance continued. "He had a wonderful conception, but he died very early. He played good jazz fiddle for those days and we'd do things featuring two fiddles and clarinet—Leroy Harris had a beautiful tone. The job that brought us recognition was at Dave's Café at 51st and Michigan on the South Side. We were there two years and the place was packed nearly every night. We had dancing and a floorshow, and besides playing we sang in four- and five-part harmony. This was in 1932 and 1933, and we never recorded. It wasn't so easy then. I had done a bit of dancing when they used to have Charleston contests around Chicago, and I would come out in front of the band and do a little dance even in those days.

"The guys didn't like leaving Chicago, but I persuaded them once to go to Buffalo, where I had got a job. That was the first time I saw Stuff Smith in person. He had a *swinging* ten-piece band at the Vendome nightclub," and Nance emphasized "swinging" almost fiercely. "We noticed that the tempos were so different from what we had been playing out West. Theirs were right in the groove, and they never played anything faster than this," and he snapped his fingers at a medium tempo. "They played like that all night long, where we had been playing fast or slow, and we were astonished.

"We got stranded up there, but it was worth it to hear Stuff, who made a big impression on me. That was the first time I missed a whole lot of meals, and finally I had to telegraph my father and mother. They sent the money for me to get home.

"Before this, I had heard Joe Venuti. I appreciated what he played, but it wasn't what I wanted to pattern my style on. He had a lot of records going for him, and Eddie South had one or two, but Stuff was virtually unknown. I used to go to Eddie South's rehearsals when Milt Hinton began playing bass for him. Milt introduced me and it was a real thrill for me to be in the same room as Eddie. He had been taught by some of the greatest European teachers, and with his tone and technique he was a really well-rounded violinist.

"There was so much more scope for violinists then. Erskine Tate had an orchestra of thirty pieces in the pit of the Vendome theatre in Chicago, and my mother used to take me to hear him every week. Now everything is amplified, but then they used strings so that you could sit at your table, hear yourselves talk, and still enjoy music. Well, Stuff Smith is the Swing King of the instrument and he has an almost violent approach to it. Mine is more orthodox, and closer, I guess, to Eddie South's. Still, I was sorry Stuff and I didn't get to make that album together in 1964, but maybe we'll do it this year. And I hope the records I made with Svend Asmussen and Stephane Grappelly in Europe—which Duke Ellington supervised, by the way—will soon be issued."

Nance's little band operated successfully until the early part of 1937, when he began to feel he wanted "to branch out and do a little traveling." Unfortunately, the other members were not for it. "They'd begun to fall in love or get married—the same old story!" he remarked wryly. "So we broke up when I couldn't persuade them to leave town."

Before this, he had had several offers from Earl Hines, but had turned them down. Now he joined the pianist-leader at the Grand Terrace, and gained a "world of experience," traveling for the first time as part of a big band right across the country to California, and then to New York, where they played the Apollo and Loew's State. Jimmy Mundy was doing the arrangements and Darnell Howard took the violin solos. "He played good jazz fiddle," Nance said, "and judging from the way he played he had had good schooling, too. I don't remember ever playing fiddle in that band at all, but I recorded my first vocal with it on a Vocalion record called *Jack Climbed the Beanstalk*. Walter Fuller was the regular singer then, and he sang a lot like Louis Armstrong.

"Earl was wonderful to work for and he's still one of my favorite pianists. I love the way he plays. To me, he's the Louis Armstrong of the piano. Working so long around Chicago, he never had the recognition he would have had if he'd been working out of New York, but he was very big all through the Middle West. Those dancehalls used to be packed."

Trummy Young was also in the Hines band, and he and Nance were roommates. Jimmie Lunceford was riding high at that time, but when Young received a telegram from him he was uncertain whether he should leave Hines.

"You think I should go?" he asked.

"To make sure you go," Nance replied, "I'll put you on the train myself tonight." And he did.

Another musician in the band whom he much admired was George Dixon.

"I used to look at him with amazement," he said. "Here was a guy who liked to play the saxes more than trumpet, but he seemed to play trumpet so *easily*. I think he was one of the most underrated musicians I've ever known. He has a day job now, but I think he still gigs around Chicago."

136 At the beginning of 1939, Nance decided he wanted to stay

home and not go out on the road again, so he left Hines and joined Horace Henderson, who had a band at Swingland on the South Side. Later, they moved north to the 5100 Club, and it was during this engagement that he recorded his first violin solo, again on Vocalion. The number was called *Kitty on Toast*, and in two thirty-two-bar choruses he exhibited all the resources that Ellington was to employ so successfully a little later.

Besides his old friends Jesse Simpkins and Oliver Coleman, the band included Pee Wee Jackson, whom he had brought up from Cleveland with Freddie Webster when Hines needed trumpet players. Jackson played first and Nance shared the solo work with Emmett Berry. "It was hard to tell the difference between us, because we played so much alike then," he said.

When Henderson began to get ready to make a long road trip, he decided to stay home, much as he enjoyed the band. He got a job on the South Side at Joe Hughes' club, where female impersonators were featured, and he came out during the floorshow, singing, dancing, and playing both trumpet and fiddle.

"This was where I got a chance to do more dancing than I had before, but it had always been more for kicks than anything else," he explained. "I never really worked on it, because I wanted to play, not dance." (Here his wife intervened to reveal that with the help of another dancer, Lawrence Jackson, he actually got to the stage where he could do no-hand back flips!) "Most of the dances I do consist of steps taken from dances from 'way back. When we were playing the Grand Terrace, I'd see things the chorus girls, the shake dancers, and the belly dancers did. I remember Jota Cook, one of the greatest. She used to stand flat-footed, but she had such control of her muscles that what she did with her stomach would make you seasick. All that kind of thing, that show world, was beginning to fade as early as 1935. I think it had something to do with the change in conditions and people after the Depression."

While he was at Joe Hughes' place, Cootie Williams left Duke Ellington. People like Johnny Hodges, Toby Hardwick, and Freddie Jenkins had been in the habit of dropping in at breakfast dances when Nance had his own band in Chicago, so they all knew him. Now Duke Ellington sent Billy Strayhorn out to the club to see him.

"One morning, I'm at home," Nance continued. "It's Strayhorn on the telephone. 'Duke wants to see you down at his hotel,' he says. I was so thrilled to think that I was even considered for the job, and that's when I joined, in November, 1940. Just to be connected with Duke Ellington was the greatest thing that ever happened to me. I'd admired the band so long, and I used to skip school when it was at the Oriental Theatre. In fact, kids all over the South Side did. You couldn't find five kids in any class when that band was there."

"Raymond? He has perfect taste."

That was how Duke Ellington answered a question about different members of his trumpet section a few years ago. Certainly, Ellington was one person who thoroughly appreciated his trumpet player's artistic ability, as well as his modesty, dignity, and humor. Unlike many people small in stature, Nance has no inferiority complex, and therefore no need to adopt an outwardly aggressive personality. When he dances and sings, he may seem to resemble another predecessor in the Ellington band, Freddy Jenkins, alias Little Posey, but the singing and dancing are an act. In what he likes to do best, in playing his horn and violin, he is essentially a quiet, serious, and intent artist.

Like many other jazz musicians today, he is often at his best in the record studio. He is quick to grasp the words and spirit of lyrics, and when a problem of tempo arises he will sometimes insist on stomping it off right. Very conscious of sound values, he will take off his sweater and stuff it in a derby to get exactly the mellow quality he wants. Sometimes Ellington used to incorporate him in the reed section. Once, when Jimmy Hamilton was suddenly called upon to play a clarinet lead, the leader called across the studio, "Ray, can you play a tenor part now?" At other times, the instructions were simple and instantly understood, the result of two decades of association: "Raymond, give me a two-bar introduction, and don't forget you're Louis Armstrong!" (on *When It's Sleepy Time Down South*); or, "Ray, you be Tyree Glenn!" (on a remake of *Hy'a Sue*).

But recording is the one area in which he is critical of Ellington. "If only he would say, two weeks in advance, 'What do you want to do?' Or, 'Here's the music: get yourself ready.' He doesn't operate that way, and he can catch you at a disadvantage. He must think he's right, and I believe he likes to take chances in the studio, likes the feeling of spontaneity. But we'd like to show our best, and sometimes, after you heard the record, you knew you could have done better. Take that *Afro-Bossa* album. Instead of letting us work on the arrangements for two or three weeks, he sprang them on us right away. When we tried out new material at dances or on the job, it paid off. *Suite Thursday* was an example. We'd played that in the hotel in Boston and at Monterey before we recorded it.

"None of this alters my opinion that his music is the greatest jazz today, from an all-around point of view—not just from the point of view of swinging, but from that of basic musical value. Technically, you may be a bitch, but to play his music you've also got to feel it."

That Nance has a mind of his own was shown in 1944, when he got leave of absence for nine months from Ellington. "We were at the Hurricane, up over where the Turf was on Broadway," he said, "and all we were doing was playing shows—eight-thirty, midnight, and two. We were in there so long, not playing much Ellington music, that I was about ready to shoot myself. So I went out with a quartet—Ted Smith and Bill De Arango on guitars, and Junior Raglin on bass—and we did pretty well, particularly at a place in Washington called the Casbah."

After his return, and after the long engagements at the Hurricane and the Zanzibar, the band went into the Aquarium, where Ellington began to pull out arrangements like *Harlem Airshaft* and *Ko-ko*. Ray Nance was happy again.

Four years later he accompanied Ellington on an unusual visit to England, where they appeared with Kay Davis, Pearl Bailey, and local musicians at the London Palladium and elsewhere. As a singer and dancer, he was exempt from the union rulings that then prevented American musicians from working there. He and Ellington played their instruments as participant and accompanist in a "variety act." It was during this trip that he introduced the leader to Thelonious Monk.

"I had bought myself a portable gramophone," he said, humorously emphasizing the English term for phonograph. "I was on my way to Bournemouth, Hampshire, by train, and in my compartment I put on one of my Thelonious Monk records. Duke was passing by in the corridor, and he stopped and asked, 'Who's that playing?' I told him. 'Sounds like he's stealing some of my stuff,' he said. So he sat down and listened to my records, and he was very interested. He understood what Monk was doing."

One of the teammates in the band Nance most admired was Shorty Baker. They were featured together on a number called *Mr. Gentle and Mr. Cool*, which was presented at Newport in 1958.

"We never did figure out who was Mr. Cool," Nance continued. "But I love Shorty. The first time I heard him was with the Crackerjacks in East St. Louis, Missouri, about 1935. I had enlarged my small band for the date and we were alternating in this ballroom. They had a very precise and wonderful group, and as they began to play *Stardust* I heard this beautiful sound coming from the other side of the room. I went over and asked who the trumpet player was, and they told me, and introduced us."

Asked about those who influenced him most as a trumpet player, he answered at once:

"Naturally, I particularly admire Louis Armstrong, because he was the great forerunner. Louis Armstrong, Art Tatum, Duke Ellington, and Jimmy Blanton—you just put geniuses like that to one side and go on from there. My mind doesn't run in Dizzy Gillespie's direction, although I'd like to be able to play the horn with his facility. I think I play with more of an emotional impulse than anything else, on the horn and the violin. Jazz is feeling, in my opinion. But then take a man like Clark Terry: he can bend any way, play any type of jazz, for he's a very unusual, well-equipped player. He can play out of his head, out of his heart, or out of his head and heart together. Besides being a wonderful musician, he's also a wonderful person, and—like Duke says—you can't categorize Clark. He can do everything well."

Ray Nance himself does many things well, the most obvious being the way he now plays the cornet.

"I've been playing cornet since about 1960," he said. "I think it has a warmer tone than the trumpet. In fact, I know it has. A trumpet produces a more brilliant, piercing sound. Because it's shorter, the cornet is also more comfortable for me to use, since I use the plunger so much and my arms are not long. Another reason I took it up, and my own idea, was because I played all the lower parts in the trumpet section, and it made a better blend between the trumpets and trombones."

Back in the days of "all reet" and "all root," Ben Webster gave Ray Nance the nickname of "Root," which is still used by some of his intimates. It is curiously appropriate as an adjective to many of those qualities which distinguish him. Warmth, feeling, and emotion are terms which could also conceivably be unfashionable momentarily in any art, but the heart has its reasons, and good taste is never out of season.

[*1966*]

Jimmy Hamilton [*clarinet and tenor saxophone*]

The importance of the clarinet in the Ellington orchestra was established by Barney Bigard. Although his style owed much to the musical tradition of his birthplace, New Orleans, it was full of highly individual traits, so that he was always one of the most easily identifiable players. During the fourteen years he was with Ellington, the leader came to rely upon his facility and imagination, and to savor his "woody" sound. When he left, it was extremely difficult to replace him. For a short time, his chair was filled by Chauncey Haughton, a capable tenor saxophonist who also played clarinet. Then early in 1943, Ellington persuaded Jimmy Hamilton to join him.

" 'Would you like to come with the band?' he asked me," Hamilton recalled. "He had been trying to get me for a month, but I didn't want to leave town and travel. From my listening, I'd been as much influenced by Lunceford's band as by Duke's, and I hadn't intended going out with any of them. I was wrapped up in studying the clarinet at the time, doing legitimate studies, which I think help bring out any original talent you may have. I had a hotel job with Dave Martin— the pianist who had been with Eddie South—and he advised me to try out with Duke.

"Right off the bat, Duke told me I'd have to play tenor. Not only did I not want to travel, but I didn't want to play tenor either! Clarinet was my instrument, but on saxophone I was more of an alto player. That didn't matter to him. What he wanted to find out was whether I had an ear, so that I could follow the harmonic structure and live with it. Right away, he realized I had an ear!

"I took the job, and everything was nice, except that I didn't like the tenor. I thought it was holding me back, because of the difference in mouthpiece. I'd work on it between shows at the Hurricane, where we were playing, but it was a handicap to my clarinet study. The characters of the two instruments are quite different. The tenor is more flexible so far as bending notes is concerned, and it is very easy to play, so you are less tense and can take more liberties. Of course, I soon found I was learning so much in Duke's band. He has great imagination, and comes up with new things all the time. He never stops. He's never lost for material. Everything that happens around him is material."

That was how Jimmy Hamilton became committed to the Ellington cause—for a quarter of a century. Temperamentally more phlegmatic than most of his colleagues, he was a musician dedicated to the clarinet. Although his style was quite different from Bigard's, owing more to Benny Goodman in its phraseology than to New Orleans, he was a virtuoso whom Ellington used to ever-increasing advantage.

The oldest of three children, Hamilton was born in 1917 in Dillon, South Carolina. He was five when his parents moved to Philadelphia, where he was raised. His father played clarinet every Sunday in a brass band, and often brought different instruments back to the house. One day, his six-year-old son "started fooling around" with a baritone horn, and found out the combination of valves to play *America*. There was no stopping him then. For the rest of the day, the household was subjected to his earnest explorations of the big horn's possibilities. He began to take lessons on it the following year, and when he was eight he was playing in brass bands. Later, he took up trumpet and played in many local bands around Philadelphia, including that of Frank Fairfax, among whose trumpet players were Dizzy Gillespie and Charlie Shavers. Hamilton's professional career really began in 1934 when he joined the Fairfax band, and it was during the years he was a member of it that he made the switch to clarinet.

"I liked anything that was a challenge," he explained, "and Benny Goodman had a great influence on me. I had heard a little of Jimmie Noone on records, and I listened to Barney Bigard, Buster Bailey, and Artie Shaw, but it was Benny who inspired me, and soon I could play many of his solos note for note."

After he moved to New York, he was with Teddy Wilson at Uptown Café Society, where Wilson liked to feature a trio of similar instrumentation to that in which he had worked with Goodman. One of the numbers they played was *Body and Soul,* and Hamilton recalled that Timme Rosencrantz, the Danish critic, recorded their version live one night. Years later, he asked Hamilton to confirm that the clarinet playing was his, because he had had so many arguments with friends and other musicians who were convinced it was Goodman.

"After I joined Duke," Hamilton continued, "I was featured more and more. My approach was different from that of Barney, who was influenced by the type of clarinet playing popular in his era. I appreciate Barney. I believe he is the most technically gifted in that style, and he has the imagination and the facility to do more than most. Following someone like that, who had been so long in the band, comparisons were naturally made, but there are many kinds of jazz and you cannot make comparisons *all over* the field. My way of playing was influenced by the trend in my era, and it still incorporates contemporary developments.

"I don't think there was another band where I could have done so much, where I could have brought out the kind of playing I was qualified to do. Often, like in *Chinoiserie,* my part virtually demanded a legitimate technique. There are things done in a studio, for instance, that people don't see or recognize, and some things that came to me—like cadenzas—I couldn't have done if I hadn't had a legitimate-type training. Now you may go into a studio, you know, and here's the music right in front of you! You don't have any chance to practice it, and that's a difficult situation for any musician. People listening may think it's pretty, but they don't realize it's not easy. When Duke writes, he just writes, and doesn't think anything about how difficult it is. We often got things from him that *seemed* impractical. He would put things in front of me sometimes and say, 'Okay, you've got it!' And then I would lend my own character to what he had written. Our sax section had some tough things to handle, and we could really have enjoyed ourselves playing some of the things other arrangers wrote, because they would have seemed so simple.

"When I first went into the band, I was far from being an arranger, but I got a chance to write things here and there. I contributed special choruses to several arrangements—cooperative efforts you might say. And being around some of the greatest arrangers in the business, like Ellington and Strayhorn, I always listened and learned. It was like a school to me. Music is my life, and as I learned more I got to feel so much more comfortable and confident. And although I was in a band that worked all the time, I still had time to write."

Hamilton was responsible for the delicate backgrounds to Ellington's famous monolog, *Pretty and the Wolf.* Another example of his ability to think in terms of unusual colors occurred when Matthew Gee was playing baritone horn in the band.

"I heard him playing his baritone solo," Hamilton recalled, "and it struck me that three of those horns would sound good, so I wrote up about sixteen bars while we were playing in Pittsburgh. Booty Wood and Britt Woodman got horns from an instrument maker Booty knew in Dayton, and when we got to Vegas we tried it out. The first time, it wasn't the way we wanted it, because we had an intonation problem, but after getting together a few times it really began to sound good."

This trio never performed publicly, but with Dave Wells in Matthew Gee's place, Hamilton recorded it for an Everest album entitled *Swing Low, Sweet Chariot.*

"I used the horns mostly for counter-melodies," he said. "In a brass band, it's the baritones that get most of the work, and they can move very fast. Three make a big sound, but it is warm, not overpowering. Because it is so big, it doesn't sound as flexible as it really is. I'd played baritone and trumpet, and I knew a section could swing. Horns like that very definitely have possibilities in a band such as Duke's. They could lend a lot of weight. Although the trombone is a beautiful instrument, it doesn't have the carrying power. French horns have a quality of their own, but I think they have more limitations."

Hamilton contributed arrangements to the Ellington book from time to time, and also wrote for several of the small-band recording dates made under Johnny Hodges' name. Although clarinet always remained his chief instrument, he practiced flute assiduously and became very proficient on it during his last years with Ellington, but that leader never elected to make use of this new skill.

143

When Hamilton left in 1968, it was after a good deal of soul-searching. He was tired of the nomadic existence in hotel rooms and band buses, and he had a number of personal goals he wanted to attain. He freelanced around New York, played a prominent part in several New Jersey festivals, large and small, and the following year was rewarded with overdue public recognition when he was voted top clarinetist in the annual readers' poll of *Down Beat*.

[*1969*]

Cat Anderson   [*trumpet*]

Cat Anderson made his first appearance with Duke Ellington at the Earle Theatre, Philadelphia, on September 1st, 1944. He had already acquired with other well-known bands a considerable professional reputation for playing in the upper register, but in the years that followed, his name became indelibly associated with Ellington's.

The pyrotechnics of *Trumpet No End, The Eighth Veil, El Gato,* and *El Viti* were the bright, surface area of his contribution. The nonchalant reversal of the horn at the end of *Jam with Sam,* as he exclaims "That's the one!" after hitting a high note, has been seen by thousands, and probably millions, of TV viewers. His ascension to high gothic roofs in cathedrals here and abroad has been a vital part of the original *Sacred Concert.* "That's as high as we go," Ellington announces as the peak is reached.

Anderson does a remarkable job in this role, and it has inevitably typed him, but he is a far more versatile musician than is perhaps generally recognized. At his first Ellington rehearsal, he was gratified when the maestro switched the books and gave him the lead parts to play. And in 1967 he had an opportunity that he had long desired.

"Although I had been in small bands before," he said, "the engagement at the Rainbow Grill was something extra. In this Ellington small band, I got a chance to do some plunger work, which I really love. I also got a chance to play in the lower register, and that was a kick, because not too many people have heard me play in it.

"I don't find any problem in using the plunger, because I've been lucky enough to hear so much by great artists like Cootie Williams and Ray Nance. I mustn't forget Rex Stewart, and I know Bubber Miley from recordings. I enjoy doing it, because I've listened to those guys and liked what they were doing. It's very interesting and it broadens the musician's scope."

Often forgotten is the fact that the first Ellington showcase for Anderson, *A Gathering in a Clearing*, featured him with plunger. (This has been reissued in RCA Victor's Vintage Series.) In November, when the band was recording in San Francisco, Cat's plunger was again much in evidence on Billy Strayhorn's previously unrecorded *Charpoy*. On two other dates in the same city, with Johnny Hodges and Earl Hines, he supplemented his collection of mutes with one made out of an electric bulb carton. Earlier records made in Europe (Columbia FPX-116 and FPX-259, and Philips B77.731L) also more than hinted at the diversification made evident in public appearances during 1967.

Cat Anderson's parents both died when he was four, and he and a two-year-old brother were placed in the Jenkins Orphan Home School, Charleston, South Carolina.

"All the upbringing I remember was received there," he said. "I even got my nickname there. When I was small, there was a fight every day. I could never win these fights, and I got tired of being whipped. One day, I ran up against the bully of the yard. There would be about four hundred of us out there, playing ball and shooting marbles. Although he didn't fall, this guy must have stumbled, and then I was on his back, scratching and tearing at him. He'd been beating me up for five or six years, but when I finished he was lying on the ground. 'Hey,' the kids all around said, 'you fight like a cat!' That tag stayed with me right up to today, although my real name is William Alonzo Anderson, Jr."

There were usually seven or eight bands in the school, each with its own teacher, and Anderson began playing when he was seven. By the time he was ten, he could play several instruments. One means by which the school supported itself was by sending the bands out on the streets and taking up collections.

"The Number One and Number Two bands used to travel a lot," Anderson resumed, "always with a superintendent from the school in attendance. They would play dance music, overtures, and marches on the street, and after each tune the superintendent would make a speech, and tell what the school was for and what it was doing. Then a hat would be passed through the audience. It was the same principle as the Salvation Army's. The bands were usually fifteen or sixteen pieces, sometimes more.

"I began on trombone, but my arms weren't long enough for the sixth and seventh positions. From that, I went to the baritone horn and the upright bass horn. I also played drums, cymbals, kettle drums, the alto and E flat horn, and the mellophone. What made me go for trumpet was when the Number One band came off the road and I

145

heard what men like Jabbo Jenkins, Jabbo Smith, and Peanuts Holland were doing on it. I'd never heard anything like that before. Both Jabbos were very good trumpet players. I never heard Jabbo Smith's early records until recently in London. His technique was very good and showed a concert background, the kind they taught in the school then.

"The teaching was stern, and we got many whippings. We had to do exactly what the teachers said. To kids today the way they used a whip might seem cruel, but it was part of the times. Having gone through that, it always seemed a darned shame to me that so many fine musicians gave up afterwards. One guy who didn't, who's still around New York, is E. V. Perry.

"As I look back on the teaching now, I know that it was inadequate in some places, that even the rudiments were not always taught properly. But the school was run on charity and the pay was small, so there was a limit to what could be expected. The school specialized in brass, and one very good teacher was Alonzo Mills, a trumpet player. Amos Gilliard was a fantastic trombonist, more of a concert than a jazz player, and he returned and taught at the school for a while.

"They had plenty of instruments there, and if you showed determination they would let you play the instrument you chose. When

Johnny Hodges, Paul Gonsalves, Jimmy Hamilton

you had that, they sat you in front of a blackboard on which were the scales and the five lines and spaces of the staff. I don't remember them teaching about breathing or correct embouchure, but we all helped one another, and to a large extent we were self-taught. We'd sit down and talk, and find things out ourselves. That accounts for a lot of individuality.

"I first went out on the road in 1929. It was a wonderful experience, like going to a ball game. We would travel three months, go to school three months, and then maybe head north for another three. One time, when we got into New York, all the trumpet players ran away. I was playing trombone then, but I told the superintendent I would play trumpet if he got me one. He did that, and because one of the missing boys had been leader, I now became leader of the band."

By the time they were sixteen to eighteen years old, the boys at the school were supposed to have learned a trade. There were opportunities to learn farming or shoemaking, or to work in the printing department. Those in the bands had the regular curriculum, and at certain seasons had to work on the farm. As they grew older, they could go out at night, and Anderson played many weekend jobs around Charleston, the money he made being his to keep or spend.

"We were all good buddies in Band Number Five," he continued,

Cat Anderson

"and we formed a band so that we could play dances. It began at a picnic, where we were setting riffs and each taking a 'Boston,' as they called solos then. It sounded good. There were about fourteen of us, and we started getting country jobs and work back o' town. One Monday, they said there would be no school and that most of us had to go up to the farm and pick cotton. The guys in the older bands didn't have to go, and the next day they started calling us 'The Cotton Pickers.' The name stuck, and eventually we became the Carolina Cotton Pickers. We didn't know anything about McKinney's Cotton Pickers then because even when we were out playing the streets of cities like Boston, Providence, and New York, we had to be in bed by sundown. So we didn't know what was going on in the music field. There were records at the school, but in those days the only ones that interested me were Louis Armstrong's.

"We decided to try our luck in Texas, but we sat there two months and didn't play a job. We couldn't get any work. We were new, and didn't have any transportation, or a name like Papa Celestin and Joseph Robichaux and those other bands out of New Orleans. The school sent a bus to fetch us back.

"When we tried another crack at it, we went to Florida and stayed nine months, but we didn't make any real money. It seemed every time we would be playing, somebody like Cab Calloway, Duke Ellington, or Jimmie Lunceford, or the Mills Blue Rhythm Band, would be in town, and we'd end up with a dollar or two to buy gas for the little raggedy car we had. That was something to see with about twelve of us in it, and a little trailer on the back! Maybe we'd have enough to get a pad of rolls at the baker's, and some green oranges. We lived like that nine months. There was no leader, because we were like a cooperative, and there was no one guy with enough git-up-and-go to go out and get something. The older fellows made the decisions, and I was a young one who had no say-so. It was all right with me, too, because all I wanted to do was play.

"We used to play stocks, and things we copied off records. Our uniforms were sweaters and white trousers. The trumpets wore green sweaters, the saxophones blue, and the rhythm some other color. The band continued quite a while after I left, but although it made some Vocalion records, it never got anywhere because it didn't have a leader who would speak up, instead of dealing with a shyster, some booking agent who didn't have a license. It was always a matter of take it or leave it. We were hungry, and if he had five dollars, it meant everybody ate."

The Carolina Cotton Pickers were still working where they could in Florida, Louisiana, and Georgia when the president of the school died in 1937. Anderson felt it was time to make a decision, for he had already had several offers. He accepted what seemed the most secure, for $17 a week, more money than he had ever had before, from Hartley Toots in Florida. Toots was a guitar player, "a very good musician, although not a jazz player." Snookum Russell made all the arrangements for his big band, and Melrose Colbert, Ray Nance's first wife, was its excellent singer.

"It was a territory band and not as polished as those in the East," Anderson recalled, "but we went to play the Apollo Theatre in New York—a big deal. Mr. Tom Whaley, my good friend today, was music director there then. Now it seemed that when territory bands went into the Apollo, they were given the hardest shows to play. They gave us *Mexican Hat Dance,* and it was too much, because the guys didn't know the short cuts, and their reading was bad, but I was up on that kind of stuff because it was what we did in school. The day before the show was to open, they decided they'd have to get another band. 'This band can't cut the show,' they said.

"I'd only been to New York before with the school band, and this time I wanted to stay at least a week, so I told Tom Whaley, 'If you give me the first trumpet parts, I can play them. I see there's a weakness there, because he (the lead trumpet) has all the other things to play, but I'm a new fellow in the band and can't go over his head.' When Tom decided to switch the parts, I played all through that number, and we made the week.

"That was in the pit. After that, we had to come up on stage and do the band's specialities. I had written a number called *Stop Now, You Did Enough to Me,* and I was amazed by the applause my high trumpet playing was getting. I'd end with a high flare, and the whole band would shout, 'Stop now, you did enough to me!' Of course, that was the kind of thing that was popular then, but I didn't have anything else to play.

"The reason I'd come to play so high was because at school there were guys who could do it much better than I could. They used to take my girls from me with their high notes. This happened every Friday night at dances. Finally, I got angry and started playing everything in the upper register. They didn't play after me this time. 'Hey, you know what you were doing there?' they asked. It turned out that I'd been playing note for note an octave above what they did.

"To play really high, you must have this need for recognition, this desire to be recognized. Then you try to find a way for yourself. They'd been coming in week after week, and outplaying me, and this drove me to discover a hidden talent. Many guys who would like to do it could do it, if they had the will power. They must think in that direction, and they must sacrifice. You have to be like a boss or a rugged person on a job. You must have complete determination. It may take many hours, many days, many years. Teeth and bone structure may have something to do with it, but anyone can bring this talent out if they have the will.

"Some people get disgusted. Before it happened to me, I was playing another way altogether. We had played all Louis Armstrong's things note for note long before Jimmie Lunceford began featuring Tommy Stevenson. In the school, all the trumpet players played *Shine*, and made a hundred C's with the F on top. We were young and wanted to play. We weren't trying to prove anything.

"When I say you have to sacrifice to accomplish it up there, I don't mean tone. There's a flaw in it unless it can be done smoothly, as you would in the lower register, where you phrase melodically. The rhythmic effect of jazz can be lost. The main thing is to make the high notes effective when you play them. You mustn't crowd in too many. Sometimes it may get out of hand. It may go sharp or it may go flat. That will depend on the state of mind the individual is in, and how much work he has done before he gets a chance to make this play. In my opinion, you can't think the same way up there as you do below. Some may argue about this, but I believe the thinking is altogether different. You've got to simplify to make it clean."

Before he went to the Apollo with Hartley Toots, Anderson had been making $17 a week. Bill Rivers, a nightclub owner in Miami, also owned the band. At the end of the week, the men were paid off by a union official downstairs. The trumpet player was surprised to receive $81.27.

"Is this mine?"

"Oh, yes. Sign here. All that's yours. You're not supposed to kick-back anybody."

At that time, Anderson didn't know what "kickback" meant, but when he got upstairs Rivers had already relieved the others of everything over their Florida salaries.

"Cat, what are you going to do?" he asked.

"What do you mean?"

"You know your salary is only $17."

"The man downstairs said this money was all mine."

"What man?"

"The union delegate."

"You know, all the other fellows have given me their money...."

"I'm going to keep this." *

"Then you'll have to lose your job," Rivers said.

150   There was one more show to play.

"I played it with one hand, with my left hand in my pocket holding that money," Anderson recalled. "I would have stayed with that band if he had just taken half, but he wanted too much!"

Anderson worked around New York for a time, played with Claude Hopkins, and then joined the Sunset Royals in 1938. He had known all the musicians in this cooperative band in Florida, and two of them, E. V. Perry and Julius Watson, had been schoolmates of his. At different times, the band was fronted by Steve Washington ("a good guitar player from Pittsburgh"), pianist Ace Harris, and Sol Albright. For a big tour of the South with the Ink Spots, Doc Wheeler became the front man, and the band was billed as Doc Wheeler and the Sunset Royals. Anderson stayed until 1941, the year he wrote *How 'Bout That Mess,* which the band recorded for Bluebird.

"It was quite a success," the trumpet player remembered. "Lucky Millinder and Sam Price recorded it, too, but I didn't make much from it, because I didn't know anything about publishing companies, and Moe Gale took care of it. Years later, when I recorded it with my own band in 1947, I changed the title to *Swinging the Cat.*"

After Pearl Harbor, Anderson was in a Special Services band which played many Army camps and bases. Engagements with Lucky Millinder and Erskine Hawkins followed.

"Erskine Hawkins didn't know I played so much in the upper register," he continued. "We were doing the same kind of thing. He always had good trumpet players, and Bill Johnson wrote an arrangement called *Frost* to feature them. The others were Reunald Jones, C. H. Jones, and Sammy Lowe. At rehearsal, while they were getting organized, nobody played what they were going to do later on, but when we got on stage at the Earle Theatre in Philadelphia, all the trumpet players were really *playing.* When it got to my part, I went up in the stratosphere and started doing the octave things. When Erskine came in, he wasn't playing that high, and he was a little shocked to find what talent he had in his section. At the end of the show, he looked at me kind of strange, and I knew I was about to leave.

"Gladys Hampton was in the audience that night, and she wanted me to go over to Lionel's band. It was a very good band then, with Earl Bostic, Ray Perry, Rudy Rutherford, Arnett Cobb, Charlie Fowlkes, Fred Becket, Booty Wood, Al Hayse, Joe Morris, Lamar Wright, Jr., Joe Newman, Billy Mackel, and Milt Buckner. It was a wonderful experience, and there was a lot of excitement, but the work was too hard, and underpaid. I didn't hold that against Lionel, because we weren't businessmen. It was a challenge, and I did my job."

151

Anderson next joined Sabby Lewis for a short time (before Paul Gonsalves). Then he went back to Lionel Hampton. In between, he often sat in with Cootie Williams' band at the Savoy ballroom. Driving home together afterwards, Williams sometimes suggested he join Duke Ellington.

"One day," he said, "Harry Carney came by where I was playing with Lionel. He was on vacation, and he asked me if I wanted to join Ellington. At first, I jumped at the opportunity, but when I thought it over, I decided not to change, Duke sent Willie Manning down to get me, but I went out on the road again with Lionel. Later, in 1944, we were in Chicago, and Lionel was getting ready to go to California by train, and I found everybody would have a *chair* to ride in. No sleeper! I made up my mind I was going to join Ellington, and I got on the phone and found he was in Sioux City, Iowa. He told me he would be in Chicago the very next day. I went to Philadelphia—in a sleeper!—the night after that, and opened with him at the Earle Theatre.

"At rehearsal, he switched the books so that I had all the lead parts. I listened very carefully. Instead of starting at the top, we'd start at the bottom, play two bars at the top, go to the middle of the arrangement for eight bars, and then back to A. I made my sketches and had it all marked out, so I was ready. Then I found the band wasn't using stands on the stage, so I had to lay the music out on the floor. The moment the curtains parted, all the lights went out! 'How am I going to play this music?' I asked. 'Baby, you'll have to learn it,' one of the guys said. By the next day, I had memorized all the music in the show and didn't need to see it anymore."

That was the beginning of Anderson's long association with Ellington. He didn't replace anyone, but came in as a new voice, as Ben Webster had done. Ellington had had good reports of his working ability beforehand, but besides Rex Stewart, he also had Taft Jordan, Shelton Hemphill, and Ray Nance at the time.

"At the Earle Theatre, the band used to play Mary Lou Williams' arrangement of *Blue Skies*," Anderson continued. "It wasn't just a trumpet feature then. There was a chorus of clarinet by Jimmy Hamilton, a chorus of tenor by Al Sears, a release by Claude Jones, and Rex Stewart used to play the ending. We were at a theatre in Canton, Ohio, when Rex didn't show. After listening to it all week—and I'm a great listener to anything good, especially on trumpet—I knew his solo. So when Duke asked if anybody wanted to play it, and nobody volunteered, he said, 'What about the new trumpet player?' I told him I'd try, and after the other solos I came down front and played it an octave higher. When I ended up on a double C, and the people were applauding, Duke said, 'Good, we'll keep it just like that.' As luck would have it, Rex came in the stage door as I was blasting away. He didn't speak to me for fifteen years. He was highly strung, and so am I."

Despite this mischance, Anderson maintained a great admiration for Stewart's work, and he became one of the few who could effectively simulate his half-valve style. "That made a big impression on me," he admitted. "It takes a lot of skill to do it. And again it's a matter of your thinking, and concentrating."

After Stewart had left the band, *Blue Skies* became, in 1946, a showcase for the trumpet section with the new title, *Trumpets No End.* Shelton Hemphill played the lead part, and Shorty Baker, Francis Williams, Taft Jordan, Ray Nance, and Anderson took the solos. As the sole survivor of that remarkable sextet in the section today, Anderson is still very much the virtuoso, but his adaptability and experience brought new responsibilities in roles formerly allotted to others, as in the Rainbow Grill engagement, a subject to which he returned zestfully.

"I enjoy having a floor full of dancers," he said. "It seems to me that everybody enjoys the music more, even those who are not dancing but just standing there watching the dancers. We play more swinging things then than we would at a concert, because people like to get up and move about in rhythm. I think that's wonderful. Some of the people on the floor may not be good dancers, but when the music has that beat to it they swing right along with it. Whether they're looking and listening, or dancing and listening, my main concern is that they're enjoying themselves."

[*1967*]

Russell Procope [*alto saxophone and clarinet*]

"I was born on August 11, 1908, at 218 West 64th Street, New York City. My earliest memory, right from the time I was crawling around on the floor, is of the music my parents were playing. I liked music even then, because I would stop whatever I was doing and listen. We had a piano at home and my mother, who had played as a child in church, always played classical music, and no jazz. My father played violin—also classical—and together they'd play things like *Poet and Peasant* and Brahms' *Lullaby.*

"When I was six, my father bought violins for my brother and me. (My brother was a year older than I.) So I started studying, and even then I liked it. I liked the violin itself, but I think I would have liked any other instrument, because it was the music that appealed to me. I studied violin until I was fourteen, and I was one of the first violins in my Junior High School Orchestra, and I was very proud when we won first prize for Greater New York. The music we played for the contest was a selection from *Carmen*. I always remember the first part as very intricate and it required a lot of skill from kids like we were. That was one of the biggest things that happened to me up to that time. Music really was a part of me. Player-pianos were the vogue when I was eleven or twelve, and I remember once somebody down the street was playing *The Hallelujah Chorus* from *The Messiah*. It moved me so much that I cried.

"The next step was to a teacher called Michaels. Professor Michaels, we used to call him, but officially he was Lieutenant Eugene Michaels. He was a very, very good trumpet player and he had been director of the 15th Infantry band in Europe during World War I. At that time it was one of the most famous military bands in the world. He had originally taught at the famous Jenkins Orphanage Home in South Carolina. He had two sons, Eugene and Otto (Gene is still active musically), who played clarinets and saxophones, and he decided he was going to form a boys' band. He called it the 369th Cadet Band and the boys all got uniforms like soldiers. Because I was a violin player, I couldn't join, but I knew something about music and when he found he was short of clarinet players he tried to get my father to buy me a clarinet. My father absolutely refused. 'I've bought him a violin and spent all this money on lessons' he said, 'and I think he should continue to be a violin player.' But I began to lose interest in violin then, because I had seen a lot of clarinet players and had begun to want a clarinet.

"One Saturday afternoon, I went to the studio where Lieutenant Michaels taught. It was on the street that later became famous as 'Swing Street'—52nd Street. There was always music on that street. Lieutenant Michaels took a sort of interest in me and now he gave me a ticket. 'Take it,' he said, 'and go down to Carl Fischer's Music Shop. Give them the ticket and they'll give you a clarinet.' That was how I got my first clarinet, and I started hemming and hawing on it right away.

"It was the thing I now wanted to do, and I studied with him for a time, learned to play the scales, and so on. It was the same system I play now—the Albert system. People have told me through the years that they thought an Albert clarinet was more adaptable to jazz than a Boehm. I don't know about this, because I've heard some pretty good people play Boehm, like Albert Nicholas and Buster Bailey, Benny Goodman, and Artie Shaw play Boehm, too. Do you

think if Barney Bigard had played Boehm he would sound different to the way he does now? After all, it's just a different system of fingering. Simeon Bellson, one of the greatest legitimate clarinet players in symphony, played Albert. Boehm offers the most technically, because you have more keys and more ways of making any given passage. The only reason I prefer the Albert system is because it's the only one I've ever known. I'm pretty sure the Albert system existed before Boehm, and today it has been much improved. The one I have is the most advanced Albert. Frankly, if I were going to recommend a clarinet to a youngster, I'd recommend Boehm. For one thing, an Albert is hard to find. I'd have a devil of a time finding one, or I'd have to go to the factory to have one made. The other day, I was down at Carl Fischer's again, across the street from Carnegie Hall on 57th, and they had two brand-new German Alberts in the window. I told the fellow I was in a hurry, but would like to try one and would come back. I went back a couple of days later and they were both gone. Anyway, I think that what you hear is more a matter of the man than the system. If Barney Bigard had played Boehm, or Buster Bailey Albert, I don't think they'd have sounded very different to the way they do now. Omer Simeon and Jimmie Noone played Albert, but Darnell Howard plays Boehm. How about that?

"Back with Lieutenant Michaels, we started playing the marches, and before long I got to parade with the clarinet. At about the same time, my brother got a trumpet and played in the band (he didn't go on to become a professional). The clarinet didn't come easy to me at all, and I remember listening to him on trumpet and thinking he played his instrument much better than I did mine. But I don't think it would have made any difference to me which horn it was, because I liked them all.

"I wrestled with the clarinet for a year, but with no idea of jazz, because I had gone fron longhair music to military band music. The jazz awakening happened out of a clear blue sky. I had gone uptown with a little girl friend of mine, and we were supposed to be attending a dance at the Manhattan Casino, which is now the Rockland Palace.* There was great band on the stage—Fletcher Henderson's —and in it were Louis Armstrong, Charlie Green, Coleman Hawkins, Don Redman, Buster Bailey, Charlie Dixon, and Kaiser Marshall. At that time, everybody danced, and they liked fast tempos, and there was a lot of fast music that wasn't easy to play. 'Swing' was years in the future, but Louis was certainly swinging then on numbers like

* At that time, Harlem wasn't as big as it is now. Now it extends from 110th St. to 155th, and practically river to river, but then it was from 135th to maybe 145th, and from Lenox to maybe Eighth Avenue. So a place like the Manhattan Casino was far uptown, and the Audubon Ballroom was in Washington Heights and more or less off the scene.

Shanghai Shuffle. I don't think anything before or since made such an impression on me as that band, and I think it decided for me what I was going to do with my life. You're more impressionable at that age and I'm glad it happened when I was that young, but as a teen-ager I had a very full schedule. Everything I did was more or less supervised. I had to take my music lessons and I played basketball in the church team. In the summer, I'd play ball in the park, and sometimes I'd go away with my mother. My life was regulated and I was fortunate to have a good family life. We always stuck together. When I became interested in jazz, my father wasn't for it. He insisted that I had to finish school, and I went along with him as far as I could, but people began to come to me and offer ten to fifteen dollars to play a dance at night. It seemed quite a bit of money to me then.

"I don't quite know why I dropped violin, but I think I thought I could never approach anything like jazz on it. There wasn't much feeling for violins then, and little for a violin to do, because vaudeville was going out of style. I did try to get back with it one time when I was with Fletcher Henderson at Connie's Inn and Edgar Sampson was in the band. I used to like to hear other people play jazz on violin. There used to be a Chinese restaurant called World Tea Garden on Lenox Avenue, and there was a man called Charlie Grimes there who played the weirdest jazz-type music I ever heard on a violin. I haven't heard anything of him for many years. I was still a kid then, about fifteen, and I used to get on the trolley-car and go all the way up Lenox Avenue just to hear him. He played with piano and drums and I remember going up to him and his 'orchestra' with a quarter and asking, 'Will you please play *Sweet Georgia Brown?*' So they did that, and at fifteen that made me feel very good. Finding him then, all by myself, was like discovering a goldmine or a rainbow.

"But after hearing the Henderson band .... There were other boys in the neighborhood who had saxophones and trumpets, and other instruments bought by doting parents. Some were meant to be musicians and some were not, but we'd get together. Again it was with Lieutenant Michaels and his sons, and in their house, that we got into it, into jazz. When the Savoy opened, Otto Michaels was one of the three saxophonists in the band called the Savoy Bearcats. Freddie Jenkins was in the Junior High School Orchestra when I was, and even as a boy he was a marvelous trumpet player. He was adapted to the instrument and could play it very well when he was twelve. Bubber Miley lived on 63rd Street. I knew of him and Bobby Stark when I was in school. Bobby used to do that growling like Bubber, too—Bubber was his idol when he was young—but later he wanted to change and he got away from it. Two more real jazz guys were Jake Green, a trombone player, and Jimmy Welch, a clarinet player. Joe Nanton came from uptown, from 137th Street. He could always play, even when he was a kid in Boy Scouts.

"Benny Carter and I went to school together, but I don't remember his playing anything when we were eleven or twelve. My first inkling of his having anything to do with music came one day when I was walking up Eighth Avenue after a music lesson, heading home to 64th Street, and he was going down Eighth (he lived on 63rd) with an alto saxophone in a corduroy bag under his arm.

" 'What're you doing, Benny?' I asked.

" 'I'm going to take some lessons on this saxophone,' he said.

"I didn't think anymore about it, but within about six months Benny Carter was the top of the whole neighborhood. He took to saxophone like a duck to water. By this time I was playing clarinet, but Benny just swept us all away with his phenomenal ability to play his instrument. He was one of the first of us youngsters to become a professional, and he was soon working uptown in clubs and on other jobs. Soon after that, he was writing arrangements and playing quite a bit of piano, and before long he could play trumpet and trombone, too. He was just a marvelous, natural-born musician. I think if he had concentrated more on clarinet, there's no knowing what he might have done, because I believe there's so much more you can do on a clarinet than on a saxophone or trumpet.

"In the first place, you have so much more register on clarinet, so much difference of tone: the low tone, the chalumeau; the middle, which they call throat tone; the medium-high; and the altissimo. They're all on the same instrument and it's like having four horns in one. I believe that men with all the ideas Benny and Coleman Hawkins had would have found much more room to express themselves on clarinet. It's just a theory, and it might not have worked out that way, but the saxophone is more limited. I remember discussing it once with Coleman Hawkins when we were working together, and I believe he agreed with me, but he had played cello when he was young and I guess the voice of the tenor appealed to him. No doubt Benny Carter played alto because he liked it, but I've equally no doubt that he could have been just as good a trumpet player, a trombone player, or a clarinet player.

"I liked saxophone, too, but my father was still against the horns because he had spent all that money on violin training. Now, my mother was always the go-between, saying, 'Don't worry about it; everything will turn out all right.' One year, just a couple of nights before Christmas, she said, 'Look in the closet. There's something there for you.' And when I looked there was a brand-new alto saxophone in a case. She had bought it for me, because she knew how much I wanted it. As my father, bless him, came to see that I could

157

handle these things, and might amount to something with them, he came around, too. He was in my corner to the extent that at one time he thought I should further my career with piano lessons, but I didn't have time.

"I think my first professional job was at a store-opening, where they wanted some people and music to ballyhoo. I got twelve dollars and it seemed such a lot of money. I jobbed around after that and I got a Sunday night gig while I was still in high school. I would go to school Monday morning without much sleep. We had a gym instructor who was a pretty hard man, and sometimes I wouldn't feel like going through all the exercises. There were plenty of boys who had extracurricular duties in those days, so the Monday morning class often wasn't too much. You'd go to this instructor and tell him you'd been to a party the night before and that your stomach was bad, and he'd say, 'Okay, let me look at you.' He'd take you in his office and look at your eyes and so on, and then get a big tumbler of Epsom salts and tell you to drink it down. So I'd stand in front of him, drink it down, and go home.

"I stayed with the saxophone and by this time we had moved uptown to 99th Street from the San Juan Hill area. One day, a booking agent told me he had a job for me in a dancing school on 116th Street and Lexington Avenue, a dime-a-dance deal. That was my first regular job and I played alto and clarinet, although after getting the saxophone I tended to neglect the other. Writers even then didn't write too much for clarinet. Fletcher's band was supposed to have been the first to feature clarinet trios, but those were in special arrangements and no one else had them. The six-piece group I was playing in had a tenor player, Bubber Wheat, who played better clarinet than I did, real blues clarinet. He works on a ship now, but then he was strictly a jazzman, not too much of a legitimate musician. That was what I was interested in, jazz, for I had had my fill of the other kind, and I didn't want to play just strict dance music. We also had a great jazz trumpet player called Fred Douglas (not Freddie), who played along the lines of Bubber Miley and Bobby Stark. He died soon afterwards, but he was a very learned trumpet player.

"I stayed on this job a year and a half, and it was good experience. From there I went uptown to the Bamboo Inn, Harry Carney had played there before I did, and for the same guy. It was a big band for those days—ten pieces, three saxes, three brass, and four rhythm. It had some of Fletcher Henderson's arrangements and Freddy Johnson was playing piano. Ward Pinkett, Langston Curl, Jimmy Archey, Joe Garland, and Manzie Johnson were some of the others in it. Sapero—I'm not sure of the spelling—played banjo and was the leader.

"Next, I went to another dancing school, the Rose Danceland on 125th, and a band led by Charlie Skeets, a pianist. He had Joe Garland, Tommy Benford, Bill Benford, Lee Blair, Gene Johnson, who played with Machito for a long time, Ward Pinkett, Ed Swayzee, and Bill Cato. While I was working there, the proprietor hired Jelly Roll Morton to take the band over. He had record contracts, which was how we came to record for Victor. He had his favorite people, too, and he sent to Chicago for Omer Simeon and some others. This was good for me, to be with people like that and to be influenced by them, particularly Simeon. Working side by side with him for several months, I couldn't help being influenced by him. Prior to that it had been Buster Bailey. I liked what Omer was doing, liked his message, loved and respected him.

"Jelly Roll had a tremendous influence on me, too. When he first came there, we were only kids, but we were thinking, 'Who is this guy, telling us what to do?' After a while he told us, 'I'm either going to run this band or I'm going to break it up!' I think I must have been rebellious at one point, because he fired me, but two or three days later he called and told me to come on back. That was a disciplinary measure! I liked what he was doing. It was strictly jazz, and he'd bring in special pieces he'd written himself, where before we'd mostly been playing stocks. He really knew about the blues, too. He was around with a band in New York for several years, and I can remember him playing piano as late as 1938 at the Onyx Club.

"When I got into this business, I wanted to learn *jazz!* I didn't just pick up a horn and start 'wailin,' as they say now. I didn't know the twelve-bar blues. I had to learn, and since this was my education, I used to pick my spots and try to go to the right school. Jelly Roll's was one. I wanted to work with *musicians,* not just a singer or a dancer who happened to have a band.

"Joe Oliver's band came to town about this time. To my mind, he was one of the greatest, although he was getting to be a pretty old man. But you could tell from what he did do how wonderful he had been. He made some good records while he was in New York and he had with him a young man called Barney Bigard. The band broke up in New York and Joe went back to Chicago—so did Omer Simeon— but Barney and Red Allen stayed. I thought Barney was the greatest man I ever heard play clarinet. His sound and notes impressed me very much, and the mood he created and his approach did too. Everyone is influenced by someone else, but though I didn't consciously copy the man, I realized that this was how I wanted to play.

"I worked next with Benny Carter at the Arcadia Ballroom, which is now the Riviera on Broadway and 53rd. He had a number of fellows with him from Wilberforce University, who had been in

Horace Henderson's band originally. This would be 1928 or 1929, and I remember Bob Carroll, the tenor player, Joe Turner, the pianist, and Charlie Green. I batted around after that, and even played a one-nighter in Baltimore with Duke Ellington. There were a whole lot of jobs in those days and it was a matter of finding the people to fill them. It's just the reverse today.

"In the winter of 1929–30, I joined Chick Webb. We had Toby Hardwick and Elmer Williams to begin with, and when Toby left we had Hilton Jefferson. Jeff was an inspiration. He was one of the greatest alto players, and he still is. Chick Webb, if not *the* greatest, was one of the-two or three greatest drummers who ever lived. Believe that. We played at the Savoy and Roseland ballrooms and worked around New York. In those days you didn't have to do one-nighters often. The band stayed together and began to get some recognition. Don Kirkpatrick was on piano and John Trueheart on guitar. The trumpets were Louis Bacon, Louis Hunt, and Scad Hemphill, and on trombones from time to time we had Benny Morton and Charlie Green. Chick and Fletcher used to battle each other and exchange arrangements. So besides pleasure, it was educational. One night, when I was playing opposite Fletcher, Benny Carter didn't show up and I played alto in both bands. While we were at Roseland, Chick made a deal with Fletcher and got Jimmy Harrison and Benny Carter in exchange for Benny Morton and Russell Procope. I'm afraid Fletcher got the worst of that deal!

"I was with Fletcher from 1931 to 1934. Those were the days of what Duke Ellington calls the Great Drinkers—guys who could drink *and* play. I didn't learn to drink in that band, however, because I was twenty-three years old and had learned several years before that. It's what I like to call Big John's Era. All the musicians used to go to Big John's bar. (He still works uptown, at the Victoria.) At that time, Fletcher was the mainstay of the Roseland Ballroom and he worked there about six months out of the year, or maybe longer. He'd do some one-nighters, and then when the season opened after Labor Day, he'd go back to Roseland. He gave that up eventually to go uptown to Connie's Inn, which Connie Immerman and his brother owned. Duke Ellington was then at the Cotton Club, and he was beginning to take over, because Fletcher was becoming less ambitious than he had been.

"When we were touring, I used to ride with Russell Smith. They called him 'Pop,' and they used to call us 'Big Pop' and 'Little Pop.' Pop wasn't a great jazzman. In fact, he didn't play any at all. He said he used to, but had stopped. He had done a lot of show work before and he was the kind of man you wanted for a lead. Rex Stewart and Bobby Stark were the other two trumpets, and they were great.

"After a while, Fletcher's band got into a bad way from the point of view of music *and* work. Money didn't matter too much to me then, because I could always go home to sleep and eat, but at Connie's Inn we were earning a hundred dollars a week, or a little more, and that was good money then. There were a lot of theatres to work, too, and we used to double in the Lafayette, which was upstairs, above Connie's.

"Fletcher would have a singer from time to time, but he never really featured one. His was primarily a dance band, and at Roseland he played tangos, waltzes, fox-trots, college songs, current hits, excerpts from the classics in dance tempos, just about everything. His was, nevertheless, the first really well-known, *big* jazz band. Most of his record dates at that time were around nine o'clock in the morning. We used to finish work at three, and by the time we'd make the rounds of the ginmills, speakeasies, flats, and things, it would be time for the record date. Probably you'd still have your tuxedo on, but you might not be in peak condition.

"With the name he had, and the men he had, Fletcher wasn't doing what he should have done, so I got a bit disgusted, and that's why I left. There were other good bands by this time, too. Duke was getting well established. Earl Hines and Charlie Johnson had good bands. Then there were McKinney's Cotton Pickers and lots and lots of bands in the Mid-West and all around.

"So now I worked for a time with Tiny Bradshaw, who had been with Luis Russell's band at Roseland, and I even went to Chicago with him. But then my mother was ill and I didn't want to leave New York. The Savoy was just around the corner, so Teddy Hill's band was a logical step. Bill Coleman, Frank Newton, Roy Eldridge, Dizzy Gillespie, Dicky Wells, Chu Berry, and Bob Carroll all played in that band. Though by this time I was most known as an alto saxophonist, I played clarinet with Teddy, too. I went to London, Dublin, and Paris with him in 1937. When we came back, I was a big man. I'd been all over the world and I knew everything. So I got married and I was very happy about it, because now everything seemed to fall into place with my work and everything.

"I joined John Kirby's band at the Onyx on 52nd Street in 1938, and that was my gig for six years until I went into the Army. At the time of our first engagement, Stuff Smith was more or less the house band at the Onyx, but when he was coming back the proprietor, Joe Helbock, didn't really want to let us out. This was unheard of, but he put us on half salary to rehearse five afternoons a week. It was the making of the Kirby band. We didn't have too much music, but we'd sit around in a circle and make up things. The next time Stuff Smith went out, we went in, and Stuff never came back. Later, Ernie By-

161

field, who owned the Ambassador Hotel in Chicago, heard us and booked us into the hotel for two weeks. We stayed there nine months, went to California, and came back to Café Society Uptown. We were on the upgrade then, had a radio commercial in 'Duffy's Tavern,' record and transcription dates. This was a period I enjoyed very much, and though bandleaders had known about me quite a while, I think it was now I got a little public recognition. I had an offer from Artie Shaw and another from Jimmie Lunceford, but I liked what we were doing and wanted to be in New York as much as possible. The war broke the group up. Billy Kyle was the first to go, but we got Clyde Hart. I joined the Army in 1943. Kirby felt this kind of thing shouldn't happen to him, but it was happening to everybody. He tried again after the war, but it wasn't the same. When I got out of the Army, he was working at the Copacabana Lounge in New York with Sarah Vaughan, and I went back to him. He had Freddy Webster, Buster Bailey, Hank Jones, and Bill Beason.

"Things had finally gone bad with Kirby when Duke asked me to come with him. Otto Hardwick had wandered off and got lost, and Duke didn't know where he would find him. When I joined, it was just on a temporary basis for a broadcast he had to make in Worcester, Massachusetts. He asked me to take a train up, and I had no idea I would be with him one week or a month later, but here I am seventeen years later! I was in terrible shape the morning he called, too, and wouldn't have done it for anyone but Duke. After the broadcast, he said, 'You might as well stay for a dance we have tonight in Providence.' I don't think I could have been any luckier than to have been sitting in the house at that time and hear the phone ring. A lot of people get gigs, but not seventeen-year gigs!

"Jimmy Hamilton was playing clarinet when I joined, and just how I came to get featured on clarinet as well is hard to explain. I guess it just happened, but when I was with Teddy Hill I tried to play in an idiom appropriate to his arrangements. The more bluesy style wouldn't have fitted. In Duke's band, I could play more in the styles by which I had genuinely been influenced, and I was familiar with the clarinet tradition in his compositions and arrangements. I had come into the band as a first saxophone player, but as time went on I'd play a bar of clarinet here and there which contributed to the flavor. I never tried to be a star clarinet player, but since Barney Bigard wasn't there anymore, I did try to maintain a tradition of the orchestra. You remember when Duke remade *The Mooche* with me playing the solo and Jimmy Hamilton playing the obbligato? That was Duke's idea and I thought it came off.

"Although I had worked with big bands like Fletcher's and 162 Teddy Hill's, their music was so much simpler than Duke's. To me,

Duke Ellington is the epitome of music in the jazz field. There are so many other things he can do, as he proves every day, that he really doesn't have to confine himself to jazz. (Nowadays, you have to do more than one thing, which is what restricts most of the other bands.) The man has so much talent at his fingertips that when we play a concert it really is a concert. He has such a variety of material to draw on, whether it's in a dancehall, a club, a theatre, or a concert hall.

"Fletcher Henderson and John Kirby were great musicians, but they didn't have much initiative. They were both easygoing men who would turn their backs on responsibility. Duke Ellington, in comparison, and in the jargon of the street, is a hustler. He'll forego a meal or eight hours' sleep where they wouldn't, and musically, of course, he is more talented. Kirby may have looked like a disciplinarian, but I don't think he knew what the word 'discipline' meant. Duke most definitely does. In order to put up with undisciplined people the way he does, you have to know what discipline means. I think he rules with an iron hand in a mink glove.

"You might say I usually lead the section, but certainly not all the time. Our section is a whole thing in itself. We don't have a first saxophone player, or second saxophone player, or third saxophone player. We have things where anybody might be playing the lead. Have you any idea who plays the lead on *Satin Doll?* It's Paul Gonsalves, a tenor lead. Sometimes you have clarinet on top. Johnny Hodges plays quite a bit of lead, and there are some arrangements where he plays lead in the first half and I do in the second half. This is just one of the things that give variety. The people sitting there listening can't put their finger on it, don't realize exactly what's going on, but they *hear* the difference. There's a word Duke uses for it— 'mixtures.' It's like somebody baking a cake or scrambling eggs, You mix it up, and that's why he calls it 'mixtures.'

"I don't think there has ever been a sax section together as long as this one—not even Guy Lombardo's! *Suite Thursday,* now, was a work where the sax section really had a major role. I always used to kid Willie Cook a lot, and he me, and one night when we got through playing it, I called back to him, 'Hey, Willie, how did the band sound tonight?' He knew what I meant! And don't forget that Duke has the privilege of indulging himself when he's writing for his own band.

"When I went to London with Duke the first time, all these people came back after the first concert, screaming, saying, 'Duke, what are you doing? Everything's wrong!' People came back carrying the programs of concerts he'd played there in 1933! I was talking to Harry Carney a day or so later about it, and I said, 'I don't know about those old programs, but in 1933 you cats must really have *played* to have left such an impression on the people.' But it was a mistake

163

trying to tell Duke the program was wrong. You have to use reverse psychology.

"Today, I don't care whether we have five thousand people sitting and listening or five thousand people dancing, just so long as they show up! So far as the Savoy was concerned, you have to remember that a lot of people just went there to dance and didn't have much interest in what the band was doing. They didn't care so long as there was a regular beat. You mustn't forget, either, that Guy Lombardo drew one of the biggest crowds that ever was at the Savoy. A band like the Savoy Sultans was a good dance band. They gave the people the tempos they wanted. Tempos didn't mean so much to people sitting at a concert. Some are interested in what you're doing and others just want to be entertained. When Roy Eldridge or Frankie Newton got up to take a solo with Teddy Hill's band, not many people on the floor may have given them much consideration, but that doesn't mean they played any the less. They knew at least ten people in the band were listening to what they were doing. They didn't have to consider their, shall we say, deportment the way they would on the concert stage, and that was an assist to music. Most soloists at dances, too, would not even stand up, but somewhere along the way show business and the band business came together."

[*1962*]

Shorty Baker [*trumpet*]

"I believe in melody. You must have a lead, a guide."

That was how Harold "Shorty" Baker concluded a long discussion on his life, times, and music. It was not said with defiance, but with the positive conviction of long experience. Nor was he arguing on behalf of schmaltz, for he believes in jazz freedom and improvisation; but he also believes that melody should be projected correctly, so that it doesn't emerge as a kind of mangled message meaningful only to its creator.

"What's the use of talking Chinese to someone who only understands English?" he asked.

Baker's own smoothly flowing lyricism communicates easily enough. His trumpet tone is certainly one of the most eloquently attractive in jazz today. His solo statements are well and neatly turned, complete in themselves, yet appropriately related to their context. His clean articulation and impeccable execution, both indicative of a deep basic assurance, give to his performances at any tempo a notable degree of poise and elegance. When he played "Mr. Cool" to Ray Nance's "Mr. Gentle," in his own composition for the Ellington orchestra, "cool" hadn't the usual jazz connotation, but rather what the word once had when adjacent to "calm and collected." Shorty doesn't put his heart on his sleeve when he plays, but there is no lack of emotional warmth in his music. It is merely that he consistently exercises a kind of exterior control.

These and other valuable attributes have made him a rare kind of musician for many years. Within the profession, he has long been one of the most respected trumpet players. Recognition has been slower from a public only too prone to mistake exhibitionism and eccentricity for quality.

St. Louis, where Shorty Baker was born and bred, should be famous in jazz for more than Handy's blues. It sheltered the most formidable school of trumpet players the music has probably known. Charlie Creath, whom Don Redman remembers as a master of the blues, was one of the founders, and undoubtedly an influence on the subsequently influential trumpet styles of Joe Smith and Tommy Ladnier. There was also the great teacher, P. G. Langford, whose five sons all played different instruments. It was he who taught Louis Metcalf, Joe Thomas, and Shorty Baker. Later came the dazzling virtuosity of Clark Terry, now an alumnus like Baker of the supreme jazz academy —Duke Ellington's.

Louis Armstrong was Baker's first influence. He played a dance date in St. Louis just after Baker had been persuaded by his brother Winfield to switch from drums to cornet. After that, Baker had no doubt at all which instrument he wanted to play.

His next influence was Joe Smith. "Joe was outstanding," he said, "and terrific playing waltzes with a plunger. He played almost like a voice, like a true singing voice, with clean, clear notes. Anybody who ever heard Joe Smith, if they played the same instrument, would want to play like him. What he did with a melody was a great surprise to me as a kid, but if a musician can make you like a waltz, he's doing something. He's really getting next to you."

Every Sunday, Baker used to play his cornet in church, and in the voice of a lady who sang there he found his third source of inspiration: "She had one of the finest voices, a very nice tone, and smooth vibrato. It gave me something to concentrate on. I'd been thinking in these terms after hearing Louis and Joe Smith, and I've never forgotten them. They've been a guide to me all through life."

In his brother's band, the trumpet section consisted of Baker, Joe Anderson, and Irving "Broz" Wood. They alternated on the first

Russell Procope

parts, worked hard to get a good section sound, and paid particular attention to maintaining matched vibrato, whether fast, medium or slow, that was appropriate to the different numbers and tempos.

Despite this experience, when he joined Don Redman, "It was," he said, "just like going to school. With someone like Don to sit down, talk, and explain things, you automatically improved so much on your instrument. If you love something you're doing, you observe and always remember. Don was another big influence on my musical thinking."

From Redman, he went to Teddy Wilson's big band in 1939. Despite its short life, he recalled it with enthusiasm as "one of the finest-sounding bands" he ever played with, Teddy being another admirable and understanding teacher. After that, he joined Andy Kirk. In all of these bands he played most of the lead trumpet parts.

In 1942, he began a long and occasionally interrupted career with Duke Ellington. Here, too, he played first parts, but the material was more varied and the lead was switched around more. "There are different types of first-trumpet players," he said. "Where one arrangement would fit me, another would fit the fellow next to me, because his conception of that type of tune would be better than mine."

Two of the many outstanding trumpets whom he worked along-

Shorty Baker

side in Duke's band, and whose names happened to come up in conversation, were Rex Stewart and Taft Jordan. Stewart, Baker felt, made a remarkably imaginative contribution within the Ellington context while retaining his own personal form of expression at all times. Jordan's ability to trick a person brought a grin and this comment: "He plays a variety of styles from Louis on down. Most instrumentalists have their pattern which you can recognize in four or five notes, but with Taft you may need eight or sixteen bars."

A musician's education is a lifelong matter, but Baker regarded experience with Ellington as a peak in the jazz field. "When you leave Duke's organization," he said, "you feel very confident playing in any band. You have the greatest confidence in yourself. He helps you. He's quick to recognize your best qualities and he'll bring out what you have in you. And years afterwards, you say, 'Yes, that's right. Duke did such-and-such a thing, Duke did this, and Duke did that. He made me do it.' Sometimes, I remember, I'd get peeved and lie in bed thinking about it. But I'd finally see the picture, see that he was helping me, not hurting me. And I'm very grateful, and thank him for what I call a million dollars' worth of experience."

Baker remembered the days when he ran around with Roy Eldridge, Charlie Shavers, and Dizzy, when they kidded and ribbed Dizzy. The bop trumpet style created by Dizzy was great, he ceded, "but after you've found out the short cuts of it, you sit back and laugh. It's part of your schooling, what Dizzy created for the entertainment business—check your book, Part One up to Part Four or Five."

About the changes bop brought to rhythm sections, he was far less happy: "It turned a lot of jazz into a kind of debate. The drummer would step in whenever he liked, step out, and step back if he heard something he disagreed with. The school of music I came up in believed in working together!"

As for the musician's attitude vis-à-vis the audience, and the theory that the boppers made it safe for jazzmen to play "pure music," to be musicians rather than entertainers, he said:

"I've heard that so many times. The music business has been very confused for almost twenty years. There are too many detours now. A whole lot of guys would like to get back on the track. But let me say that when you finish your tune and take your bow, it's ridiculous to look as though someone just passed away in the family. You smile, because you're glad the people appreciate what you have done."

Baker was a great admirer of the small group John Kirby led: "They played all types of music and they had a very good, clean sound." He felt there was still room for such a small combination, as distinct from the prevalent trios and quartets, the Dixieland bands, and the loose associations of experimentalists in outer space.

[*1960*]

Paul Gonsalves [*tenor saxophone*]

"*Paul Gonsalves is a wonderful musician,*" *said Duke Ellington.* "*Highly skilled, with tremendous imagination, he is equipped to perform whatever comes into his mind. That is rare, of course, and a good way beyond what was found in jazz at the beginning. In those days, guys couldn't deliver all the ideas that occurred to them. They had to be smart and resourceful, and limit their performances to where they had complete authority. Paul doesn't have to worry about limitations of that kind.*"

"Even when I take a jazz solo now," Paul Gonsalves said, "I may reach far back to some of the things I played in my childhood."

Gonsalves' parents came from Cape Verde and his father taught him and his two brothers to play guitar. They learned to play music for Portuguese folk dances, and they picked up hillbilly and Hawaiian styles from radio and records. On weekends, friends and relatives of the family would come visiting, and the boys had to be around the house to entertain. This grievously interfered with Gonsalves' athletic activities and the trio became a chore. "I built up this thing within me where I came to hate music," he recalled, "especially the humdrum kind we often had to play."

Luckily, his oldest brother, Joseph, had an insight into jazz, and Gonsalves remembered how they were both attracted by an Ellington record a deejay used for his theme early in the morning when Joseph was dressing to go to work. They would also listen to live band broadcasts at night, and on Saturdays Joseph would always spend part of his paycheck on records by Ellington, Henderson, and Lunceford. Gonsalves got to recognize all the great soloists of that era, but he remained more interested in listening than in playing until, when he was sixteen, Joseph took him to a midnight show at the RKO theatre in Providence.

"The feeling that came over me when the movie ended, and all the lights went out, and the curtains parted, and I saw Jimmie Lunceford's band—man! Of course, I knew all their records, knew all Willie Smith's solos, and liked the band next to Duke's. When I went home that night I was so thrilled, and I decided from that time on I wanted to play saxophone. So I worried my father until he went out and bought me one, a fifty-dollar tenor in pretty bad shape, but still a saxophone.

"Coleman Hawkins was my main influence. There was something in his music that coincided with Duke's, that for me denoted class. Apart from his musicianship, there was something about him personally—the way he held his horn, the way he dressed. I called him 'the Duke Ellington of the saxophone.' His style seemed more musical than that of other tenors, a kind of classic way of playing. I admired Lester Young, but Coleman Hawkins was *it* for me.

"When I graduated from high school in 1938, we finally gave up the trio. I was going to be a commercial artist and had the chance to get a scholarship to one of the best commercial art schools in the country, the Rhode Island School of Design, but I had become proficient enough to double on sax and guitar and I got a job in Providence. It was my first professional job, in a tuxedo, playing from five in the afternoon to one in the morning. I made an impression on local musicians and that added to my ego."

Gonsalves was fortunate in finding a tutor who had taught in the Boston Conservatory and who took a real interest in him. He did not look down on jazz and he was such an inspiration that Gonsalves used to practice diligently—"eight hours a day, four in the morning and four in the afternoon." After three years his technical proficiency encompassed everything his teacher could impart, but on the latter's advice he studied clarinet for a further year. (Many years later, in Canada, he picked up Harry Carney's clarinet and blew some arpeggios. Ellington came out of his dressing room at once. "Who's that playing clarinet?" he wanted to know. Gonsalves had modeled his style on Barney Bigard's.)

Although he didn't study harmony and theory as his teacher suggested, Gonsalves found his background of guitar playing stood him in good stead when it came to the new chord progressions. "And I always had a tendency to play a lot of notes, because I had plenty of technical ability. Musicians used to say, 'Why not play less complicated?' But I always felt I should play as much as I could play, and that, you might say, has shaped my style. Although I've been influenced by some great musicians, I feel today that I've devoted enough time and study to the instrument to inject my own feelings into what I play.

"My teacher also taught me that since jazz was largely improvised, you could incorporate from all types of music. He encouraged me to listen and broaden my scope, and I found this to be true. So many of the comical quotes and tags in jazz come out of different musical experiences, such as being in a little pit band. You can hear classical tags on records by Louis, Bird, and Dizzy. When a jazz musician gets up to play a chorus, to tell a story, all these ideas are in his mind and liable to pop up at any moment. The real art is in how he utilizes these things."

Gonsalves' first band experience was in an eight-piece group in Providence led by Henry McCoy and called the Jitterbugs. When that broke up he joined Phil Edmonds in New Bedford.

"It was then I found out about the hardships when you're away from home," he said, "but these expriences add to your playing. What had to be added to the music, after you'd studied all those books, was something you had to live. So we were a bunch of young kids, and if we didn't have anything to eat next day we'd chalk it up as part of the game. I'm glad I had those experiences. There were so many opportunities in those days, even if the pay was only three dollars a night. There were places to play, places to jam, and places, so to say, to go to school. You might get a job where you had to accompany vaudeville acts, and that was experience, too. The opportunity to play was all important. Musicians would play regardless of the money, and then go some place afterwards to jam. The big bands were schools, too, and every little town or locality had them. Around Boston, there must have been twenty fourteen- or fifteen-piece bands. Fellows used to rehearse for nothing and the conversation at those rehearsals would be very much concerned with the solos of famous artists on records. There's so much stress on conforming to business now that it's become more cut and dried. Those times won't happen again." From the time he left high school, Gonsalves found he was able to make a living in music. He was in the Army from 1942 to 1945. When he came back from India, he joined Sabby Lewis and his fame began to spread. Visiting musicians passed on the word about "the young tenor player at the Savoy in Boston." Eventually, when Jacquet left, he had a telephone call from Count Basie, whom he joined at the Royal Theatre in Baltimore, He brought the house down playing Jacquet's *Mutton Leg*.

After four years with Basie, he returned for a while to Sabby Lewis. Then Dizzy Gillespie called him. "I wondered about myself, because I didn't consider myself a 'modern' artist, but if Dizzy saw something in my playing . . . well, maybe I ought to go." He stayed until the band folded ("it was one of the best Dizzy ever had") and then headed for New York with his savings.

"I didn't know if I could make it in the Big City. I thought I would starve, you know, like an artist in a garret. But what really happened was that I had a ball every day. I used to go to that place on 110th Street and jam, and Charlie Parker used to come by there, and maybe in the daytime Gene Ammons, Charlie, and I would go out in rowboats.

"September rolled around, and it was starting to get a little cold, and I decided I ought to get a job. I woke up one morning with just $7.20 in the world. I couldn't sleep and all through that day something kept telling me to get up, and get dressed, and go to Birdland. It got to be eleven o'clock at night before I finally did just that. There was a crowd around a table where Duke was sitting. By the time he got up to leave, I'd had a few drinks. Normally, I'm kind of shy, but now I had nerve enough to say:

" 'Hi, Duke, how are you?'
" 'Say, aren't you Paul Gonsalves?'
" 'Yes.'
" 'Hey, sweetie, I've been looking for you. Why don't you come down to the office tomorrow?'

"The result was that he asked me to go out on a string of dates with the band. Secretly, I was thinking, 'I've got this job, because I know all Ben Webster's solos from the records.' The first thing Duke played was *C Jam Blues*, and then *Settin' and a-Rockin'*. So I asked him if he still had *Chelsea Bridge*, and as I stood up to play my solo I overheard him say to Quentin Jackson:

" 'This so-and-so sounds just like Ben!'
"So I got the job.

"If I die tomorrow, I'll consider I've been successful, because when I began to study music it was with the idea of being in that band. I've tried to keep a tone that fits it during my ten years. My teacher told me that while you have to have technique to facilitate your ideas, primarily you should try for a good tone. That's why I always admired Coleman Hawkins, Don Byas, and Ben Webster, and why, when I doubled on alto with Sabby Lewis, I always tried to sound like Johnny Hodges.

"When Charlie Parker and the modernists came on the scene a kind of straight tone became a necessity, and not only in order to play fast. With the closer harmonies that came with the modern concept of jazz, the style of playing with a lot of wide vibrato had to go or the music would have sounded out of tune. I think that music reflected the times. There was more tension, speed, neuroticism. Jazz was getting stereotyped and I can remember being bored while I was with Basie's band. Changes like that don't happen only in music. The importance of art is the way it affects practical things. We don't have the money to buy a Picasso, but his work can affect the lines of, say, a lamp. Lines are derived from those paintings and you can see beauty in things now that you couldn't ten years ago. Maybe that explains why I liked jazz so much, preferred it to classical music. There was a freedom in it and I could interpret my *own* ideas.

"Now you can maybe name a band that puts down more consistently precise performances, but not one that plays such complicated, unorthodox music as Duke writes. He is still progressing himself. Some of the fellows don't always understand all the things he brings in to the band today. They feel it's a little advanced and they say, 'What's he trying to do? What's this?' But Duke knows his band consists of fifteen musicians, and he knows they're human beings, too. He is prepared for performances to vary, according to the way the guys feel, and according to what he can draw out of them. One night we may stink, but the next night we may sound wonderful. When there's that fusion between guys who all feel like playing, when everything's going down right, and we're playing his music the way it should be played, then it's the greatest jazz band there is. I heard Duke tell someone, 'You can't stand over a band of this sort with a whip and expect to get music out of it.' I worked a couple of weeks with Tommy Dorsey once, and Tommy was a wonderful guy, but there was no feeling at all and musically it was miserable.

"The real story behind the success of *Diminuendo and Crescendo in Blue* is relevant here, I think. There had been a big controversy among New York musicians when we went into Birdland about what we were going to do in a predominantly 'modern' house. 'Duke's band will die in there,' they were saying, but we were really swinging at that time. Out of a clear blue sky, Duke says, 'Get out 107, 108.' I'd never played it although I had the original record at home. This particular time, when they got through playing the first part, I leaned over to him and said:

" 'Let me take some choruses in here.'

" 'Go ahead,' he said.

"I don't know how many choruses I played, but I know it caused some excitement. People were standing on their chairs. We didn't play it again until that time at Newport. We were getting ready to go on when Duke called me in the wings.

" 'Paul, do you remember that number we played at Birdland—107, 108?'

" 'Yes,' I said.

" 'That's what I want you to play tonight. When we get through the first part, you go out there and play as long as you like.'

"When the record came out, there was a lot on the album cover about Jo Jones that I felt was very wrong. It happened that there was a real competitive feeling in the band that night, and we went out there to play the very best we could. After all the little groups, the impact of a big band is what you want for a festival's finale. Paul Desmond told me shortly afterwards, 'What you and the band played was the most honest statement that night.'

"Of course, I thought I had only played a couple of minutes. I've never tried to memorize the record. I don't have it home and have never listened to it. It has become harder and harder to do, night after night, because the people expect me to play a long time. The length is really determined by the way the rhythm section is working and how everything is building up. The climax may come after ten or after five choruses, but if you go beyond it you destroy everything. One night in Des Moines, Iowa, a guy in front of the stand made me angry.

" 'Hm, you, Paul Gonsalves . . . I don't think you can play that long like on the record,' he said.

"So I played sixty-six choruses. Some nights I play it and ideas come, but sometimes they won't."

As Ellington and Johnny Hodges are always at pains to point out, however, Gonsalves is at his creative best on ballads and slow mood pieces. He is frequently heard in a rich, rhapsodic version of *In a Sentimental Mood* with the band, and he has recorded attractive versions of two of Hodges' features, *Warm Valley* and *Day Dream*, as well as Quincy Jones' *The Midnight Sun Never Sets*. On numbers at fast tempos he satisfies the public conception of the frenzied, driving tenor man, but behind the sacrificial image there remains one of the most exciting soloists in the field. His sympathy with the "modern" element has, it is hoped, been made evident here. Yet his taste in jazz is extremely broad, albeit critically selective. When the band was playing Boston's Storyville, he would insist, during intermissions, on escorting his friends downstairs to hear Memphis Slim and Willie Dixon. "This is authentic," he would say, meaning that within their idiom they were genuine artists.

While Duke Ellington was in France, working on the movie, *Paris Blues*, Gonsalves, like other members of the band, spent much of his vacation in record studios. He recorded with John Lewis, with Nat Adderley, with a percussion unit, and with Booty Wood. Leading a group that included Sir Charles Thompson, Ray Nance, Harold Ashby, Aaron Bell, and Jo Jones on two sessions, he not only played tenor, but guitar as well, for the first time on record.

"Who does that remind you of?" he asked, grinning. "Teddy Bunn?"

[*1961*]

Willie Cook   [*trumpet*]

"Has Duke still got that good trumpet player?"

The question was asked by Irving Goodman, Benny Goodman's trumpet-playing brother, when he was making one of his infrequent visits to New York. The members of Ellington's current trumpet section were named, and rejected in turn as not being the one he had in mind. At length, after several of those previously in the band had been discussed, Willie Cook was mentioned, and Goodman smiled.

"That's the one I mean," he said. "He can play."

It was typical of the respect and recognition Cook had won within the profession, although his name had never exactly become a household word to the audience. Ellington, however, did not forget his capabilities, nor his achievements. When he had Dizzy Gillespie as a guest on a record session in 1959, the number he chose for him to play was one Cook had distinguished himself on three years before, *Upper Manhattan Medical Group*. Gillespie did not find it easy.

In 1968, a few days after Cook had again returned to his band, Ellington found himself facing insistent demands for an encore in São Paolo, Brazil, when most of his musicians had left the stage. Seeing Cook still in the wings, he called him down front to perform with just the rhythm section. The trumpet player improvised versions of *Tea for Two* and *St. Louis Blues* with a harmon mute on microphone, and he and the accompanying trio not only upheld the band's honor, but sent the large crowd away happy into the night. A year later, at a special concert in Berkeley, California, it was Cook whom the leader entrusted with the seldom-heard solo on *Black Beauty*, a number originally played by Artie Whetsol and dedicated to Florence Mills. And it was Cook, again, who was chosen as the sole trumpet for the prestigious and highly successful engagement at the Rainbow Grill in New York during the summer of 1969.

An excellent first trumpet player, he is a flexible soloist capable of interpreting many of the specialized Ellington trumpet roles, but above all he continues the tradition of sensitive, melodic statement that was created by Artie Whetsol and fostered by Shorty Baker.

Willie Cook was born in Tangipahoa, Louisiana, on November 11th, 1923. When he was four, his parents moved to East Chicago, Indiana.

"At that time," he recalled, "most of the people from Louisiana either went to Chicago or Los Angeles. The southern route, on the Southern Line, goes straight to California, and the Illinois Central runs from New Orleans straight up to Chicago. My father worked on the railroad."

Cook went to school in East Chicago—seven miles from Hammond, eighteen from Chicago. An older brother played trumpet in the school orchestra and, when he brought the instrument home, young Willie, then in third grade, used to practice on it.

"When I got to fourth grade," he continued, "I started playing violin, but I still practiced on the trumpet. I liked violin, but I didn't go far enough with it. I have some knowledge of it—the fingering, etc. —and I got so I could play little elementary songs. But after two grades, I really started playing trumpet, and I let the violin go. I stayed with the trumpet all the way through high school. The teaching there was very good. We had a teacher named Nick Young, who had played with Stan Kenton in California when he was in college there. I also had a private teacher, Fred Riggins, who used to go out with bands like Tiny Bradshaw's until his wife decided she didn't want him to travel.

"When I was fifteen, I began playing with the Jesse Evans family band—three brothers, a sister, and the father—in Gary, Indiana. It was like a Dixieland band. As soon as I got out of school, Riggins came and asked my mother if I could go out on the road in the band he was playing with—King Perry's.

"This band had fourteen pieces: five saxophones, three trombones, four trumpets, and three rhythm. The saxophone player, Morris Lane, was about the only man who did anything, apart from King Perry. We copied Fletcher Henderson's style, and everything we played was like the Henderson band. We went to Cincinnati, Pittsburgh, Milwaukee, and Indianapolis between February and July, 1942. We were booked by the Ferguson Brothers out of Indianapolis, and they had a lot of what were called 'territory' bands. After about six months with Perry, I went with Jay McShann.

"Walter Brown was singing in this band, and McShann also had John Jackson, the alto player, and Paul Quinichette on tenor. When we recorded for Decca, it was my first record date, and I had a little solo on the channel of Gene Ramey's *Say Forward, I'll March*, a number you may know as *Hamp's Got a Duke*.

"Earl Hines was playing in Washington, D.C., and he heard us there. His musical director, Jesse Stone, came by and took five musicians out of Jay's band—myself, Bob Merrill, two of the trombones (Arnett Sparrow and Rudy Morrison), and the other vocalist, Earl Coleman. It was heartbreaking when it happened to Jay, because he wasn't working too much at the time. We'd have three or four days to lay off in little towns like Norfolk and Newport News, and he almost cried when the guys left. That sort of thing isn't very ethical, but it happens all the time, and it's a matter of giving the fellows a better story, of making them think you have better bookings.

Paul Gonsalves and Stanley Dance

"I started arranging in 1944. The first arrangement I made was *Let's Get Started*. I took the first sixteen bars of that same tune of Gene Ramey's and put my own middle to it. Earl recorded this, *Bambi*, and a couple more for A.R.A., but they were never issued here. Wardell Gray soloed on *Bambi*, and Benny Green on one of the others.

"I really taught myself arranging. The other piano player in the band, Cliff Smalls, was a good arranger, and he showed me how to voice the instruments. I did it through trial and error. I'd write something, and if it didn't sound right I'd change it. When we were at the El Grotto in Chicago, we used to do whole concerts on the work of one composer—Jerome Kern, Fats Waller, George Gershwin, people like that. I wrote some numbers in there, but Bugs Roberts did most of the writing, and it was very beautiful. He had a little band in St. Louis later, and he died of lung trouble. When Ernie Wilkins joined the band, he did some of the writing, and I remember he did one of the last concerts.

"The band was never too successful, because Earl had had a lot of trouble with his booking agent, a man named Fox. When he was at the Grand Terrace, he had more air time than any other orchestra in the country, but eventually he found out that he had been terribly underpaid, and he was very angry about it. He didn't know how

Willie Cook recording in Buenos Aires, 1968

powerful the people were, and the agents didn't give him good bookings. But during the '40s, he got a big band together, with a harp, five violins, four girl singers, etc., and he came out of that heavily in debt to the booking agency. That's when the band broke up, and he had to go out again with Louis Armstrong. When he had paid off all his debts to the booking agency, and to his musicians, he got his own group together again, a small band.

"Playing trumpet beside me in Earl's band was Shorty McConnell. He got sick a couple of times and became very religious; he just goes back and forth to the church now. He and Ray Nance were about the same age, and he was a very good trumpet player, a good soloist, but he lost his teeth, and that interfered with his high playing. That happens to a lot of people. It just seems to be a physical disability, because I didn't take very good care of my teeth, and I've never had a toothache yet. Until last year, I never even had any cavities. Other trumpet players in that band were Benny Harris, Rostelle Reese, and Ira Pettiford, a brother of Oscar the bass player.

"I worked with another of the Pettiford brothers in McShann's band. That was Alfonso, and he was really a trumpet player, but he was playing valve trombone then. He was older than Oscar and the best musician of all of them. They had a seven-piece family band that used to play up and down the Mississippi on the riverboats. Margie, the sister, used to play alto, and Harry's still in Minneapolis, but Oscar and Alfonso died.

"My first real influence on trumpet was Harry James, then Louis Armstrong, and, a little later on, Charlie Spivak. My godfather, John Vinson, was a friend of Louis Armstrong's in New Orleans. He was not a musician, but Louis used to come in this poolroom where my godfather was one of the main attractions. When he heard I was going out to play, he gave me an introduction to give to Louis. I kept it a number of years, but I never used it.

"I always did like melodic playing and I guess I intended to be a first horn player from the beginning. Pops Smith was my favorite first trumpet man. I had the pleasure of meeting him, and we used to talk all the time. After I listened to him, I realized how great a trumpet player he was—such beautiful lines. He took very good care of himself, and he used to say, 'Look, if you want to play a horn, eat plenty of beans and greens!' Another of my favorite lead trumpets was Snooky Young. I liked the way he played—strong, flexible—and I used to try to imitate him.

"After the first phase, I ended up in the Roy Eldridge style, and I started copying his solos. I heard him jamming with Jabbo Smith in Milwaukee once, and I remember, back in 1942, Fats Navarro and I sitting up all night long with Roy's record of *Rockin' Chair*. We'd keep turning that needle back until we got it down. Fats was real big then, but very young, and he'd been working in Snookum Russell's band.

"Roy was the main influence before Dizzy Gillespie, but Dizzy had finished studying with Costello by then and was with Cab Calloway. I didn't take to bop right away. Because I didn't understand it, it seemed as though they were kind of messing up music. Sonny Stitt was the first one who took me over to a juke box and made me listen to Charlie Parker. 'This is going to be the man,' he said. At that time, Sonny played like Johnny Hodges when he was drinking, and like Benny Carter when he wasn't. He was good at both of them. He was just a good musician, and he and Charlie Parker used to be together a lot. Sonny was very intelligent, and he was always fast, even when he was just a kid. He could analyze and dissect chords and everything. He knew what everybody was doing when they played. Benny Harris is the cause of a lot of guys playing in that style, too.

"Yardbird [Parker] had that western, soulful blues touch to his playing, you know. Everybody in Kansas City used to play like that. Then, when he and Dizzy got together, they went further out with chord structures and progressions. Instead of minor sevenths, they'd build a minor seventh off a dominant seventh. In other words, they put two chords where there used to be only one.

"At one time, Benny Green and I were supposed to quit Hines and join Cab Calloway's band, but we wouldn't leave. Earl used psychology. He had everybody loving that band. He'd give you a speech that would make you stay! And the band sounded so good we really didn't want to leave. Then the Army was taking so many musicians that things started to break up.

"Actually, that's one reason why I got the chance to go with Earl in the first place. I probably wasn't properly prepared for the job, but I was the youngest guy in the band, and I wanted to learn. So I didn't say much; I just listened and tried to learn as much as possible. Earl has a good musical mind, and I think I learned quite a bit there. He puts out a good show. He can look at people and figure what they want to hear. We used to work in the El Grotto for six months at a time, and each night one of the guys in the band had to act as bandleader before Earl came out in the first set. We had to call the tunes, and we used to see who could get the people on the floor first, by playing the right tunes, danceable tunes. Scoops Carry was the straw boss, but every night a different guy would have to be the leader. It gave everybody experience.

"We were in Portland when Jimmie Lunceford died, and we played the same place where it happened. After Earl's band broke up in 1947, I went home to Pittsburgh, where I had been living since

I married in 1943. I got a call from Ed Wilcox and Joe Thomas who were leading the Lunceford band, and I joined them in Toledo, Ohio. I had left my horn in Chicago, and I sent a telegram and asked for it to be sent to Cleveland. I hadn't touched it in three months, and I was wondering how I would make it. The difference between then and now would depend on how much time I had put in on the horn when I was twenty-three. If I had my muscles built up to a certain degree, I could lay off three months, and then just go right to playing. Now, if I laid off, it would take two or three weeks, playing every day, to build them properly. But then, I was very surprised! I went right in and played the book. It wasn't really rough. Wilcox wrote most of it, and we played all those dances.

"I took Joe Wilder's place, and Paul Webster and Bob Mitchell were the other trumpets. Freddie Webster had left by then. Outside of Louis Armstrong, he was the first big name I met. While I was still with King Perry, I ran into him and Jimmy Crawford on the street in Indianapolis one day when the Lunceford band came through. We used to catch all that band's broadcasts to hear Freddie, and Lunceford used to have him play *Embraceable You* a lot.

"I was with the Wilcox-Thomas band about six months. Joe wanted to leave and form his own band, and I was supposed to quit and join him in two weeks, but it took him more like six months or a year to get his band together. In the meantime, Dizzy Gillespie came by and wanted me to play with *his* band, and after I got there I didn't want to leave. I stayed with Dizzy until the band broke up in June, 1950. Working in that band, I really learned a lot. It was out of tune and everything, but there was so much spirit you didn't even notice that.

"After that, Gerald Wilson called me. He wanted me to be straw boss of a band he was getting together to work behind Billie Holiday. We rehearsed for about two weeks in Philadelphia, and went on a southern tour. The band got stranded in Greensboro, North Carolina. It was a big band: Gerald, Johnny Coles, and myself were the trumpets; Melba Liston was on trombone; Danny Turner was on alto; Carrington Visor—and this was the first time I heard his big sound —was on tenor; and Philly Joe Jones was on drums. John Levy was the manager of the band, and he didn't have the money to send the whole band home at once, so they had to sleep in the bus, and he sent them back one at a time. We had played five or six engagements, but we didn't have any people at them. It was a bad affair all over, and probably a case where they had borrowed money from someone and had to get it back right quick.

"Billie Holiday didn't mean so much down there as in other parts of the country. This was 1950, and we played for black audiences. At

180

that time, if black people had dances, the whites could be spectators, but they couldn't dance together. They liked rhythm-and-blues bands, and Buddy Johnson was king down there, but ours was a kind of modern-sounding band. Gerald, I remember, had a bad feeling about Kenton's band then. Why? You compare his *Yard Dog Mazurka*, which Lunceford recorded in 1941, with *Artistry in Rhythm*.

"I was with Billie about a year. When the band broke up, I traveled with her as musical director and played on a few gigs. Lester Young worked some places with us, and we had Billy Valentine on piano, Joe Shulman on bass, and Harold West on drums.

"By this time I had a family, so I went back to Pittsburgh and got a construction job, because it paid the most money. I'd become a little disgusted with the way I'd been working, and after spending that time with Billie I'd gotten into a bad mood period. This job was the only way I could support my family, and I did it from the latter part of 1950 until Duke called me around October of 1951.

"Paul Gonsalves and I had worked together in Dizzy Gillespie's band. When I went to a concert they played in Pittsburgh, Paul and Ray Nance took me into Duke's dressing room. He had heard me play something with Dizzy's band, and about two weeks later he called me and told me to meet him in Detroit. They were doing the *Big Show of '51*, one of those package shows with Nat Cole and Sarah Vaughan. Shorty Baker had disappeared from the band for some days, but he came back the night I arrived. I was sick! 'I guess I'll go back home,' I said, but Duke told me to stay on. 'No, you stay anyway,' he said.

"Shorty left about a week after that. He was quality. He used to play everything so pretty. I always wanted him back in there so bad. I'd been hired to play his book, but we didn't have any rehearsal or anything. He had been playing *Mood Indigo* and *Jam with Sam*, so now I played them. Shorty didn't think he was getting enough.

"Sometimes, when I'd been drinking, I'd talk to Duke like he was just another bandleader. 'I think I'm pretty fair,' he'd say. 'I know what a man does, and I pay him accordingly.' And he was probably right, because he is pretty fair.

"I was out of the band several times up until '58—maybe three months, three weeks, or five weeks—and then I left for a year and a half. I came back in '60 for a little while, and then again in '61. In '62, I went back for about three weeks, and then it was a long time to September 1st, 1968, just before the South American tour. Oh, yes, I wanted to be back very bad, but I didn't want to ask Duke to come back again. Somehow it happened that he must have been thinking about me, and decided that I might by the right person with both Ray Nance and Shorty gone.

"Mostly, I'm playing the parts now, and copying and extracting since Herbie Jones left. I like that, because it gives me a chance to see how the maestro constructs. One thing I always wanted to play was *Someone*, but he's got so many numbers in the book he could play that would still sound good. He probably forgets a lot about them himself, but I think he has tried to pick out the ones that he considers the best, and the ones that fit the guys more.

"When I came in his band, there wasn't much room for arranging, because he and Strayhorn would always do the things. Then, too, if you didn't write something that sounded like Duke Ellington, he might play it sometimes, but he wouldn't play it on important occasions. Jimmy Hamilton got himself to the stage where he could write very well, so I heard, by the time he left the band. Jim was such a technical fellow. Real small details were very important to him, and consequently he used to write very well. Especially on that little clarinet piece, *Pretty and the Wolf*. I liked that.

"Paul Gonsalves and I want to do some recording together. I'd like to do something with a small band, and get Benny Green in it. I have some ideas of my own, and I'd write the arrangements myself. I think it should be about time for it."

It should be. Now should always be the time to hear musicians of his talent, experience, and taste. Yet as he said that, in August, 1969, it was impossible not to reflect that good taste was out of season so far as the record companies were concerned.

[*1969*]

Clark Terry [*trumpet and flugelhorn*]

"My instrument was a length of water hose, coiled two or three times and tucked under my arm, with a funnel at the end that looked like the mouthpiece of a horn. When I blew on the edge of that funnel, I got a sound something like blowing into a jug."

This was the unlikely beginning of Clark Terry's brilliant career, a career which has brought him to a position where he is admired and respected throughout his profession. Great musical talent was involved, but also resource, courage, and determination.

The seventh child and the youngest boy in a large but poor St. Louis family, Terry was drawn to music at an early age, primarily because his oldest sister's husband, Sy Mackfield, played tuba in Dewey Jackson's band. His mother died when he was six and his father, faced with so many problems, became somewhat tyrannical.

He didn't want his son to be a musician and there was no money for an instrument, but his wishes were circumvented when his son and a bunch of neighborhood kids formed a little "jazz" band. Clark played the contraption described above. There was a "tuba" made from the hosing of an old vacuum cleaner, a jug for mellower bass sounds, and "drums" in the form of an upturned bushel basket beaten upon with chair rounds.

This enterprising combination was not long satisfied with the scene of its debut, the backyard. "At night," Terry recalled, "when our parents were sitting on the front porch watching the cars go by, we'd sneak off to the nearest tavern and gather a few coins. Sometimes we'd come home with as much as a buck or two, and then they'd want to know, 'Where did you get this money?' "

It was at the school picnics, held each year just before vacation time, that he became fascinated by the trumpet. "They'd always have a marching band," he said, "which would end up playing for dancing in a pavilion. I wasn't much interested in the dancing, but I'd always find myself behind the brass section, where I would single out a trumpet player. 'Mister, let me just blow your horn,' I begged a guy called Louis Cauldwell one day. I begged so hard he let me. Usually, a kid can't make a sound when he first blows a horn, but through some quirk I did. Louis was surprised and from then on he always encouraged me, and I never forgot him. Later on, he had a candy store and when I got started on trumpet I'd go by to buy candy. He had become a great fat cat by then, but we'd sit down and talk with him straddling his chair, the back of it in front of him. I don't know whether he is still alive, but he was a very good trumpet player as well as a kind man. Since then I've learned the truth of the saying that 'you never stand so tall as when you stoop to help a child.' "

At high school, Terry eventually got into the band, but there was no trumpet available and the teacher advised him to take valve trombone because the fingering was the same. "When you're young," Terry said, "valve doesn't look as attractive as slide trombone. You're fingering away right there with tubing about half a block in front of you and half a block behind." Luckily, it was not long before a trumpet was handed down to him.

"I was under the tutorship of Charles Hayden Wilson who, in later years, taught my son. (I started him off on trumpet and he plays well and gets a good tone, but every teacher I sent him to would say, 'Why don't you get your dad to teach you?' Now I think he'd rather not be a musician. He used to dig the way things happened, how I'd come home off the road, after being away so long, and how I'd be tired and beat.) Wilson was a very busy man who really preferred teaching piano and vocals, so he assigned me to Leonard Small, an apt young trumpet player. Small was actually the nearest thing to a 'private' tutor I've ever had in all my life. I've done some conscientious studying since then, but always more or less on my own. I never could afford the famous St. Louis teacher, Gustaph, but I would go and ask him questions and he would never turn me down. He knew who I was, a kid from a poor neighborhood, and he helped me with my problems. Small was bitterly against me puffing my cheeks as I did when I first went to him. 'Don't puff your cheeks! Put that mouthpiece right in the center there,' he'd say. 'You've got nice teeth, so keep it right there. And keep the tips of your fingers right on the valves.' Naturally, that helps speed from the physical viewpoint, and for years I used to feel my fingers should stay glued to the valves."

Within the school band, which played mostly marches and overtures, a little jazz group was formed. Its pianist, Walter Ray, was learning to write and he discovered he could put on paper the things he heard on Fats Waller's popular records. Besides Terry in this combination were Ocie Reece (drums), Benny Nelson (clarinet), and James Borrow (guitar).

"More or less every trumpet player at that time was being influenced by Pops [Armstrong] and Roy [Eldridge]," Terry remembered, "but later I was much influenced by the trumpet players of my own town. For instance, Levi Madison, who I think played one of the prettiest trumpets I ever heard. He was older than Shorty Baker, but he had a very similar tone. Then there were Dewey Jackson, George Hudson, Crack Stanley, Mouse Randolph, Bobby Merrill, Sleepy Tomlin, who was with Jimmie Lunceford at one period, and Joe Thomas, who lives in New York now. Sleepy would always kid me, but he gave me constructive criticism, too. I remember when I was experimenting with mouthpieces and had a very fuzzy-type sound. 'Hey, Fuzzy,' he'd say. 'One of these days you'll get that fuzz out of there. You'll be all right!' "

Terry's home life meanwhile had been more than strict. He had seldom been able to go swimming, biking, or skating like the other kids, who jeered him—"You've gotta go home and tend your old man!" But he was anxious to get ahead and had worked very hard from the time his mother died. "I worked myself up a paper route, and another for hauling ashes and tin cans, even going out of my own neighborhood, maybe a mile away. I worked in a bowling alley setting pins. Every night and weekends I'd be working. Eventually, out of my savings, I bought a fifteen-dollar bike—ten down and a dollar a month. This was my undoing. We were supposed to hand over the money we earned and when he heard about it my father was furious. 'Whoever sees him first,' he told the others, 'tell him now he's got a bike to keep riding on it!' He meant it, definitely, and it seems I've been riding ever since, because I never went home from that point on. I thought he treated me unfairly, but since I've been a grown man I've understood more and forgiven him, because he worked so hard, for long hours, and he must have been terribly taxed, physically and mentally.

"So I rode on up to my oldest sister's house and she took me in. While I was there, my brother-in-law got me my first real job, at the Lincoln Inn on Market Street. The hours were tremendous, the pay seventy-five cents a night. I was still at high school and used to get no more than four or five hours of sleep. I used the school horn at first, and it was very bad, but later a neighbor who ran a cleaning and pressing establishment bought me my first horn and case, for ten dollars."

Terry had also shown considerable promise as a boxer and had been taught by Kid Carter. "One night I received a busted lip and was knocked out. I had wanted to impress a chick at a dance on trumpet, and it was then I decided the two don't go together, trumpet and boxing." (Many years later, Archie Moore was to express his appreciation of Terry's playing and demonstrate, incidentally, how one noble art may profitably draw inspiration from another.)

"My sister and her husband worked days," Terry continued, "and they left chores for me. When I came home from school, I'd open the window and sit there practicing. The kids would gather around and I'd assign them to different tasks, my chores. 'You sweep, you do this, you do that, while I play,' I'd tell them."

When Terry's schooling ended, Mackfield arranged for him to go out with the Reuben and Cherry carnival in a band led by Willie Austin. After about a year, they became part of Ida Cox's *Darktown Scandals*, and subsequently they were with a small show which folded in Harrisburg, Mississippi. "*The Merry-Go-Round Broke Down* was popular then and it actually happened to us," Terry said. "We were flat broke, but Willie arranged for us to travel back to St. Louis with a man who owned the monkey show and a truck. Willie rode up front in the cab, but we were in the back with the monkeys for this eight-hundred-mile trip from Mississippi. The monkeys were running all over us and we were scared to death, but after a few hundred miles we made a joke of it and said, 'What the hell? We're going home!'

"Then I started working with Benny Reed, a one-legged pianist. We'd take his cork leg at night and hide it, so that we could eat breakfast before he got out of bed. We had three horns and three rhythm, and we played nightclubs like the Spinning Wheel in Carbondale, in southern Illinois. One day we played a dance on a picnic ground. There had been an athletic competition between high schools, and along with the teams had come the school bands. The bandleader of one from East St. Louis was an old buddy of mine and he wanted me to meet a little trumpet player he much admired. So here comes this little kid asking questions, 'How do you do such and such a thing?,' and so on, and it dawned on me that this was the same kind of thing as when I used to stand behind Louis Cauldwell, but I was young and single, didn't give a damn about anything, and was only interested in music and girls, in that order. Though we talked, my mind was really on some girls dancing around a maypole, and I kind of fluffed the kid off.

"Six months or a year later, I went up to the Elks Club where we used to go to jam and keep up with the latest. There was a long flight of stairs and as I went up I heard this trumpet player flying about on his horn in a way I couldn't recognize. Eddie Randall had the band and I knew everyone in it but this little trumpet player. I went over to the stand.

" 'Aren't you . . .?' I began.

" 'Yes,' he said, 'I'm the guy you fluffed off in Carbondale.'

"It was Miles Davis. We've often laughed about that since.

"I volunteered for the Navy in 1942, went to Great Lakes and straight into the orchestra. I was playing pretty fair jazz then, but I polished up my technique while I was in the Navy. I practiced very diligently. In fact, people used to say, 'If you want Clark, look for him in the head!' It was the one place I could practice without disturbing anybody—there or in the shower-room which led off it. It has a psychological effect on you if you think you are bugging somebody, but there I could blow my heart out. The book I most enjoyed practicing out of was for clarinet. A guy in the reed section had this old, ragged book with very interesting and moving exercises. Maybe I should mention here that I also listened to the Basie band for years, and while Pres [Lester Young] influenced nearly all the tenor players, he also influenced me!

"There were people like Gerald Wilson, Willie Smith, Big George Matthews, and Ernie Wilkins in that Navy band. Ernie and I used to have little private jam sessions. He'd blow while I beat on the wall, and vice versa. Every day or so there would be real sessions that might last three or four hours, and where guys would just blow until they fell out. It was a concentrated music period for me, because when we were there there was not much else to do.

"I got out in 1945 and George Hudson, a trumpet player, asked me to join a big band he was forming in St. Louis. I had had plenty of section work in the Navy and George put the full weight of the band on me. I played all the lead and all the trumpet solos, rehearsed the band, suggested numbers, routines, and everything. Pops caught a couple of our shows when we were at the Apollo. I was featured on

Poor Butterfly in an arrangement Stan Kenton had given George, and I was very proud when Pops (Armstrong) came backstage and said, 'I like the way that boy played that horn.' Later, when he was putting down some be-boppers in an article, he praised me. Clifford Brown came and asked me, 'How come Pops likes you and not us?' I dig Pops and I told Clifford, 'Because we've always laughed at each other's jokes!'

"Charlie Barnet called me from California while I was working the Riviera, a big, plush sort of place where Ellington swears he originally wrote *Sophisticated Lady*. I didn't know a soul in Charlie's band and the only person I knew in L.A. was Gerald Wilson. He took me over to where the band was playing and I walked up to the bandstand. The band was on the air and Charlie motioned to me to go round the back and onto the stand. Next thing, he was announcing, 'Now we'll hear from our new trumpet player, Clark Terry, who has just arrived.' It was one of his originals, *Charleston Alley*, or something like that, and it wasn't too difficult, but it was a big chance to take, on the air, coast to coast. Ellington does things like that, too. I stayed with the band for one of the happiest years of my life, until Charlie got lonesome for his swimming pools, private plane, and yacht. Charlie's the most wonderful person in the world."

After short periods with George Hudson again, Charlie Ventura, and Eddie Vinson, Terry joined Count Basie in 1948 at a rehearsal in Nola Studio. "Basie was running through a few things, trying to find out what kind of cat he had picked up. He gave me a very difficult part that had a high A which had to be held for three or four beats. I knew it was do or die, so I hit and held that high A for three or four beats, and I haven't done it since."

When Basie broke up his big band, Terry remained in the small group which was to include Buddy De Franco, Wardell Gray, and Charlie Rouse. While they were playing Seattle for a couple of weeks, Terry encountered another young trumpet player. This was Quincy Jones and he came to Terry's hotel almost every day to discuss music and the trumpet. Terry encouraged him in his playing and arranging, and Quincy has never forgotten it.

Eventually, Terry grew tired of traveling and went home. Before he left, he had found places with Basie for at least three St. Louis musicians—Bob Graf and Ernie and Jimmy Wilkins. But he was not allowed to rest long. His next call was from Duke Ellington.

"Everything previous was like elementary school," Clark insisted. "The time I was with Ellington was like college. I think he is a very rare, naturally gifted person who knows things ahead of other people. He explains certain basic facts to his men. If guys want to have an argument, he'll say, 'Look, fellows. I thought everyone knew I am *not* a disciplinarian. I hired you because you are superb in your field and I want you with me because of that fact. Apart from being excellent musicians, you are all *men*, so govern yourselves accordingly.' And he gives everyone enough rope to hang himself.

"I remember one day on the bus, Oscar Pettiford—God bless him!—was in a rage, walking the aisle and raising an uproar. When the bus stopped he moved off into the forest shouting, 'I'm an Indian. I understand the wolves and animals of the forest. They talk with me.' It was fifteen or twenty minutes before we could locate him, capture him, conquer him, and bring him back, but when he was on the bus again, still raging, he wanted to talk to anyone and everyone about anything and everything. So he picked out Duke! It was one of those rare occasions when Duke was riding the bus, up front, instead of with Harry Carney, because we were going through a mountainous area and he likes to be with the bunch when hazardous trips are involved. Oscar walked up to him and began:

" 'Duke, you so-and-so, I want you to know one thing, blah, blah, blah . . .'

"One word led to another, but Duke tried to cool him:

" 'Yeah, man. Solid, man. Yeah, crazy, man!'

"Oscar got violent and took up the subject of money.

" 'I don't want to hear all this,' Duke said. 'Talk to Al Celley. He's hired to take this grief off me.'

"Oscar became even more furious, because he couldn't understand why, if he worked for Duke Ellington, he couldn't talk to Duke Ellington about what he wanted to talk about, which happened at this point to be money. So Duke closed his eyes and went to sleep on him. He has a phenomenal knack of being able to exclude himself when he wants."

Late in 1959, Terry joined Quincy Jones in Europe, to play in the Harold Arlen show, *Free and Easy,* and with high hopes it would come back to New York. Among the musicians, he had the biggest acting role. "I enjoyed it so much," he said, "I looked forward to going to work every night." Great as the show was, circumstances were against it, including one of the Algerian crises. "I think if that show had reached Broadway it would have run five years," Quincy has said, "and it would have been a big thing for Clark, because he was one of the real stars." When the show folded, the band decided, after a vote, to continue operations in Europe. During this period, the second opportunity presented itself for Terry to join the staff of musicians at NBC. "I talked it over with Quincy, because I really hated leaving him, and I felt worse about it than anything I'd done in years, but he understood.

"So I joined NBC in March, 1960. I have to play all kinds of music, which I don't mind at all, because it's good experience. It also affords me plenty of time to do many things in and out of music that I've always wanted to do, and I can be at home, sleep in my own bed, and enjoy my wife's cooking."

Clark Terry esteems versatility. "I'm equipped, I think, to play in more than one vein. Anyway, I've been branded as a be-bopper, a copier of Rex Stewart, a musician's musician, and even, in a book, as 'an erratic musician with a peashooter tone!' I can play fast, and there was a time when that seemed to be all that was wanted from me. But I can play softly, slowly, and melodically, too, and I love to use a plunger." Five years ago, he took up flugelhorn, on which darker-toned instrument he now plays with great artistry and authority. "The flugelhorn is like a woman," he says. "It cannot be forced. It requires pampering."

The past year has seen Terry's versatility demonstrated in many contexts, but his uninhibited, tearaway solo on Gerry Mulligan's *Let My People Go* was an especial surprise to those who regarded him as a suave virtuoso or a poised, unemotional technician. The broad scope of his performance at a Duke Ellington Jazz Society concert in New York was also a revelation. Due soon are two contrasting albums under his name which he liked making. One of ballads was for Prestige with Junior Mance, Joe Benjamin, and Charlie Persip. A second, more ambitious, was for Candid with an octet and arrangements by Budd Johnson, Al Cohn, and Yusef Lateef.

As this was written, Terry's trumpet and flugelhorn were united with Bob Brookmeyer's valve trombone in one of the most distinguished new combos to appear in New York for a long time. During an intermission at the Half Note, Terry and bassist Joe Benjamin were sipping their second cup of tea.

"You seem to be enjoying yourselves up there," they were told.

"We are," Terry answered.

"You don't look bitter about anything!"

"Isn't that a drag?" said Benjamin.

[*1961*]

Sam Woodyard [*drums*]

"The night before I joined the Ellington band in 1955," Sam Woodyard said, "Max Roach and I went by a club in Philly where Count Basie was playing. Bill Graham was in the band then, and he

Clark Terry

grabbed me, and he, Basie, Freddie Greene, Marshall Royal, Eddie Jones, Max, and I went to a room in a hotel around the corner where some of them were staying. We sat up all night.

"I was scared, figuring there would be a hell of a drum book in Duke's band. How was I going to sight-read it? I had never been to a drum teacher in my life. All I had learned had been from people who had confidence in me and had sat down and shown me things. Now, we were all drinking whiskey and those cats were getting juiced, but I was so scared I was cold sober.

" 'To hell with it,' they said, trying to calm me down, 'just go in there and swing it!'

" 'Well, I don't know about that . . .

" 'Just go in there and listen, and play like you've been doing.'

"The next day, Milt Buckner drove me all the way into New York with my drums, and he came upstairs with me to the rehearsal at Nola Studios. Jimmy Woode, the bass player, came over as I was setting up and said, 'Hey, baby, glad to have you in the band!' I told him how I felt and he said, 'Forget it. Everybody feels like that the first day.' And that's what I've said to a lot of new cats as they've come in the band since.

"When I looked around, Max Roach was sitting there, but he was in my corner, anyway. Art Blakey and Shadow Wilson were there,

*Percussionists's parley: Chatur Lal
and Sam Woodyard, India, 1963*

too. Though they were friends of mine, that didn't make it any easier for me.

"The first number Duke called was *Harlem Airshaft*. I didn't know it, but I soon figured where the tune was going, and Clark Terry leaned over and said, 'I gotcha,' and told me things as we went along. When we got through the number, Duke walked over to the band and said:

" 'Gentlemen, have you met Sam Woodyard?'

" 'Yeah, I've met him,' Paul Gonsalves said. He turned with a smile and that was his way of saying I'd been swinging a bit. And that made me feel better.

"After we'd played a few things, Duke called something they hadn't played in six months. The band had been doing an aquashow all summer and Johnny Hodges had rejoined that very day. 'Watch this,' Clark Terry said. 'Everybody will be scuffling,' I had figured everyone knew what to do but me, but now I found out who was and who wasn't playing his part.

"The first night with the band, Duke asked me, 'How familiar are you with *Skin Deep?*' I didn't really know it and the kind of solos I'd been doing with Milt Buckner were very free. I was worried about dragging Duke and the cats and I think my performance was pretty weird, but Clark encouraged me again. 'You know, we're scuffling,

191

too,' he said, 'and tomorrow you'll be three hundred miles from here.' He taught me the whole book in about a week. and he had a very good way of teaching without hollering and making you feel conspicuous, so that people out front wouldn't be thinking, 'Well, they've got a new drummer.' He'd indicate things with his hand, or say, 'You've got four bars at the end of the chorus,' and so on. He sat at the end of the trumpet section, next to me.

"Clark, Paul, Jimmy Woode, and Willie Cook were in my corner from the first, but even those who weren't speaking soon came around, and we'd have a little taste, and they'd say they'd like me to play like this or like that behind them. and so we all got together. They found I wanted to play for the band, and that it didn't make any difference to me if it was with sticks, brushes, or hands. There's no sense in your building a house and my building a garage for it if we're not on the same property."

Sam Woodyard was born in Elizabeth, New Jersey, on January 7th, 1925. His mother remembered that when he was quite young he used to beat out rhythms on chairs and furniture in the house. His father played drums at weekends, and that was how his son broke in, too.

"I wanted to get in the school bands," Woodyard recalled, "but they wouldn't let me in. They had a dance orchestra and a band that played for what they called 'Assembly.' I could have gotten in just about the time I quit school, and that was on my sixteenth birthday, but I wanted to help my mother then, and once you go ahead and make it you just can't turn back. One day leads into the next, into a week, into a month, and a year, another year, and another year. . . .

"When I left school, I got a day job and played Saturday nights, with sometimes a matinée thrown in. Then I got lucky and worked with a trio three nights a week, using brushes. That was one of the good things I learned early on. Most drummers don't like playing with brushes. Nearly all the trios then consisted of saxophone, piano, and drums, so time-wise everything depended on the drummer. The *boom-boom* of the bass drum was important, but it could get pretty mysterious, because I didn't have the qualifications then to get an overall good sound.

"The first name of real promise I worked with was Milt Buckner, in his organ trio. I met him in Pep's Bar and Grill in Philly in 1953. I had gone down there with a saxophonist from Jersey named Joe Holiday and the two groups used to work behind the big bar, one each end. When Milt was leaving for the Band Box in New York, a place near Birdland that is now called the International, he asked if I would be interested in joining him. 'Swell,' I said. 'I'm with you!'"

Woodyard was with him two and a half years. At first the group included guitarist Ernest Williams, but later, Danny Turner, the alto saxophonist, took his place. In view of his subsequent career, the period with this trio was of inestimable value to Woodyard. Though a Jersey band called the Barons of Rhythm had inspired him as a kid —both Bobby Plater and Ike Quebec were in it—he had no experience with big bands other than very occasional weekend gigs.The best experience was playing with Milt Buckner, because that was very much like being with a big band.

"Some organists play horn style, but Milt played locked-hands style and as many 'instruments' as he could get going," Woodyard said. "When I went to Atlantic City with him, Wild Bill Davis used to be around the corner and he had Chris Columbus on drums. Chris took me under his wing. We used to get off at four, but they often played much later. Between sets, I'd go round and listen to him, and maybe sit around in his dressing room, and sometimes he'd come around on my job and sit at the drums. He's forgotten more than most drummers will ever know and he showed me so many things, especially about playing with an organ. You have to listen to the sounds as they come back, because it's an electronic thing. When the organist is playing the bass, you hear the sound of his foot hitting the pedals, so that you more or less have to get in between the beats. Then you have to be steady, because his leg will tire after an hour or so and the tempo may begin to fall back a bit.

"Playing with an organ is really something on its own, and a lot of drummers find it impossible. Some organists get around one difficulty by recording with a bass player, because the organ bass is hard to pick up properly. From what Wild Bill Davis, Bill Doggett, and Milt told me, the closest you can get to the real bass sound is by playing the same notes in the left hand as with the left foot. You couldn't use a bass player in person, because you'd never hear him. I broke more bass drum heads in the time I was with Milt than in all the time I've been with Duke Ellington, because you have to play with such power with an organ. They have that volume pedal on it and when they get halfway happy you see the toe go down—and you can wait for it to come up! And they have those speakers all around the joint, and the sound always goes up around one or two in the morning, and you've got to go along strong with the man. In some of those intimate rooms, you can see the bottles and glasses shaking on the shelves. The people absorb some of the sound when the room gets crowded, but open the door and you can be heard a block away.

"Milt Buckner was a wonderful cat to work for and he had a heart as big as this world. When you went to work, anything you'd got in you, you'd give it, even when you felt bad. He was enthusiastic and

193

inspiring, on and off the bandstand, and you never knew what was going to happen from one day to the next. Even the mistakes you made would be different! We used to play one- or two-week engagements in Philly, Cleveland, Detroit, Toledo, and 'way out on the South Side of Chicago. Before I was with Milt, I was with Paul Gayten, and we used to do the southern route—shuffle and backbeat all the time. So it wasn't new to me when I came to do things like *Asphalt Jungle* with Duke.

"It's funny how shuffle rhythm stirs people up, and I've got a little bounce I add to it. Chris Columbus used to do it at the Club Harlem, and he would jump up and down—everything in correct time—on a little bicycle seat he had. People used to try to get near him, and they'd stay there watching him maybe till nine or ten in the morning, and when they came out the sun would be shining bright.

"Drums can be very exciting. People used to go to battle to the sound of drums. Drums made them feel like fighting. After a while they'd point the guns in a certain direction, turn everybody loose, shout 'Charge!,' and they'd go for that wall or anything that stood in the way.

"Now, when I play my drum solo the band walks off and leaves me. If there were band riffs in the course of it, it would put me in a kind of vise and I'd have to play cues to bring them back in. That would mean telling the same story Friday you told Monday. And the band going off is a kind of commercial gimmick, like when Duke introduces his 'first-chair percussionist' and I look around as though he were surely going to bring another drummer on. It breaks a few people up. I could sit there stony-faced, but it is more warming that way. There are a great many people who start running for the men's and ladies' rooms. It's very disheartening to see people get up and go, though I know there are others who regard the drum solo as the highspot. I never know what I'm going to do. What I play on the tom-toms tonight I'll play on the snare drum tomorrow night, and on the cymbals the next night. When I run up on something that I think blends with what the band is doing, I keep it in. I really do try to think of the band first, and sometimes when it comes time for my solo I don't truly have the energy to play it. It's not always a case of being tired physically, but emotionally, because I can get my kicks when the band is playing a ballad, too.

"I've never been able to read fast, but there's never more than just so much you can get out of a book. You've got to get out and do it sometime. I have a fast ear and if I hear a thing down once I'll play it the second time, I don't care what it is. A teacher may say, 'Now you're qualified to play,' but you get in a band, and the tempo drops, and the leader says, 'What's the matter with you? Just play! You're a drummer. Listen, and keep swinging.' And you can't do it. What the teacher taught you was correct procedure, but what does 'correct' mean in a situation like that?

"There aren't many opportunities today for young drummers to get experience in carrying the weight of a band like Duke Ellington's. You sit there behind the drums, look around the bandstand, and there are those fourteen musicians, and it's an awful lot of musical weight. Everybody's patting his foot, and *thinking* right, but you've actually got fourteen different tempos, because everybody's got his own way of patting his foot. One's a little bit behind the beat and another's on top of it. It would be easy to be swayed, but you can't let yourself be. You've got to think, too, in terms of sections and the overall scheme. To keep the whole thing going, plus pleasing the bandleader, often means sacrificing yourself.

"I had the chance to play with Basie's band one night when we were laying off. This scared me, too, as long as I'd been with Duke's band. You might think it would be the other way 'round, the kind of arrangements and the way we play in this band, but I didn't want to be a drag and it had been so long since I played with a guitarist. When I got on the bandstand—I soon felt the difference between four rhythm and our three—often two when Duke is conducting. I didn't know the arrangements, but Freddie Greene was sitting right in front of the bass drum and Thad Jones was on my left, and between the two of them they cued me in, just like Clark Terry used to do.

"When you've got someone like Freddie Greene in the section, there's no sweat, because he listens and he's never stiff. Out front, you may not always hear him, but you feel him. The musicians certainly do. With a guitar player like him, I could play *Diminuendo and Crescendo in Blue* with brushes instead of sticks and get the same fire going behind Paul Gonsalves. That's the kind of a cat Freddie is, and that's the kind of thing that hits people without their knowing what it is. Sometimes we play *Diminuendo* and it doesn't get off the ground. Maybe we've been riding the bus all day and the guys are tired. You can't play it every night the way we did in 1956. It's hard on Paul, too, because he has to play to satisfy an audience and himself. Of course, there are little personal marks of identification that you keep, because you like to hear them yourself. But being free you turn this around, or go after that a different way, just to see what happens. When we made the record, it was only the third time I'd played it, or rather numbers 107 and 108 in the book. On that occasion, as Duke said over the microphone, a 'wailing interval by Paul Gonsalves' came between them. Because I was unfamiliar with it, there are some real bad breaks on the record and some sloppy work, but one well-known critic gave me a very good write-up. Who should know better than me if I was wrong or not? Pretty weird!

"No one is perfect. To me, anybody who can sit, stand, lean against a wall, or hang by his toes and say he's perfect is a damn liar. Because man made it, even a metronome isn't perfect. In a rhythm section, it's all a matter of listening. The tempo varies for many reasons. Maybe it's fatigue. It may drop through disinterest or go up through enthusiasm. Sometimes the tempo doesn't change, but the color of the tune changes. It may take fire in the last choruses and the extra excitement makes listeners think the tempo went up. You go with the change of feeling, but the tempo hasn't necessarily changed. The main thing is if you've got it off the ground and are still swinging. There is, though, a tendency for musicians to start climbing together, and before you know it color and dynamics go out the window—and if there isn't a window, then they make one.

"A rhythm section is often criticized from different angles by people with different conceptions of how it should play. A drummer may have a four-bar break in an arrangement, but if someone doesn't come in on time afterwards, some people will say it's the drummer's fault, because they didn't really listen to what he played. They'll say he should have played something more simple, but those were the drummer's four bars and as long as he got back for the first beat of the fifth bar he could have gone out and run around the block. It's not his fault if someone else can't keep time.

"I've come up through those grooves where there are not so many in the rhythm section, where the drummer has got to be the strong one all the time. Jimmie Crawford, to me, was one of the greatest drummers in the world. What that cat got under the Jimmie Lunceford band was something else. Papa Jo Jones is another one. I heard Chick Webb mostly on records, but I stood outside the Savoy once when I was too young to go in and they had the windows open. He was the first drummer who made sense in a big band, and that stuck with me. His time was right *there*. He knew how to shade and color, and how to bring a band up and keep it there. Big Sid Catlett was like that, too. I heard him at Frank Dailey's Meadowbrook in New Jersey when he was with Benny Goodman. The difference was that Chick was a bandleader and obliged to do things that you wouldn't do as a sideman, not that he wasn't a great accompanist. Sid was a big man and anytime he wanted to get powerful you knew it, but the personal touch, in the sound of his drums and in his style, was very crisp and tasteful. Dave Tough influenced me, too, with his simplicity. If there was any way he could get out of taking solos, he would. He had a good sound to his drums and he always kept his bass drum under the bass fiddle, so that you could hear the tune the bassist was playing. In fact, you could feel his bass drum rather than hear it, and it didn't conflict with the rest of the band. Even on those old Chick Webb records, you could often feel the bass drum as much as you could hear it, and that's how it was at the Savoy. It's very easy to get overenthused at the drums and overshadow other people in the band, especially if you've got the drums too tight so that you sound like a machine gun back there. Then you start playing rimshots and all the people near you begin to flinch."

"Sam Woodyard? He's a swinger."

Duke Ellington was delivering some capsule estimates of his men, and this three-word summing-up of the drummer who has been with him longer than any save Sonny Greer reflected his appreciation of one of Woodyard's cardinal virtues. It was also partly explanatory of the quick understanding that exists between them, one which becomes most evident in the recording studio when they are working on new material. Ellington may mime his requirements from the control room, dance them on the studio floor, or detail them verbally.

"Chang, chang, chang," he will call, requesting cymbals.

"Play four bars introduction, Sam," as he sets up a routine, "sixteen bars of exoticity, and then swing the bridge."

"Gutbucket, right from the beginning. You got it! I'm going to conduct, Sam."

"Put a little more sex in there."

Once, when Ellington had retreated to the control room during a second take, he sounded a note of disappointment at the results:

"Sam, you were swinging when I was out there."

"That's because you're not here," was the drummer's reply. "Crazy, baby, I'm with you."

There were no parts for the percussionists on the recordings in the *Afro-Bossa* album, complicated though their roles often were, and a certain amount of mock disaffection with this state of affairs was sounded on one occasion.

"Where's my part?" Billy Strayhorn (on "second cowbell") demanded of Tom Whaley.

"And where's mine?" asked Woodyard, who never gets one.

A few seconds later, Whaley handed him a sheet of manuscript paper with a big letter B on it.

"What's that mean?"

"Be natural!"

"Be ready, I thought."

"Be here!" Johnny Hodges called.

197   Another day, when they were recording a collection of band

themes for a Reprise package, Woodyard insists that Ellington requested him to "get in the alley" on Wayne King's *The Waltz You Saved for Me*. This was significantly different from his frequent request for the drummer to "put the pots and pans on."

"It's an old Southern expression," Woodyard explained. "Give the man some hamhocks, greens, and cornbread! Originally, when the man came home for dinner and there wasn't anything ready, he'd say, 'Well, put the pots and pans on!' What we mean by it in the band is, 'Swing and get off the ground—and stay off until you're ready to come down!' I could add that the prettiest meal in the world isn't anything unless you have salt and pepper to go with it, and that's how it is with a band if the rhythm section isn't right.

"Every day you learn something new. It's not always how to do something, but how not to do it. I had such an awful time with that shuffle when we recorded *Artistry in Rhythm*. I stayed up half the night playing on the chairs and the bed. Duke often has his ideas about what he wants you to play and he'll walk up and say. 'Do that with this hand and this with that hand.' And it can be difficult to put together time-wise and make it relate to the arrangement. I had never played a shuffle with my hands like that before and it wasn't hard the way I wanted to do it, but what he wanted was something else. Playing with my hands, I can't project where the beat is with much power to the band. It's coming over the microphone loud enough, but not to the musicians, and you get tense. Recording always has its own problems.

"The first time I went into Columbia with this band, a guy came out of control with a blanket before we ever started playing. I broke him out of that.

" 'Put it over your bass drum,' he said.

" 'For what?'

" 'We do it for all the drummers who come in here. If you don't cover the bass drum the needle starts jumping.'

" 'That's your business. Don't tell me how to play my drums. You just move the microphone back, because I'm going to play the way I usually play for the band.'

"The band may be swinging along on the level and you get to a part where it really starts smoking, and you all come up together. You're supposed to be there. If the drummer doesn't do it, the guys in the band say, 'Man, what happened to you?' But the engineer comes out and says you made the needle jump, you with three hundred dollars worth of his microphones right in your lap, so that you can't really get around your drums to play four bars.

"Anyone can always come to me and say, 'Give me a little flavor here, or do this there.' Or they can tell me where to come up and

where to go down. Just don't tell me what drum to play it on!
"I love everybody who's playing from the heart. I just dig people
who like to live. There are only twenty-four hours in a day and you'll
never get them back, so you do the best you can however you can
and wherever you can. 'Wherever' has been a big word for our band
the past few years, we've traveled so much, but everybody really
speaks the same language. It's just a matter of putting the pots on!"

[*1965*]

Booty Wood [*trombone*]

Mitchell "Booty" Wood joined Duke Ellington on Labor Day,
1959. He took the place of John Sanders in the band and immediately
set forth on a European tour.

"I never had a chance to rehearse or anything." he recalled.
"There were only about five of us on the boat, anyway. We opened
in Amsterdam. The music wasn't too hard to read, but the circumstances you had to work under were something else. Some of those
big halls over there had their own ideas about lighting effects. They'd
shove a spotlight on a soloist, black the whole band out—and I'm
supposed to be reading music! It wasn't too easy, but Britt [Wood-
man] and Butter [Jackson] were a big help. And whenever I could see
the music it was much better!"

At the conclusion of the tour, Quentin Jackson left the band and
Ellington casually intimated to Wood that he wanted him to take on
the plunger work. Wood had little interest in it, and very little experience of it beyond what he had heard Jackson do.

Back in New York, most of the band went into the Columbia
studio to make the *Blues in Orbit* album. Duke called on Wood for
the lengthy plunger treatment of *Sweet and Pungent*, and he obliged
with visible reluctance.

"Why would he have *me* play that . . .?" he asked disgustedly a
few minutes later when a successful take had been accomplished.

It is a different story today. Wood declaims in the dramatic
plunger roles with enough zest and artistry to bring an appreciative
grin even onto Johnny Hodges' poker face.

"Listen to him talking," Hodges said.

"Booty Wood is one of the best plunger trombonists I ever
heard," said Ellington.

It would be hard to name more authoritative judges of the growling horn than those two. Yet one wonders how Ellington *knew* Wood could do superlatively something for which he expressed no liking.

No one else in Wood's family was musical. His first instrument was harmonica in a grade school band. He didn't go for the official method, nor did the teacher go for his, which consisted, as he remembered, of "playing it by ear and picking my own melodies and keys."

Next, he developed an obession for trombone. It was the usual thing, the look of it in parades, that attracted him, but when he eventually got it he didn't like it. "I didn't like the parts I had to play in the school band—all oom-pah and backgrounds—but I couldn't afford another horn, so I had to stay with it. After a while I began playing in a little jazz group and things got better."

At that time he was thirteen and there was a shortage of trombone players in Dayton, Ohio, where he was raised. He was influenced more by trumpet than trombone players, and he remembers being particularly impressed by the brothers Young, Snooky, and Granville. Snooky got him a job in a local twelve-piece band. "I'd had the horn only a few months then, but my teacher was very good and I hadn't found it hard to learn to read. So they were quite impressed and I worked with them a year or more. But at first I couldn't solo one note if you took me away from the music."

Thereafter, for nearly seven years, his education was interrupted by jazz forays with different bands. He went back to school for the last time when he was nineteen and graduated with a sister three years younger than himself. Meanwhile, he had had adventures a-plenty in Florida with the bands of Porkchops Curry and Walter Johnson, and he had played in New York and Boston as one of Chick Carter's Dixie Rhythm Boys alongside Gerald Wilson, Snooky Young, Ray Perry, and Eddie Byrd.

After graduation, he joined Jimmy Raschel's band, in which he met musicians like Howard McGhee, Milt Buckner, Wardell Gray, Big Nick Nicholas, Bernie Peacock, and James Wormick. "Those bands out in the Mid-West," Wood said, "were not great for polish, because they'd always include some guys who had no intention of making music a career, as well as those that had. So naturally they didn't attain the highest standards, but there were usually some guys in them who were outstanding."

Friendships were made in those days. Howard McGhee came looking for Wood in Dayton to join Andy Kirk, but he was out of town and when he caught up with the band in Chicago the chair had been filled. After scuffling there for a while, he took Chippy Outcalt's place with Tiny Bradshaw. Tiny's big band was enjoying considerable success then, its lead alto, Bobby Plater, having just written *Jersey*

Bounce. After a year and a half in that berth, Milt Buckner got Wood into Lionel Hampton's band, which at that time was about the best of Hampton's career. Fred Beckett was leading the trombone section and Wood admitted to learning a lot. "I used to practice six or seven hours a day," he said. "I thought I was really going to be somebody!"

In 1944, he entered the Navy and the band at Great Lakes under Willie Smith's leadership: "It was a terrific band, one of the finest I ever worked in. You had plenty of time to work on your horn, and you were surrounded by the best. By this time, I had come strongly under Trummy Young's influence. I thought he was the greatest. Carter Smith, Trombone Smitty, was at the Lakes too, and he was a wonderful player."

After his discharge, he went back with Hampton until 1947. Though the personnel remained good, the material and its mode of presentation were deteriorating. "I wasn't too happy when clapping your hands became more important than what you played, so when Arnett Cobb decided to leave, I left with him." Cobb was dogged by ill luck, but Wood was with him until he fell sick the third time. In between, he played two lengthy engagements with Erskine Hawkins. "I think I had more fun in that band than any other," he said. "Erskine was such a nice guy to work for and the personnel was more like a bunch of brothers." Wood's two exciting and well-constructed choruses on Hawkins' *Beale Street Blues* give a good idea of his ability at that time.

He went home to his wife and family after six months with Basie in 1951. His intention was to return to the Count again when he re-formed his big band, but in Dayton, Snooky Young had a little band that played seven nights a week. There was a place for Wood and he took it, as well as a daytime post-office job. When Basie called, things were going too well financially for him to leave.

Although far from inactive musically, it was 1959, eight years later, before Wood stepped out of Dayton into the wider world of jazz again.

"Duke came through to play a dance," Wood said, "and Clark and Britt came by the house and we had dinner. Then we all went to the dance together. During the evening, Jamie Woode got sick and couldn't play anymore. So Butter started to play the bass and Clark called to me, 'Come on up and play this chair!' Duke didn't ask me, but I'd been drinking, too, and was a little bit high, and just went up and played it. I just sat in, even took some solos. So the next night they were playing fifty miles away in Newport, Kentucky, and Clark came out and said, 'We want you to make the gig tonight, because Jamie is still sick.' So I said, 'Okay.'

"Three or four days later, Duke called me and asked if I wanted to join the band. They were getting ready to go to Europe and I decided I'd try it."

Thus fortuitously, a skilled and conscientious musician was returned to his rightful milieu, that of the big band. Wood maintained the precious Ellington heritage of plunger trombone while contributing something fresh. Besides the recordings with Ellington, his trombone was to be heard in albums by Johnny Hodges and Harry Carney —and his euphonium in one by Jimmy Hamilton!

[*1960*]

Aaron Bell   [*bass*]

Aaron Bell was born in Muskogee, Oklahoma, on April 24th, 1922. His mother was a music teacher, and all her nine children received piano lessons. His twin sister, who played particularly well, later also became a teacher. In high school, he became interested in the band. An older brother played trumpet in it, and young Aaron used to take his horn upstairs and blow it whenever he had a chance.

The band's instruments were furnished by the city, and when an opening occurred on tuba, he applied for that instrument and got it. The bandmaster helped him, but it was then more a matter of group than individual instruction. As he sought to solve for himself the problems of the instrument, and to express himself musically, his mother's knowledge was of great assistance. She played piano and organ, and gave vocal tuition. One of her pupils was the well-known pianist and bandleader, Jay McShann.

The school band, which consisted of about forty-five pieces, was of the military type, and mostly played concerts. Eventually, Bell became its first chair tuba player. "Then I got interested in jazz," he said. "I'd heard records, and there was a little jazz group around town led by T. Holder. Barney Kessel, the guitar player—they used to call him 'Fruit Cake'—would jam with them, but I couldn't do that on tuba. They had good piano players, so I couldn't get in on piano either, but I was very interested, and I stood around and watched. The whole Pettiford family had just left Oklahoma for Minneapolis, and I didn't get to hear them until I came East. Don Byas was from Muskogee, although older than I. He saved my life once, when he pulled me out of an old gravel pit where we used to swim. He had two brothers, Vincent and Jack, who both played clarinet, but they went into teaching and didn't stay in music. There was also a very good guitar player named Oliver Green, who later went to Los Angeles and worked as a cameraman. Don Byas lived about a couple of houses from me, and when he and Oliver got together for little sessions, I'd go over and listen."

When he was seventeen, Bell went to Xavier University in New Orleans. His mother was from that city and a Catholic, who had brought up her children in the same faith. Relatives were able to help at first with room and board. In his application, he styled himself an arranger as well as a tuba player on the strength of some writing he had done for the hometown jazz group.

"They didn't give me a scholarship," he recalled, "but they told me to come down and they'd help pay my tuition. There was a bass viol there that belonged to the university, and I told them I was interested in learning it. A nun gave me tuition, and I did such a lot of practicing that I made the band on bass in my sophomore year.

"It was not like the conservatory, where all the subjects are music. It was a liberal arts course with a music major. I minored in languages, French and German. I had philosophy, sociology, psychology, and, of course, in a Catholic school, religion. They also required mathematics in the first year. The young music instructor, Allegretto Alexander, conducted the concert and military bands, played piano and trumpet, and was a very good arranger. He taught me an awful lot about jazz. I got into arranging early, and did quite a bit for the college band."

Besides playing with the university band, Bell had opportunities to work with professional groups in the city, such as Herb Leary and His Society Syncopators, and pianist Fats Pichon's band. The former was strictly a dance band, whereas Pichon's played jazz. It wasn't Dixieland, however. The band, usually of ten or twelve pieces, played typical big-band arrangements. Later, it was taken over by the trumpet player, Dave Bartholomew, who eventually went into rock 'n' roll with Fats Domino.

Bell enjoyed life in New Orleans. "They had jam sessions quite often down there," he said. "There was always a lot of work—and a lot of musicians—but there was a *friendly* spirit of competition. You could ask questions and they'd help you out. Little Al, the regular bass player with Pichon when I first went down there, showed me so much about the bass. It's not right to think of a city like New Orleans as a musical backwater. There are always guys in places like that who just don't want to leave home. I remember particularly an alto player called Wiggles. That's the only way I ever knew him, as Wiggles. And this guy could play—oh, I mean he could *play!*—and I heard him before I ever heard Charlie Parker, and this guy was *terrible*. I don't know who came first, but his lines were quite similar to Parker's. It's like Buster Smith, another fine alto player, who won't leave the Dallas area. They say he inspired Charlie, but I don't know who inspired Wiggles. Then there were two piano players down there, brothers, Big Cato and Little Cato, and they were both terrific. Big Cato was a great pianist, and he stuck more to the older style, but Little Cato was one of the first fellows I heard really playing modern. Had he come East, he would probably have been the Bud Powell of his time. That Dave Bartholomew was a brilliant trumpet player—he had everything—and he did leave for about a month with Jimmie Lunceford's band, but then he went back home."

Bell finished at Xavier in June, 1943, and that August entered the Navy for nearly four years. He was assigned to a band that was sent to the naval base at Peru, Indiana. Among the musicians in it that he remembers with special admiration was Benton Banks, "a great pianist, great violinist, and great arranger." Because he slept so much, Banks was then known as "Rip."

After he got out of the Navy, Bell married, and was home in Oklahoma when Andy Kirk's band came to Tulsa. He sat in with the band on bass, and Kirk offered him the job. After a year with Kirk, he returned home and taught music at his old high school, where he was put in charge of the band. He also taught privately in his mother's

Booty Wood

music studio, and became musical director of the local radio station. The following summer, he went to New York and entered New York University under the G.I. Bill of Rights to get his master's degree. While waiting for his union card, he worked as an orderly in Harlem Hopsital to supplement his meager allowance. Once he was a member of Local 802, he began to get jobs, first with Lucky Millinder's band at the Savoy ballroom through the help of Lucky's lead alto, Bernie Peacock, and then, thanks to a recommendation from Budd Johnson, with Teddy Wilson. He went back to the Savoy with Eddie Wilcox and the remnants of the old Jimmie Lunceford band when it still contained Paul Webster, Elmer Crumbley, Russell Bowles, Omer Simeon, and Joe Marshall.

"All this time," he continued, "I was making connections, and I worked with some pretty big guys, like Stan Getz, but I didn't want to travel and leave the city, because by now we had a couple of children. I worked with Lester Young, and I learned an awful lot about playing with him, because he gave me more freedom. I hadn't done too much soloing on bass before, so this was good for me. Because he knew I was still at the university, he called me 'Professor.' 'Take it, Professor,' he'd say. Prez [Young] and Teddy Wilson were great guys to work with. They never bugged you, never argued, never put you down, but made you feel they appreciated what you were

Aaron Bell

doing. Sometimes, because of where I was living in the Bronx, I'd be late, and I'd charge in, taking off my coat, running to the bass. 'Hi, there!' Teddy would say. 'I'm sorry,' I'd reply. 'Oh, that's all right. Have a taste?' And he wouldn't go on the stand until I got there. Prez was the same way if I was late. 'Well, Professor, you gonna make it tomorrow?' he'd ask. 'I'm gonna *be* here tomorrow, on time,' I'd answer. They were both good for me, because they took inhibitions about playing away, and sort of bolstered my ego.

"While I was working with a pianist named Herman Chittison—a very fine fellow with a beautiful touch—at Café Society Downtown, Joya Sherrill was on the same bill, and we had to play for her. That was when I first met her, and she liked my playing. She had been working at the Hotel Concord in the Catskills, and she knew they had been looking for a trio up there. She called and asked if I could get a trio together, and I could and did—Charile Bateman on piano and Charlie Smith on drums. We went up for a weekend and stayed eighteen months. Thursday nights, they had symphony concerts, and we all played in them, too. They'd call up guys from NBC in New York, and get together about sixty pieces. Charlie Smith was an excellent musician and drummer, one of the best I ever worked with. During that time, I made my first album, for Herald, with this trio that we called Three Swinging Bells."

Subsequently, Bell worked with Cy Coleman and Stan Freeman, and began to get a name as a trio bassist. Through Coleman, he got a job in a Broadway show, *Compulsion*, which ran five months. With a quartet, he played on stage in two scenes, the trumpet in the group being the veteran Henry Goodwin. During the same period, he was able to work at the Velvet Club on Second Avenue, an engagement which led to his recording albums for Victor and M-G-M under his own name. Except for a three-month tour with Cab Calloway's band, which took him to Canada and Las Vegas, he freelanced around New York, making a name for himself in recording circles, and working meanwhile towards the master's degree which he secured in 1955. From time to time, too, opportunities occurred for him to practice his hand as an arranger.

It was while he was working with Carmen McRae that critic Leonard Feather persuaded Duke Ellington to hear her bass player. Wendell Marshall was leaving the band after it completed an engagement at Birdland. "Come on and sit in, and let Duke hear you," he said to Bell, who declined, being at that time uncertain of his ability to cope with the position. Later, Feather introduced him to Ellington at the Hickory House, but when the leader requested his services, other commitments prevented his accepting for several months. Finally, on April 12th, 1960, he joined Ellington in Las Vegas.

"Jimmy Woode was still with the band at the time," Bell remembered, "but I think he wanted to leave and go to work with his father in Stockholm. Even then, I had doubts about traveling and staying with a band, but I found I liked it too much, and I got along nicely with Duke, so I decided to stay. He took my responsibilities into consideration, and fixed it so that I wouldn't have to worry about the family being taken care of.

"I think it means a lot to him to have someone he can rely on on bass, because a lot of times, when he's conducting and not playing piano, we're working with a two-man rhythm section. We have a sort of affinity for each other. I wouldn't say Duke's the greatest piano player in the world, but I would say he's one of the most distinctive. What he does, I like, and I've learned to sort of anticipate what he's going to do. Often, I just *know* what he's going to do before he does it. As a matter of fact, I've gotten so I can tell just about what number he's going to call before he calls it. Sometimes he throws us a curve, but when he varies the program it's because of the audience. And he never forgets them. They're always uppermost in his mind. From experience, and from watching him so closely, I've learned what type of audience he'll make which switch on. It usually works out the way he's going, but sometimes it doesn't. When that happens, he lets the band call the numbers. If he can't outguess the audience, he'll say, 'What shall we play?,' figuring that somebody else may hit it.

"You remember when we were at Newport, and we had to follow Quincy Jones. It was 'way late, and the crowd was leaving, because everybody else had been allowed to overrun their time. You have to give Duke credit for knowing how to meet a situation. He knew he couldn't cast the spell he usually casts. 'I'll go up and do my forty minutes,' he said, 'and everything I'm going to play is fast music.' Maybe he was thinking the faster we played the sooner we'd get off. It was the right thing to do, though, and the music had a lot of impact even at that hour. But then I've never seen Duke at a loss for words in any situation—except when you ask him for a raise. He can't understand you then; you're speaking another language. He lives purely in the realm of art. Such materialistic matters as money. . . !

"There are problems today in big, heavy bands like his, because there aren't drummers and bass players with that kind of experience. Even before the time of Jimmy Blanton, when he had Wellman Braud and the older fellows, the bass played a very prominent part in the rhythm section of Duke's band.

"The impression the general public has of his style is chiefly concerned with its melodic contours and harmonic construction, but it's that jungle effect in the rhythm section which really sets the whole thing off. The bass and drums naturally play a very important

207

part in this, and when I'm playing with Duke it stays on my mind to try to give him the depth I know he wants. I think the music sounds better when you're playing like that. Sometimes I start walking modern figures, and things that I've heard, just to keep up with the times. If I were on a record session with some of the younger guys, I'd play very differently—more of a light, skipping thing—whereas with Duke I try to anchor it, and to give him something to lean on. And that's a good function for bass, because, after all, when you say 'bass' you mean 'basic.'

"Sam Woodyard does a job in playing for Duke. I think he has the right idea, too, but he's often over-recorded. What Duke likes most is that *drive*. When I first went with Duke, everyone said, 'Wow, the band sounds good since you came in!' But I don't think I was playing well for a while. It took me a long time to get onto it. There were things I had been listening to on records, and I had preconceived ideas about what I should do to make it really swing, but there were some numbers that completely threw me, and I didn't know what to do. *Matumba* (or *Congo Square*) was one of them. It's so unorthodox, and Sam's not playing any definite rhythm. There's no bass part there, and it took me a long time to figure out what to do. Actually, I'm playing two against three on it. It took me a while to arrive at that. I didn't just come in and start doing it. The same with *Satin Doll*. There was never any writing around me. The solo is more or less my creation. The whole band is out, so if I'm playing badly that day, and not thinking, or I'm not in the right mood, then it'll be very bad and nothing will be happening. I love to play *Jack the Bear*, and I'm sure if I got to play it every night, I'd get a lot better, and be able to characterize it. What I do when we get occasional requests for it is from the record: I'm doing a Jimmy Blanton, or attempting to.

"I have the advantage that I can carry more melody than a drum. It's a worry and a fact that Sam's health is not good. It's not a put-on when he gets through with his solo and looks like he's about to drop dead. I believe he hasn't any reserve strength left at all, that he's using everything he has every time he plays. That has an emotional value to the listener, because the audience sort of feels it."

Jimmy Blanton, Ellington's famous bassist of 1939–41, is the first musician Bell names as an influence, although he heard him only on records and broadcasts.

"He influenced me greatly," he admits at once. "Little Al, whom I spoke about before, also influenced me a lot, and he had a sound very much like Blanton's. I'm sure if Duke had heard him, he'd have wanted him, too. Now Jimmy chiefly played 'spot' things like *Jack the Bear*. I don't think there's any record, except the duos he did with Duke, where he plays the whole chorus. Oscar Pettiford, who was with Duke from 1945 to 1948, took it from there, and went further. "He could take a song and solo on it, developing a theme chord-wise just like a horn player or pianist would. He was always clean and exact, just like Jimmy. And he was always tasty. When bass players are soloing, there are certain things that lay good on the instrument which they tend to throw in no matter what the tune. It's easily done, and it can be done on whichever chord they are on in the tune, so that it seems to fit. They're not taking a motif like Oscar did, and they're throwing in something that doesn't really belong. That is, it fits the chord, but it doesn't necessarily fit the melody of the song, the title of the song, or the words of the song. It's a gimmick to show you're good on the bass. Oscar wasn't like that. Every time he played a solo, he was telling a story. The trouble is the general public can't hear down in that range like a bass player who's attuned to it. There are even many musicians who can't really tell the difference between bass players. One of the members of Duke's band is an example. 'What difference does it make?' he would say. 'A bass player's a bass player.' To others—and to Duke, thank God!—it means a helluva lot of difference, because they listen to the bass line.

"I remember once when I was working in a New York nightclub, and a lady patron came up and said, 'You seem like you're enjoying yourself so much.' 'Well,' I said, 'I do some nights.' She laughed and replied, 'I can understand how the pianist and even a drummer can enjoy himself, but I can't understand how you can enjoy yourself standing there and going *boom-boom-boom-boom-boom* all night long!' To her, I wasn't getting any variation, but she could *see* the drummer going to the cymbals, the light drum and the heavy drum with sticks, brushes, and sometimes mallets."

Although Pettiford is clearly Bell's favorite bass player, he is appreciative of many others. He expressed admiration for Walter Page's "great walkin' feeling," Gene Ramey's "fire and drive," Paul Chambers' "depth and buoyancy in the rhythm section," and Ray Brown's "magnificent general technique." Charles Mingus he recognized as having "one of the greatest techniques on bass in the world," and Milt Hinton as being equipped to play "just about anything in jazz and classical music." He had a healthy respect for George Duvivier, his all-around ability, his "neat, clean solos," and the way he would "develop and stick to his theme when he started playing a solo." Of the younger musicians, Wilbur Ware was one he esteemed highly: "He is one of the few modern players that still plays *bass*. He's very modern in his phrasing, in the overall conception of his lines, and in his mind, but he still plays bass. At the right time, it's always there when you need it."

209 Bell feels the line of demarcation between jazz and symphony

musicians is being steadily erased. Jazz musicians always respected their "classical" counterparts, and the latter are now looking with more interest and favor on the versatility of those in jazz. "You take a bass player like Charles Mingus," he said. "There's hardly anything written in the symphony field that he couldn't play, but those symphony bassists can't do what he can do in jazz." Oddly enough, the better jazz players can earn far more money, which is one reason why Bell did not take up an invitation to try out for the Philharmonic in New York. Another was that differences in approach still persist.

"Most 'classical' bass players," he explained, "have a very short attack. They don't hold on up here [with the left hand]. They're very good, very in-tune, exact, with perfect time, but they're not swinging. To teach a student to play classical or jazz, I think you'd have to use two different methods. In one, you vary the length of tone, and in the other you vary the attack."

Despite his dedication to the string bass, he has never lost his interest in the tuba, and on one occasion he was delighted to have the opportunity to sit in with the Ellington band on that instrument.

"You don't have to worry about having firm chops as you do in playing trumpet," he said, "but in tuba you have to learn to control the relaxation of your chops. The lower you go, the more relaxed you have to be. It doesn't take any more wind than a trumpet, although a lot of people think it does. There's no comparison with the bass violin so far as rhythm work is concerned, although the tuba can be utilized more in connection with the brass section. There's no problem in blending with the trombones, but I'm more interested in using it as a solo instrument."

When he reluctantly left Ellington in the fall of 1962, it was partly to avoid the incessant traveling, and partly to realize other ambitions. Since then he has composed, arranged, recorded (sometimes on tuba), played in several Broadway shows, and resumed a teaching career in New Jersey.

[*1962*]

Buster Cooper [*trombone*]

"A cousin of mine, George Cooper, played drums with the 'Bama State Collegians. Although my father used to play guitar in the juke joints, it was George who really got me interested in music. He used to come over every year to our home in St. Petersburg, Florida, and he made a big impression on me. Then my father decided to buy my brother a trumpet, and when we went downtown to pick it out I saw a trombone in the window that cost ten dollars.

"I was about sixteen then and I messed around on that horn for a while, but I was crazy about baseball and wanted to be a baseball player more than anything. But after my cousin had formed his own sixteen-piece band, my brother used to go off on trips with him, and when they began telling me about the good times they had I started playing again, and with more interest. Before that, I had been taught how to play in high school.

"After a while, I joined my cousin's band and went on a tour to Texas. When I left that band, I joined Nat Towles in Omaha, Nebraska. He had three trumpets, but only one trombone. Oliver Nelson and Noble Watts were in the sax section. Oliver played lead, but he would never take a solo. He was writing arrangements, too, but he had to write then more what was expected from a territory band for dancing. Up to that time, the trombone who had influenced me most was Lawrence Brown. One of the records we had at home and that I remember I liked was Duke's *Midriff*. Lawrence took a solo on it.

"I was with Nat Towles for about a year before I went to New York and studied for another year at the Harnett School of Music— harmony and counterpoint. I joined Lionel Hampton in 1953, at a time when he had a very good band. Clifford Brown, Jimmy Cleveland, Gigi Gryce, and Quincy Jones were in it. Then I played in the Apollo house band under Reuben Phillips for a couple of years, and after that I was with Lucky Millinder at the Savoy for about nine months in a band that included Jimmy Nottingham, Ernie Royal, Henderson Chambers, and George Dorsey. I was with Benny Goodman for about six months before my brother and I formed the Cooper Brothers band with Eric Dixon on tenor and Lloyd Mayers on piano. By this time, my brother Steve had given up trumpet and was playing bass. We worked around the city and then went to Paris for a year with Curley Hamner on drums. We opened at the Olympia Theatre. When we came back, we played at the Tops Club on 125th Street and later at Wells' on Seventh Avenue.

"I joined Duke Ellington on the recommendation of Clark Terry. Duke called me while we were still at Wells', but I couldn't make it then because the engagement called for several more weeks. Mercer called me about a month later and I took Leon Cox's place in June, 1962. It's an education being in that band and sitting alongside Lawrence Brown. He's the greatest. In over a year, I haven't heard him fluff once. And Chuck Connors, the man with the biggest sound in the band, is the best bass trombone player I ever heard.

"I think all the instruments—trumpet, piano, clarinet, and saxo-

211

phone—have had their eras in jazz except the trombone, so our day is coming! I played valve trombone for a while, but I didn't like it. It's easier to play, but it's a kind of cheat if you're going to play trombone. It has a foreign sound and it always seemed out of tune to me. I can get more attack and much more out of the instrument with slide than with valve. I've met older trombone players like Vic Dickenson and Benny Morton, but I haven't had much chance to hear them play. I know Trummy Young very well and like the way he can play. The mouthpiece I'm using now is one he gave me. I never pick up the plunger, because I think it would slow me down. It requires a style of its own, one you really have to specialize in.

" 'Buster?' They called me that because I weighed fifteen pounds when I was born on April 4, 1929, but my real name is George."

[*1963*]

Jimmy Jones [*piano*]

One of the most sought-after arrangers in New York today is Jimmy Jones. Among those he has written for are Sarah Vaughan, Joe Williams, Lena Horne, Harry Belafonte, Wes Montgomery, Nancy Wilson, and Duke Ellington. Not so long ago, he was also one of the most sought-after pianists for jazz record dates, but though his ability at the keyboard remains undiminished, he now has much less time for the piano. He regards the change in his position as an advancement. "It has taken me from labor to management. Writing is more on the executive side, where you put things together, and I like that. Playing the piano, you're just a prop for a setting."

Jones was born in Memphis and raised in Chicago. Because everyone in his neighborhood seemed to have one, he first began to express himself musically on four-string guitar, but his mother played piano and he switched to that instrument in his teens.

"The guitar influenced my piano harmonically," he said, "in thinking in terms of groups of notes rather than single lines. Of course, a lot of cats today are playing single-line stuff, too, but when I played guitar it was more or less in a chord style like Wes Montgomery's. It was a Mid-West type of thing and Wes reminds me of the old days when I hear him play these full chords. That was the way I played and I just transferred it to the piano. Looking back, I think if I had projected the single-note approach, which I could have done, it would have been more commercial, but once you get an established style, an identity, you hate to change it."

After high school and music college in Chicago, where he played in the junior college orchestra, Jones went to Kentucky State, where his first major was sociology and his second music.

"It was there I learned to write," he recalled, "by trial and error, where it didn't make any difference if it sounded bad. The main thing in writing is to be able to hear it. I don't care what you put on paper; you've got to hear it played to know if you like it or not."

From the very beginning, Jones insisted, his greatest inspiration was Duke Ellington, and he had been encouraged in this by his parents, who took him to hear Ellington whenever he played Chicago. In fact, long after he had embarked on a professional career, Jones continued to receive press clippings from his father relative to the Ellington band's appearances.

"Earl Hines was the prominent pianist in the city at that time, and he was wonderful," Jones admitted, "but I always liked Duke better, for his orchestra as well as his piano. When Dave Brubeck once asked me who had influenced me most, I told him the Duke Ellington *orchestra*. I tried to make the piano sound like it."

Playing in local dance groups, his career for a time ran parallel with John Levy's. He made his first records for the Session label with a sextet which included Levy on bass and the great Alvin Burroughs on drums, but it was when he joined Levy as a member of Stuff Smith's trio that his fame spread beyond Chicago. "Stuff had a good personality and we had such a ball playing that people began to have fun just watching us have fun," he remembers. "On records, we didn't have time to develop ideas, but in person we went much further in extensions."

The trio had a great success, but its unity was strained in New York by the excitements and stresses of 52nd Street, and by the demands of freelance recording. The first records made under Jones' own name, for H.R.S. in 1946, also marked his first association with members of the Ellington musical family, such as Harry Carney, Lawrence Brown, and Toby Hardwick. His writing for the date showed a strong Ellington influence. On the Street, he remembered sitting in with Coleman Hawkins, Ben Webster, Don Byas, Dizzy Gillespie, and Charlie Parker, but, despite the allure of that thoroughfare, he ended up in Café Society with J. C. Heard's group.

"Sarah Vaughan came down there and I played the audition for Barney Josephson to hear her," he said. "Then I went with her as accompanist and became her musical director. I made this change from the straight jazz scene because it was more lucrative, not that I liked it any better. But it was the better end of the business and

Buster Cooper

today I guess I like them about the same. As years went by, I found I had the flexibility to switch back and forth from jazz to show business, and that's what I worked hard on, so that I could meet any situation—playing, writing, or conducting.

"It would be about 1959, when I had rejoined Sarah, that I started studying again. I felt an urge to write, but because I also felt that some of the modern devices were getting by me, I went to New York University. My particular style of piano influenced my string writing. That big, lush album I did with Sarah was almost like amplifying my piano accompaniment for an orchestra of thirty pieces. I hadn't realized I was playing that much contrapuntally. The first time I ever heard any of my writing for strings was on a Joe Williams album, the one with Ben Webster and Sweets [Edison]. I had never written or conducted strings before, and I was nervous, for I didn't know what it was going to sound like. I was surprised! But once you can hear it, you can keep developing. Yet you're always a student. You never can say, 'This is exactly the way I want it,' because it doesn't come out like that.

"Perhaps the lack of acceptance of my piano forced me to widen my scope. It was a quiet style, but I didn't intend it to be that way. I wanted everybody to enjoy it, because the musician is where the art is and the public is where the money is! I was happily employed,

Jimmy Jones

but no one ever tried to promote me as a solo act. I have only been the leader of a trio on records, and I've often thought maybe I ought to yell or holler in the middle of a record date. One record on which I did make an impact was *How High the Moon,* with Don Byas. That was twenty years ago and I still get compliments on it. Now that I've established an 'image,' so far as the writing and conducting are concerned, I'm thinking seriously of doing more as a player, of bringing it all together with the piano."

For several years, Jones' main occupation has been recording in New York, where the quality and variety of his work have won him the respect and admiration of the whole profession. Something of his methods and ability to meet challenges emerges in his accounts of record dates with Harry Belafonte and Wes Montgomery.

"Harry runs a record date like Duke," he claimed, "and you could never relate it from hearing his music. Take that *Midnight Special* album, for example. I had a big orchestra: seven brass, five reeds, and a string section. Because Harry's image can be lost if he gets past two guitars, it took a lot of thinking, with all those trumpets and trombones, to avoid having him sound like the rest of the singers. But though he wants to keep that image, he had told me, 'Just write— overwrite if you want to!' When we got in the studio, we'd change everything around—letter A with Z—and he'd change his lyrics. He's a talent and he works like Duke with a similar production sense. He knows how to *produce* a track on a record rather than just having the arrangement played down, I've often heard a wonderful arrangement played by a wonderful band fail because it wasn't produced with a fresh, *single*, guiding thought.

"I recently finished a thing for him called *Hootin' Blues*, for the show he has on the road now. It's a sort of fast Country and Western piece, with a harmonica, two guitars, one guy making pig calls, and the dancers dancing like Katherine Dunham's ballet. I had to capture the atmosphere in sound with about forty pieces in the pit. I decided to operate like Ellington and think in terms of effects rather than notes, and it came off well. The French horns were hootin' like the guy, as though they were calling pigs, and that pig call became a theme. From the horns, it went right up to the piccolo, with the strings 'way up high, too, and the timpani below. You know how a harmonica can sound like a train, the way Duke does it. . . .

"The string album I did with Wes Montgomery was one I liked. We had about thirty pieces. Wes is the most amazing man you can see in a studio. I would take the score down once, he'd hear it, and then play as though he had a solo perfectly written out. String players will give a bow tap when they're applauding a soloist. This guy had them doing it almost every take, and I've seldom seen them do that as long as I've been in the studios. They appreciated the amazing things he was doing with his left hand. There's a kinship, of course, between the violin and the guitar, and that was another challenge. 'How can you write a string background for a string soloist?' one guy asked me. Wes was playing amplified guitar, and jazz, but there had to be a relationship as well as contrast."

Recognition of his gifts as pianist and writer is engraved on many a record, but his appointment in August (1963), as conductor for Duke Ellington's show, *My People* was another highlight in Jones' career. It began in typically casual and oblique Ellington fashion at Basin Street East.

"I was just supposed to rehearse some singers," said Jones, "but each day I was deeper into it, until all of a sudden I was in Chicago! I'm very happy I took it on, because it was a great experience and the band was wonderful. I used to kid Duke about the band, and he'd laugh, but I think he liked it, too. He said it had a different personality.!"

John Sanders, a member of that band, subsequently remarked that Ellington doesn't like to have everything written down, but always prefers a margin in which to work. As a corollary, Jimmy added.:

"The way I see it, he has a thing completely sketched out in his mind. Then what he does is like a chain reaction. Here's a section, here's a section, and here's another, and in between he begins putting the connecting links. What makes it confusing to other people is that he knows where each section belongs, but to begin with they're not necessarily in position. The amazing thing about Ellington is that he can think so fast on the spot and create so quickly. I watched Duke write once and it was astonishing. When he knows what he wants and has got it in his mind, he can write awfully fast. His is a school in itself, one you have to go through to understand, and one he's developed over a period of years. Though he is highly respected, he would drive some of the more conservative guys nuts. 'This is wrong,' they'd say, or 'That's wrong.' But it's not wrong, because it sounds good. I agree with him all the way, because if you're not careful you can get so inhibited by study. I believe people with natural ability should play by ear first. Later, if they want technique, they can study, when they've molded their own character, instead of molding it out of a textbook. A bunch of rules can swamp your true self. I think Ellington has kept his beautifully. It's a form of study, anyway, to go by trial and error, to see what you like and don't like. He knew everything, every spot, every note in that show, despite the kind of aloof appearance he wore. He was completely aware at all times as to where this or that belonged—the lighting, the dancing, the music, the scores.

"The performances of the show improved so much that it got to the point where it was automatic, almost running on its own. After everything was weeded out, and the show business logic was in order, it was really clicking. My job as a conductor was not so much when the show was going good, but a matter of what to do in an emergency. I'd be looking in the wings to see if the other acts were there, so I'd know what to do if they were not! I could never sit back and relax. It was more a matter of holding the show together. Now and then we might have a little discipline problem with some of the kids—not the kind you'd notice in the audience—and that I'd have to check with the stage manager. It always has to be checked before it gets out of hand. I had earphones on most of the time, because the singers were 'way behind me. If I had been in the pit, looking at them, it would have been different. I was coordinated with the whole place—I heard cue calls, lighting calls, conversation, as well as the singers and the band, and that was why I was soaking wet when I came off sometimes!

"When we came to record the cast album, there was a three-man team again. Ellington would stay in the booth and I would conduct. Sometimes, if he wanted to get a particular feeling, he would come out and conduct. Then Strayhorn would stay in the booth with the singers and I would go and play piano. Duke was pretty smart on me one time. There was an oldtime piano there, the kind with tacks on the hammers, and Booty Wood, Harold Ashby, and I were jamming, just loosening up with Joe Benjamin and Louis Bellson. 'Oh, I want some of that!' Duke called. It was the same group that accompanied Jimmy Grissom on the record, with Booty playing plunger trombone that was really quite close to Tricky. Booty has really got it together. It's a thing of itself—conversational, and a matter of the musician's personality. As for me, I went 'way back, to James P. Johnson and Fats Waller."

With that, one might almost say Jimmy Jones had attained his main objectives: "To be flexible, to appreciate all facets of jazz and popular entertainment, and to be able to bring them together."

[*1964*]

Jeff Castleman   [*bass*]

The Ellington band has nearly always been fortunate in its bassists, first with Bass Edwards on tuba, and then for many years with Wellman Braud on string bass. Like his fellow Louisianian, Pops Foster, Braud made his presence felt on even the early records.

"Tuba was supposed to be better for recording the low notes in the days before microphones," Ellington explained, "but Braud always made sure he could be heard. He used to stand up so close, we would have to pull him away from the horn. He had great flavor."

When Braud left in 1935, he was succeeded by Hayes Alvis, Billy Taylor, and in 1939, by Jimmy Blanton, a young musician from St. Louis who radically changed the whole conception of the bass in jazz before his untimely death in 1941. Following Blanton came Junior Raglin, Oscar Pettiford, Wendell Marshall (Blanton's cousin), Jimmy Woode, Aaron Bell, Ernie Shepard, John Lamb, Jeff Castleman, Paul Kondziela, and Victor Gaskin, a distinguished gallery on the whole. None, perhaps, had the authority and invention of Oscar Pettiford, but each had an individual quality. Like Blanton, Castleman and

218

Kondziela were very young, but unlike him and all the others, they were white.

Castleman's view of the Ellington milieu naturally differed from that of the veterans in it, but he adjusted to its conditions with unusual intelligence. His friendly disposition, good looks and manners, excellent technique, and eagerness to contribute creatively, made him a popular member of the band.

His father was a musician who played trumpet and vibraharp, and arranged. For nearly ten years, using the stage name of Billy Allen, he led his own group, mostly in Palm Springs. Then he went into the motion picture business as a producer. His son, meanwhile, had become interested in bass.

"I don't know what made me go for it," he said, "but that was my first instrument. I remember I used to listen to old Woody Herman records at a time when I also had a bow and arrows. I was about eleven, I guess, and I used to pluck on this bow! I didn't start to study until about 1962, when I took a summer class in music at junior high school. The man gave me a bass and a bass book, put me in a room, and said, 'Go!' I knew a little about music from school, from courses in choir, and I'd studied a bit at times with my father, who had had some conservatory training, but I'd never studied piano.

"Well, there in that little room, it sounded terrible, it really did. The man came in every now and then, and it was three days a week, because it was summer time. I don't remember his name, but he was a bass player himself, and he helped me. In my last year in high school, I played in the school groups. It was all hunt and peck—really a scuffle. But it's a fight with any instrument, learning to play.

"After high school, I used to stay home Saturday nights and listen to KSL in Denver. They had a jazz show that came on about eleven or twelve, and a Bill Evans record was used for a theme song. At that time, I wasn't really involved, but I heard the bass player, although I didn't know who it was. I'd never heard the bass played like that before, and it was an inspiration to play a little more. It was Scott La Faro, and I used to play along with the radio. A lot of different things were played on that show, but I used to wait for the theme, because it knocked me out. Most of the records I had were older, and they didn't have any modern bass work on them.

"I went to college in 1963, to the University of California at Riverside, for a semester, and I didn't like it at all. I felt like a number. I applied to one college, was accepted the next day, and went in as an honor student. I figured I'd go in as a king, and I was studying to be a lawyer, but it wasn't what I wanted to do, so I started working a jazz thing four nights a week in a rehearsal group. There were several players from Stan Kenton's band in it who really impressed me at that time. We got together a few times, and jammed and played, and they asked me if I wanted to work a job with them. I look back now and see it was kind of funny. They all went outside, and I guess they were voting on it. I couldn't play anything. I really scuffled with the blues, but the group was pretty good, playing better than most of those around. They all stayed in professional music afterwards, and did pretty well. Most of the players I've worked with have been older and further advanced than I have been. I always feel that if I stay in a musical environment where everybody plays better than I do, then I will progress, but where I play better than the rest, then I stagnate.

"After a few months with this group, I left and went to City College in Los Angeles, because that's the best for someone who wants to be a playing musician rather than a music teacher. They have a very good performance program where you really get to play, and they have studio musicians come in and help the students. Les McCann came out of that school.

"I was there a semester, and then I went with Si Zentner. A friend who had been in the rehearsal band joined Zentner first. As a joke, I'd said, 'If they ever need a bass player, call me.' He had been there only a few days when I got a call. I didn't think I was really prepared, but I decided to stick my neck out and try it. I'd done a few things with my father, who had a Shearing-type book—vibes, guitar, piano, bass, and drums. I'd recorded with them, and he'd helped me learn to read pretty fair. I might not sightread at that time, but I'd get it if I looked at it a couple of times.

"So I went with Zentner, and we played Fort Dix, New Jersey. I was eighteen, and I played rotten the first night, but I was gassed by what I heard. Si had a good band then, and I was overwhelmed by the sound, because I stood right up in front of the band. They had a very good drummer—Bobby Harrison, excellent, one of the best I've heard in recent years, and a beautiful time player. Pete Christlieb, Gene Goe, and several other good musicians were in the band.

"The next night, I played better, and Si and I got along pretty well. If you stay out of his hair, everything's fine. He was playing kind of semi-jazz then. It was a dance book with a lot of jazz in it. The trombone section was always excellent, because he always managed to keep four good trombone players around. He liked to play himself, and he played very well. A lot of guys put him down for business things, but they never put his playing down. He had the only real big-band hit in fifteen or twenty years. The last I heard, he was a musical conductor in Las Vegas."

220

Castleman was with Zentner a year, finished playing the Mel Tormé show with him in Las Vegas on Saturday night, and started again in City College the following Monday morning. This time he took mostly music courses, with the requirements in English and history.

"There was no bass teacher there," he continued. "It was all theory, and performance, and the stage band. I'd become interested in arranging and had done a couple of things for Si. I had previously written things for smaller groups, and some jingles for my father. Bobby Harrison and I had collaborated on *Hittin' Twelve*, which Basie has. It was basically Bobby's thing, but we worked on it together. Bobby's very underrated, and when he left to go with Frank Sinatra, Jr., I left too. Gene Goe left a little later and went with Count Basie.

"In my second semester, I began to get all frustrated and disgusted. My sightsinging teacher made music very difficult for me. She knew I'd had a little professional experience, so when there'd be something in a mezzo-soprano clef with seven sharps, she'd say, 'Castleman, sing that!' And I hated to sing a note anyway. Some people have voices, and I don't. I can do it, but I don't like to be put on the spot. School was taking so much time and I didn't get to play enough, and I decided to quit. That was three semesters I'd had. The very next day, I got a call from an acquaintance I'd played with before. Did I want to go with Louis Bellson and Pearl Bailey? I said, 'Yes,' and went out on a four-month tour.

"I really enjoyed playing with Louis. I like the atmosphere in a small group better, but Louis made the big band relaxed for me. He played so well that I never worried. He's a nice guy—an angel—and it was a wonderful experience. He opened my eyes to how nice the business could be—that you can be a nice guy and play well, too. I learned so much from him that I progressed a lot further than I would have otherwise. He called me back the following year and asked me to contract the band. So I was twenty, and the manager ! That made me feel good. The original tenor player was Chick Carter, who had gone to Europe, so Louis told me to call Harold Land. Harold couldn't make it, so I told Louis I had someone else in mind, and called Pete Christlieb. Louis fell in love with him instantly. They had a beautiful rapport. Pete is very schooled. His father, Don Christlieb, is one of the finest bassoon players.

"When I was growing up, I always heard you had to make it in the East, in New York. I found it a lot slower in the East when I came here. It seems to me that the good players are concentrated in Los Angeles now—not the hard-core jazz players, but the musicians who

221

can play 'most everything well. Pete Christlieb should really have his own group, like Gary Burton, but a lot of great players don't get the breaks, don't get the push like Burton did.

"Then there are so many people making just miserable music, while there is all the good talent going to waste. I saw it happen in Palm Springs. The sidemen in my father's group did very well and made a lot of money. Then in 1961 or '62 the rock-' n '-roll thing came in, and the guys worked under scale, and now there's no music business in that town anymore.

"Maybe some of the avant-grade jazz people don't know how to get around their instruments, but some of them play very well. There are some I like, and some I've been influenced by. I like some of the things Ornette Coleman has played, and some I don't understand, but I can understand what makes the man emote this way. My feeling is that there are a lot of so-called jazz groups who have the work, but who really aren't the true thing in jazz. Maybe they're resting on their laurels. They become stars and create an image. Most of the real playing is being done in lofts, in backyards, and in garages.

"Cannonball [Adderley] didn't know how to make it at first, but he knows now. I think he decided, 'Well, I'll sell out a little bit, and still play.' He saw it coming. To be honest, I think jazz is really going to be one of those things that is tucked away in a corner, but I don't think it will ever die. I think it's a true art form, but the players coming up to keep it alive are very few now. There's no opportunity for them to play except in a garage and a loft.

"At one time, there was entertainment value there as well as the music. It had both things going for it. It was novel, and people had heard nothing like it before. Now they go and it sounds like the same thing to them, because they don't understand the spontaneous part, the creative part of jazz. Their ears aren't trained to listen to it, and I don't think they ever will be. I think jazz will basically be listened to by the same people that listen now, those who like creative things whether they understand them or not.

"There's no survival if you do away with the paying audience. There are very few people in the business who can make their living playing jazz. I play jazz of a sort, but not the kind I would like to play. There is such a limited market for jazz. You might think that when you're playing with an ensemble your opportunities for improvisation are kind of limited, but it's not really true, because Duke has given me more freedom than I could have on any other job—freedom so far as choice of notes and rhythms are concerned. I play a little as a soloist. I'm inclined to think that, rather than an ensemble, what we have is a fifteen-piece quartet!"

After the second tour with Louis Bellson and Pearl Bailey, Castleman had returned to freelance work and recording in Hollywood. While working with the Righteous Brothers, he took up the fender bass.

"Nearly all the famous bassists in Los Angeles use the fender bass, even Ray Brown," he explained. "Everybody sold out. I'm a purist when it comes to my instrument, but I don't mind listening to fender bass if it's played well. I don't like the stand-up amplified bass, because it sound hollow: it doesn't have body or depth to it. I remember trying one at the Riverboat one night when I was there with Si Zentner. The guy had his strings about two inches off the fingerboard, and there was nothing to hold on to. Instead of pulling the string into the fingerboard to get a woody or crisp sound, he'd pull across the string, which is an older method, almost like the slap bass method. But they're making a fretless electric bass now, and I think that will be the next thing.

"To get back to my *career!* I was working at the Chez Voltaire in Beverly Hills in a duo with Joe Castro. The club is part of the Beverly Rodeo Hotel, which is where Duke stays when he's in Los Angeles. He's known Joe for years and thinks very highly of him. I told Joe I would like to meet him. Duke was flying out the door when Joe introduced me as 'my bassist.' That was all that was said. The following night we worked a party where Bob and Evelyn Udkoff, very good friends of Duke's, heard me play. We had a fine drummer with us, and both Joe and I got to play more. The next day, they took us to hear Duke's Sacred Concert. I'd never heard Duke in person before. I stood backstage and listened, and afterwards they took me downstairs to Duke's room. 'I want you to meet your new bass player,' Bob Udkoff said.

"The next night, a Friday night, I played in Duke's band at Santa Monica Civic Auditorium, where it was accompanying Tony Bennett. Just as Duke himself was ready to come out, his regular bass player arrived with his instrument, so rather than make a scene I took my bass and walked off. I felt terribly disappointed, but Duke called me the next day, said they were going to Lake Tahoe, and would I come and play Saturday and Sunday.

"It was the end of October, 1967. I went up and played the two days, and had a ball. I went in with a kind of cocky attitude, because I really didn't need the job. I got to play a lot with Joe Castro, and we worked only five afternoons a week, with Saturday and and Sunday off. We were through at eight-thirty or nine o'clock, so I could work two jobs if I wanted to. It paid well, and tips were great. But I'd always wanted to work with Sam Woodyard, and Sam was feeling good. He'd just come back in the band and was playing very well. The second night, Duke asked if I wanted to join the band. 'Well, I'll give

223

it some thought,' I said. I was really knocked out that he even thought about it, but I was still being a bit cocky. He offered me a figure, and I said, 'I can't go right now for that.'

"So I flew on home on Monday, and then he offered me some more money, and I said, 'Okay, I'll go.' There was about a week in between, and then I flew up and joined the band in Lake Tahoe. I took Bill Yancy's place. He wasn't there too long. After John Lamb left, Bill had come back and taken his place for a month or so.

"I liked the job a lot. It was the first time I ever played in a band without music, which kind of gave it the atmosphere of a small group. I had to learn what was going on, rather than rely on the paper, for there were only a few bass parts used. Even when we do new things, there are not always bass parts—maybe sixteen bars in a forty-five-minute suite. When Duke has a new tune, he'll bring it in and play it, just with me, so that I've got a pretty good idea what to do beforehand. Then he'll bring in the arrangement. Anyone who came to play in my place right now would be lost. They wouldn't know where to begin. Duke would have to teach them everything. He wants to give you as much freedom as he can, but he also feels a bassist can play a better bass part than he can write, which I don't think is true. When I've insisted that he write for me, he has written things that are terrific.

"There is a bass book, of course, a monstrous book that I drag around with me, but we almost never play it. Usually the things you pull out of the book to play are charts that Louis Bellson or other people have done. There are bass parts on a few of Duke's things, but they are mostly heads. You might have a sketch on *Solitude*, but it's like sixteen bars, and then it says, 'Bridge.' When we did *The Latin American Suite*, Herbie Jones [the trumpet player and copyist] gave me a part three pages long—three blank pages.

"Duke had played *South American Sunshine* [a section of the suite] as a piano solo for quite a while, and he never said he was going to do it differently. I learned it by listening to him, and by watching him. But when he had us play it in Buenos Aires that time, he really *made* us play it, because we hadn't much idea what to play. To him, that's jazz—the creative part. And it *is*, you know. It puts you in a compromising position—boy, you're really on the spot!

"I've been asked many times about being the only white guy in the band, but I felt more out of place because of my age than because of race. There had been other white players in the band, so I didn't have any 'first thing' feeling. So far as I am concerned, players are players, and I've played with everyone. I've never had any religious, or moral, or racial prejudices. It is a privilege and an honor to play in Duke's band.

"Of course, a lot of funny things happen. When we check into a hotel, I'm nearly always last, because they don't think I'm with the group. I just stand there until people behind the counter look at me and say, 'Can I help you?' Sometimes, when I say I'm with the band, they'll say, 'No, you're not!' Again, it's often more a matter of age than race, because they just don't expect to see some young person with the guys in the band. Then, when we're working, you hear people saying, 'Oh, lookit, there's the white boy!' I don't pay any attention, because it's only a visual thing. If they closed their eyes, they wouldn't notice any difference—at least, I hope they wouldn't. But people do wonder. Sometimes they're asking themselves, 'Is he a light-skinned Negro, or what?'

"I always rode in the back of the bus. I used to sit right in the back, under the bass, and hide from everybody. It was comfortable there, because I had three seats to myself."

While on tour in South America, Castleman and the band's singer, Trish Turner, became engaged. Both were twenty-two when they were married in Las Vegas on December 22nd, 1968. Joe Castro was best man, and the whole Ellington band was in attendance.

"We hope to be able to work together with a group of six or seven pieces," Castleman said, some weeks before he and his wife left the band to set up a home in Los Angeles. With his friend Gene Goe, then with Count Basie, he had already recorded music in the vein he hoped to explore more thoroughly in the future.

"It was happy music," he went on. "If you came in a room and we were playing that, you'd smile. You wouldn't be depressed. I find a lot of depression in jazz, and I think it comes from the grievances people have. They have to scuffle; they have to work to remain dedicated; and to play jazz every day of their lives, they lose a lot. It's hard to play happy and full of love when you're not, when you're sad, or worrying about where your meals are going to come from. I don't think things have basically changed much over the years. The musicians who play well will always work, but the artisans and specialists in certain fields—they will have trouble. Whatever branch of music they play in, the ones who are in a minority will have trouble working. Those who do the layman-type musical jobs always work, and always have a living.

"A lot of jazz players aren't interested in making the people happy. They don't even know the people are there. To be able to play jazz really spontaneously and well, you have to be able to shut everything off. You have to shut off the environment except musically, and listen to nothing except what's going on around you. If you create a show, go out and smile, and play scoobydoo solos, the people say,

225

'That's great, that's jazz!' But it's not. It's a cop-out. If you have to be thinking about smiling rather than playing, you're in trouble."

[*1968*]

Alice Babs   [*vocal*]

"Alice Babs is a performer beyond measure," Duke Ellington remarked. "She can sing anything she sees or hears. Opera, Bach— or jazz."

He was referring to the Swedish soprano who arrived in New York on January 9th, 1968, to rehearse for his second Sacred Concert. Reviewing its presentation at the Cathedral of St. John the Divine and astonished by the scope of her artistry, John S. Wilson commented in the *New York Times:* "Her voice proved to be a magnificent Ellington instrument—pure, full-bodied, amazingly lithe... with warmth and strength at both ends of a broad range."

This was not Miss Babs' first visit to the United States. In 1962, a trio called the Swe-Danes that consisted of violinist Svend Asmussen, guitarist Ulrik Neumann, and herself, undertook an extended American tour, appearing on the Ed Sullivan Show and at the Cocoanut Grove in Los Angeles. A West Coast disc-jockey, Frank Evans, an avid fan, repeatedly aired European records of hers that were unavailable this side of the Atlantic. "Suffer, my friends, for you can't buy these gems," he would lament.

An album that featured the soprano, recorded for the American market with Red Callender on bass and Shelly Manne on drums, was released in 1962. On it, the singer accompanied Asmussen's violin, singing everything that he played, negotiating difficult intervals at lightning speed. Despite the fact that one of the selections, *Scandinavian Shuffle*, caught on overnight, there was no fullscale promotion. When one considers what untold millions are poured out to build public faith in those of minimal talent, it is ironic that none could be found to bring a superior artist like Alice Babs to the general attention.

Her reappearance on the American scene resulted from an earlier collaboration between Duke Ellington and a Swedish TV producer. The composer's discerning ear and penchant for talent are well known, and in 1963 he was approached about a television show for Swedish audiences. During the search for a star to share billing with him, he was given a variety of albums featuring European singers.

ers.

"I was told," Alice Babs confessed shyly, "that when he heard mine, the search was over. On the show I sang *Come Sunday* and *Take the 'A' Train*. One chorus was wordless, and I featured phrases I recalled from recorded band solos—Rex Stewart's *Boy Meets Horn*, and Ben Webster's *Cottontail*.

"Afterwards, Duke said, 'I'd like to do an album with you . . .' 'You are very kind,' I thought, 'but this is too much.' Yet three weeks later he called from Paris and inquired, 'Would you like to come here tomorrow?'

"Still unbelieving, I replied that I required four days. Then I attempted to listen to all the records that he had done. I tried to pick the songs I would like to do. And concerned myself with the lyrics."

Not only did she memorize them perfectly, but on the album in question (as in the Sacred Concert), her accent is scarcely detectable. Yet *Serenade to Sweden* [Reprise 5024], which features Alice Babs, arrangements by Billy Strayhorn, Duke Ellington at the piano, and first-class accompaniment by a studio orchestra, is still inexplicably unavailable in the United States! Sixteen titles were recorded, of which the most memorable were: *Come Sunday, Azure, "C" Jam Blues, I Didn't Know About You, Take Love Easy,* and *Something to Live For.*

"*Come Sunday* is very beautiful," Alice said. "*Heaven* is in the same genre, I think."

Heaven is the second of the four themes in the Sacred Concert written for the soprano. Permeated by the blues, *God Has Those Angels* was the first, and served as a glorious introduction to a voice and style eminently suited to Ellingtonia. The singer's rendition of *T.G.T.T.*, a number the composer favors for its remarkable sequence of intervals and distinctive flavor, has been everywhere acclaimed a musical *tour de force*. The clarity and sober beauty of the final theme, *Praise God and Dance*, revealed the nature of the artist's personality.

"This is *great*," she said. "It has a gravity that conveys the deepest message. And the melody line is so pure. Like Bach. I can give it the same power I give to Bach. In churches at home, his are the songs I sing.

"The Sacred Concert is truly marvelous," she went on. "A real peak. The greatest writing, I feel, that Duke has ever done. It is so big—and yet consistent. All highs, no lows. *Something About Believing* is memorable, and it will live, I am sure. But *Supreme Being* is the most fantastic of all. I think Europeans, the conductors, people in the symphony orchestras, will greatly admire this work. It belongs in the world of serious classical music."

With Alice Babs in the feature role, the Sacred Concert was

performed three times. Following its première in the Cathedral, it was presented twice in Connecticut, at St. Mark's in New Canaan (where the choir earned much esteem), and at Welte Hall, Central Connecticut State College, New Britain.

"There were times during the performances," the singer recalled, "when I had difficulty controlling my emotions. In the cathedral it was very beautiful—the lighting, and the massive congregation! I had to remind myself I was not the one to be moved, that the message was designed for the listeners.

"You have to grow with these songs," she observed. "The more I sing them, the more I can get out of them." But the degree to which she had mastered their intricacies was amazing to the musicians. "Concert singers," trombonist Lawrence Brown commented, "avail themselves of every opportunity to live with a score. Here there was a heavy work load to digest in little more than a week."

Before Alice returned to Europe, Ellington set about recording the entire concert, beginning with her selections. Listening in the studio to *It's Freedom* by the A.M.E. Mother Zion Choir, Alice revealed what this composition had conveyed to her as she sang it alongside young singers for whom it had especial relevance.

"The things you read about Black Power," she said. "I hear this number and I could cry. These boys and girls could be my children

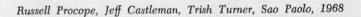

Russell Procope, Jeff Castleman, Trish Turner, Sao Paolo, 1968

—they are no older. I find I like them so much." In the background the *Freedom* chant swelled. "It's hard to believe," she went on sadly, "how such things can be. They want freedom *now*. They can't wait longer. So much talk... When I sing *Freedom*, I feel I have to change also. *We* have to change. We need to free ourselves of the thoughts we harbor about other races. When I first heard *It's Freedom*, I was happy. I told myself this would be performed all over the world. It says something the world has a need to hear. Duke has written: *Freedom is not just a word. Freedom is something we have to have.*"

She recalled the attentive congregation in New Canaan. "They found it not too unpalatable, I think. It was there in a form they could digest and less uncomfortably than might someday be the case."

Alice Babs, née Alice Nilsson, was fortunate in possessing musical parents. She credits her father with her first introduction to jazz. An orchestra leader and pianist, he developed her talents early, forming study habits she never lost. To this day she takes a weekly lesson from a professor in Stockholm, where she now lives. Musical productions in school, and in the town where she was born, were built around her, parts were especially written, and she profited from the variety of the demands on her skills.

First appearing in public at the age of twelve, she broke into Swedish movies as a teenage star and was soon recognized throug-

Alice Babs

hout Europe as an outstanding artist. Her talents ranged from the rendition of simple folksong to the music of Mozart and Bach. She performed alongside the world-famous tenor, Jussi Björling, and for the Swedish Royal Family. During World War II she traveled constantly, appearing with Sammy Davis and other stars in concerts.

"I was the first Swede to go to Finland after war broke out," she recalled. "My programs were for the soldiers. It seemed difficult at first, there were so many wounded. And I was young. But I admired the Finns greatly. They are honorable people. The Finns knew," Alice said, "that freedom was more than just a word."

Her voluntary contributions were accorded recognition when the war ended and Field Marshal Mannerheim presented her with the distinguished *Pro Benignate Humana* award.

Recalled to the microphone, she broke off smiling, "But I don't want to sound sad. I am naturally gay and happy. Perhaps that is why jazz has always exercised a great attraction for me. I heard Louis Armstrong, whom I loved, when I was only eleven."

As the recording session progressed, Duke Ellington's musicians were lavish with praise, occasionally breaking into spontaneous applause. Trumpeter Cootie Williams, usually slow to enthuse, observed succinctly, "For me, she's the *most.*"

"She has a fantastic ear, and what may be perfect pitch," Harry Carney added.

"Not perfect, fortunately," the singer corrected. "Otherwise one's career would present many problems. When you are touring, bad pianos are an ever-present hazard."

"Having all that talent," Paul Gonsalves remarked, "it's a marvel she remains the way she is. As pretty inside as out."

"She doesn't differentiate between amateurs and professionals," Ellington amplified. "With the choir, for instance, if she sees they're nervous, she'll move alongside and start singing from there."

Today Alice Babs does not accept many engagements. Happily married, the mother of three, she now prefers to live a more leisurely life. "In Sweden I sing only occasionally. When I want to sing, and there are songs I like very much," she said. "Sometimes for ten or twelve days in the summer, in Stockholm's open-air theatre."

She might not do so this summer, however, for the past six months had been more than ordinarily hectic. In the fall, with Svend Asmussen and two other Swedish artists, she had undertaken a concert tour of Asia, at the invitation of Scandinavian Airlines. "Singapore, Bangkok, Hong Kong, and Tokyo," she said. "And now Tanzania." A scheduled visit to the east coast of Africa was cutting short her American stay.

"For me, it has been an incredible time, and I cannot think," she told Duke Ellington, "that anything can await me which will surpass the excitement we have experienced here."

"What has Alice Babs got that other singers lack?" a reporter asked Ellington later.

"*Everything*," the composer replied.

[*1968*]

Harold Ashby [*tenor saxophone and clarinet*]

Harold Ashby took Jimmy Hamilton's place in the Ellington band at the beginning of July, 1968. Unlike Hamilton, he was not a clarinet virtuoso. His preferred instrument was the tenor saxophone, on which he had been much influenced by his close friend, Ben Webster, the musician who first demonstrated the tenor's potential as a solo instrument in the same band. Like Webster, Ashby expresses himself with warm lyricism on ballads and with intensely rhythmic phraseology on swinging pieces. But alto saxophonist Charlie Parker, as he will explain, was an earlier influence, and this is reflected in his partiality for an alto-like sound in the upper register.

Confronted with parts written for clarinet and formerly played by Hamilton, he conscientiously took up again an instrument he had not touched for nearly two decades. While Russell Procope now became the chief clarinet soloist, Ashby's increasing ability added to the flexibility of a reed section in which Paul Gonsalves and Harry Carney also played clarinet.

On May 26th, 1969, a program entitled *To Duke with Love* was presented at Madison Square Garden to benefit Odyssey House, an agency concerned with the rehabilitation of narcotic addicts. Governor Nelson A. Rockefeller and Mayor John V. Lindsay were the honorary chairmen, and many famous singers and musicians came to pay stage homage to the maestro before he led his band in a typical concert. Impressed with the importance of the occasion, Harold Ashby arrived early and secured a separate dressing room for himself. Having changed his clothes and readied his two instruments, he agreed to discuss his career, the importance of which he invariably minimizes with droll understatement.

"I was born in Kansas City, Missouri, March 27th, 1925," he began. "Neither of my parents was musical that I know of. My mother died when I was seven. I had four brothers and a sister. I'm the youngest, and the only one that stayed in music. One of my brothers played alto, and another played trumpet. They just worked around Kansas City, and I think one worked with George Lee once. Both of

231

them went to school with Ben Webster, and they played violin in the school band with Ben. It was the old Lincoln High School. One of them bought a clarinet, paid fifty cents for it, and when I was going to school, let me play it, let me take it to start in the school band. I was in the high school band, and I finished high school in '40. Then I went to Lincoln Junior College and played tenor. I got an hour's tuition a day from a fellow named Richie Smith, a music teacher. After I finished at Junior College in '42, I went to R. T. Cole's vocational school for a year.

"You had to take up a trade there, and I took music. Seems like that was what everyone was doing at that time. After I got out of Cole's, it was July, and then I went into the service. I bought a horn and took it into the Navy with me, but to get into the band you had to be a professional. So when I found I couldn't get in, I sold the horn. I was a steward's mate, like a waiter, you know—clean up. Between 1943 and 1945, I didn't get to go anywhere except Chicago. I used to go to the Down Beat room where Ben and Red Allen were playing. I used to go down there and listen to them.

"I didn't meet Ben then. I met him in Kansas City when he came back home one time. His people used to live there, his aunt and his grandmother, I believe—I don't really know. He came back, and there was a session, and Jay McShann had a record date. Ben didn't have his horn, because they hadn't sent it out yet. So he borrowed mine, and that's when I first met him. But I had heard him a long time before. My brother had taken me to hear him play. This was a long time ago, in a place called the Jockey Club on Tenth and LaSalle. He was up there playing with a local band, Bob Wilson's. This would be around '48 or '49. When I got to know him real well was later around Chicago, and when I came to New York.

"I went to Chicago and played with all the blues bands, like Big Willie Dixon's. We used to play dances, and I made quite a few recordings for Chess and Checker. I can't think of the names of all those bands, but I remember Willie Mabon's, and they were mostly on Chess. Another fellow who played tenor on a lot of them was Herbert Robinson. They used to call him 'Jeep.'

"I used to go down to the Union in Chicago and play cards, and gamble, and drink, until I got tired of it. I would save my money, and then lose it when I got juiced. So I tired of that scene, and said, 'Well, I got to change.' I thought that if I left, and tried something different, it would be better for me. One day, I remember, I had some money in credit at the Union. The night before, I'd been playing cards again, and I had lost. 'Well, that's all I'm going to lose,' I said to myself. I went and got the rest of my money, got on the plane, and came on to New York.

"This was December 7th, 1957. When I got here, I stayed at the Hotel St. Francis on 48th Street. Ben Webster was here then, and I met him. He came around one morning and told me I should move out on Long Island to a Miss Sutton's place, where he had a room. Another fellow, Big Miller, the singer, he had a room there, too. So I got on a train and went out there. I figured it was too far out, but after I got there, I found it was nice, peaceful, and quiet, rather than all this hustle and bustle down here. So I took a room and stayed out there all summer, and I went around to a place over there and played weekends. After the summer was over with, I came back in town and moved in with a fellow named Willard Brown, who has since died. I worked with Milt Larkins down at the Celebrity Club on 125th Street, and that's all I did.

"I had met Mercer Ellington out there on the Island with Ben, because he lived just three or four blocks around the corner. When Mercer recorded an album, Ben did it with him. And when Ben had left town, Mercer used me on the next one. About all I did around New York was play the dance scene, and the rock-and-roll scene. The first time I worked with Duke, it was around '60 or '61. He used to live at 935 St. Nicholas Avenue, and I lived at 925, and I went out with them for two nights one time, on a Monday and a Tuesday. After that, that was *it*. But I worked with Mercer on several occasions. We played dances and different things like that, and I played Birdland with him.

"I also recorded with Ben. He had a session for Verve, so he used me on it. I made a couple of sessions with Johnny Hodges. After that first time I worked with Duke, the next week Johnny used me on one of his dates, one that had Shorty Baker on it and was never issued. I made another with Johnny and one with Lawrence Brown, and then in 1960 I had made an album under my own name for English Columbia with Jimmy Jones on piano.

"So that was more or less what I was doing up to the time Jimmy Hamilton left and Mercer called me to join Duke. At that particular time I was overweight, and I was doubtful whether I should go out or not. Then Mercer said, 'Well, for a few days . . .' Because I didn't play clarinet, I figured I'd be here for just a short time.

"When we were in Chicago, Johnny Hodges went out to the Leblanc factory to check on some horns, and he brought back a clarinet for Paul Gonsalves to play. Since there had been some confusion going on because of the parts, I hadn't tried to learn the book. Paul already knew it, and it would have been a thing for me to try to switch parts. (Paul still plays the clarinet on *Creole Love Call*.) So at first I used this clarinet of Paul's to play these simple parts, you understand? I didn't think it would go this far. I play a solo on clarinet in *Harlem*, but mostly I just play clarinet in the section. In the Sacred Concert, I play one or two little passages.

"I like clarinet, just for a challenge. I would really like to play it. Since I've gone this far, I would like to try to do the best I can. When I was in Chicago, I got some assistance from the Government under the G.I. Bill and went to the Roy Knapp School of Music, and I played clarinet there in class in ensemble. I think it was the Margie Hyams Ensemble, and she did most of the playing. I did it just to do something, and I had only simple little parts to play, but I got to know something about the fingering. It's really all a matter of *playing*, and confidence.

"After I heard Ben, he was my main inspiration—on tenor. But what I had been listening to most on records at that time was Charlie Parker. On his records, in what they call the be-bop age, you know, they had Lucky Thompson and Don Byas, and after I heard Don Byas I liked the idea of tenor. Then when Ben came to town, that was *it*—the sound of the instrument, and kind of the way he phrased.

"I enjoy being with Duke. It's a different thing, a new life really. I never did get a chance to travel, and I'd never even been to Atlantic City or any of these places. Also, it's a new musical experience. I never sat down and really played with a band before, or ever really *thought* about music. I'm being truthful with you. The traveling gives you something to do, and a person's got to have something to do. When I was in South America, there was the Spanish, and I had a phrase book. Then the West Indies were a kick, too."

Duke Ellington obviously enjoys Ashby's tenor playing, because he has featured him on many different numbers, among them *Just Squeeze Me, Satin Doll, B.P. Blues,* and *Neo-Creole,* the last being the theme from the movie, *Change of Mind.* Ashby sits between two of the band's greatest stars, Johnny Hodges and Paul Gonsalves, and when he gets up to blow he seems modestly overconscious of the fact, but when he sits down the listener has been made aware that he is where he deserves to be.

[*1969*]

Wild Bill Davis [*organ*]

The man who basically deserves the credit (or blame, depending on how you look at it) for the organ boom is Bill Davis, a serious, intelligent musician once mistakenly nicknamed "Wild."

"Originally, I didn't like organ, period," Davis confessed recently. "Most of the people who played it were church people and they played basic harmony and church music. It's wonderful in church, but outside it's a different thing. Who wants a church organist in a nightclub? It was a challenge to me to play it differently, but some people still won't accept it. Generally, the organ has not been accepted by the white audience as it has been by the Negro, but I always felt that if I could get it in a place with a certain category or class of people, as on the East Side, they would say, 'This is it!' And we were very well received at Basin Street East.

"Some people come right out and tell me they don't think the organ should be played like that. They're thinking of it strictly as a church thing, which is not very broad. From the artist's point of view, it should be thought of as just an instrument. I can't go along with the critics who say they don't like the sound, because in the course of any one performance they're going to hear several different sounds."

The difference between the Hammond, which Davis plays, and the church organ is primarily one of sound. In one case it is a matter of electronics, in the other of wind—and the wind instrument duplicates a reed sound.

"It's good and it's the traditional sound," Davis admitted. "I'd like the opportunity to study and play the pipe organ as well. I couldn't play it the way I do the Hammond, which is quicker in response and gives the crisper effect I like. My main approach all along has been from the standpoint of arranging for a band and trying to duplicate its sound. My true love was arranging, but that meant sitting up and writing all night long. On the organ, I could hear it almost instantly.

"Hammonds are all supposed to be alike, but they're not. Those made after the war haven't the brilliance of the prewar ones. I own three, and several Leslie speakers. I have one organ in California, another at home in New York, and I keep one for the road. The Leslie firm is not attached to the Hammond company, but their speakers are very important to me for the crisp sound you can get from them.

"The organ is made with all the tones, generators, and that sort of thing, and it has a big cable with six or seven wires in it that goes to the speaker. The Hammond organ is very practical because you can hook up speakers in series, taking a cable from one speaker to another. There are several kinds of Hammond speakers, but the Leslie is a good deal more complex and costs about six hundred dollars. It contains a woofer and a tweeter. There are two revolving cones in V-form on the tweeter and the motor that rotates them can be turned on and off. The woofer, a fifteen-inch speaker in the bottom of the cabinet, is placed in a channel with a baffle. This speaker points down

235

Harold Ashby

into a revolving chamber controlled by a switch on the organ. It revolves at such a speed that when the music goes down through it you get a vibrato effect. The tweeter works in a similar way. In the middle is a bit of mechanism called the automatic separator, which separates the highs from the lows, and the tones go from the amplifier to this separator. If you cut off the revolving mechanism of either the tweeter or woofer, it creates a straight sound. The Leslie Vibratone Speaker, as it is called, has the 'pipe voice of the electric organ' and has been responsible for any number of organ sales, because it beautifies the sound of the Hammond organ and gives it variety.

"Recently, a lot of players have favored switching the vibrato off. I don't like the sound myself, though straight tones can have a good effect in music. For instance, when I recorded *The Love Theme from the World of Suzie Wong,* a sort of oriental thing, the straight tone fitted and was better. It made an interesting blend in this case with the guitar and saxophone, which I had in fifths. It was about the first time I had used that switch.

"Most of the other organists do it all the time. It's become a fad, popular among the younger guys. They mostly play in single-note form, whereas most of the time I play in chord form. They play like a horn, where I play like a band, or like a reed section—or a brass section, as on *Sent for You Yesterday,* which I recorded for Victor

236

Wild Bill Davis

recently. Bill Doggett is another exception; he uses his organ as an accompaniment to the horns a lot of the time, or to provide a bass line. He went after a band thing where he could play dancehalls, but I worked clubs, which I preferred. He shouldn't be underestimated because of what he plays on records. He's a terrific musician—a wonderful pianist and a wonderful organist."

William Strethen Davis was born in Glasgow, Missouri, on November 24th, 1918. While he was still an infant, his family moved to Parsons, Kansas, a small railroad town of about fifteen thousand people. He had no interest in music, but his mother, who had taught before she married, had retained her own piano. She encouraged Davis to use it. The oldest of four boys, he "turned off for a long time, put it away, and then returned to it." He and the next younger brother went to a neighborhood teacher when they were ten and eleven, but music remained a "come-and-go thing" to young Bill until a relative came to live with the Davises. He was an orphan, but he brought his victrola and some records by Fats Waller with him.

"I played those records," Davis remembered, "over and over, and they developed a new interest for me. I started to go back and practice and study in the classical books the teacher had given me. About this time, too, I began working for a drugstore, delivering packages and so on, and making enough to pay for more weekly lessons. As I progressed musically, I began to play at little parties around to make some extra change, and all the time I was getting more interested in the classics and in the limited amount of jazz I could hear on the radio. I was in a remote area and radio was in its infancy, but you heard actual performances then, not records. One night, by chance, I heard Art Tatum, and I couldn't believe it. He sounded like a person with four hands and two pianos. I could play enough by then to realize it couldn't possibly be!

"Tatum stimulated my interest in music so much that I felt I wanted to get out and do better things. Parsons was a good place to grow up in, but there was no scope for a professional musician, as Buck Clayton found out, and he was born there. I finished high school in 1937 and won a music scholarship to Tuskegee Institute in Alabama. In the summer, I tried to make it on my own and once was lucky enough to get to New York. After a couple of years, I went to Wiley College in Marshall, Texas. I had been gaining experience in the school bands, but I found early on that I could express myself better in writing than in playing. So I got a couple of good books and learned the voicing of instruments. This, some knowledge of tone qualities, and simple mathematics are the basics of writing. When they had heard some of my work at Wiley, I was offered a position with Milt Larkins' band, playing guitar, but principally as a writer."

This was Davis' first professional band and at that time (1939-42) it was the best band in Texas, including in its personnel Arnett Cobb, Eddie Vinson, Russell Jacquet, and several other musicians who later made names for themselves. The band played in dancehalls and clubs, nearly all segregated, throughout Texas. The pianist was Cedric Haywood and, though he had had little formal training, he turned out arrangements that intrigued Davis.

' "You learn to write within the limits of the musicians you have in mind, especially when you are working in a band," Davis continued. "I had heard bands on the radio and my conception had been influenced by Duke Ellington more than anyone else. I had a great respect for his voicing and what he had been able to do with his band. He seemed to use every instrument very effectively. Arranging is more of an art than some people realize. An arranger who knows the men in his band can take a musician who is really weak and put him in a position where he seems very strong. This is a characteristic of Duke's and it was something I recognized about arranging a long time ago.

"I gained a lot of experience with Milt Larkins, but eventually I knew I had had all I could get there. I wasn't concerned with music altogether. I saw the need of a degree from the point of view of social

238

life, background, and character, and I got mine in music education when I was twenty-two. That I was as sensible as that at that age was due, I think, to my home—not a broken home—and intelligent parents, who had long preached to me about learning and getting something in your head. So I looked forward not just to music, but to living a good life. I wasn't interested in just having a ball, but in accomplishing something in life regardless of what I did musically. I could have assumed a position as an instructor at Wiley, but I felt it was time to move again and I went to Chicago."

Davis worked around Chicago with different groups for a year and a half and began to get a reputation as an arranger. He wrote music for shows at the El Grotto and the Club DeLisa, and a couple of numbers for Earl Hines while Charlie Parker was in the band, as well as two vocal arrangements for Hines' singer, Sarah Vaughan.

"I finally joined Louis Jordan in 1945, just after *Caldonia,*" he recalled. "He was about at his peak then. At first I worked for him as an arranger, writing all his things like *Choo, Choo, Ch' Boogie* and *Don't Worry 'Bout That Mule.* I was with him three years, and I was very careful and got a good start financially. Louis had been doing one-night stands, but one of the first engagements I played with him was at the Zanzibar in New York. We were there three months, on the same bill as Duke Ellington, and that was when I got to know Duke. *Love You Madly* was one of two arrangements I remember doing for him. I also did quite a few big-band arrangements around that time for shows and for Louis, who would augment his normal small group when he had several acts with him. I was with him until the latter part of 1947, playing piano, and I left when I got the organ.

"I had it in mind when I joined him, and the more I thought about it the more I was attracted by the idea. The Hammond Company had been engaged on war contracts and hadn't been making organs. When I ordered mine in 1945, I had to wait almost two years to get it. It cost me $2290 and it was a gamble, absolutely. I was making $175 a week when I left Louis, but when I returned to Chicago, where I made my home, I started out on the organ making about $45 a week. But I was happy.

"I began working in the Savoy Ballroom [Chicago], and it was then a skating rink. They had an organ there and I could practice on my own at home. Then I began working nightspots in Chicago and I spent all 1948 there. John Hammond heard me and in March, 1949, he made arrangements for me to come to New York. My first record was on Mercury, and then I was on Mercer with Duke Ellington on piano. It didn't turn out as successfully as we hoped, because the organ is pretty hard to record and in those days they didn't have the recording techniques and equipment they have today. In fact, the organist had to be almost as much of a technician as the engineer himself, and in addition he had to play the music."

Davis was at Wells' on 133rd and Seventh Avenue for twelve weeks and then went to Atlantic City for the rest of the summer, appearing as a single. He came back to New York at Smalls' and picked out an organ which the management bought for the club. A big success there through the winter, he returned, as was to become his custom, to Atlantic City for the summer. In August, 1950, he rejoined Louis Jordan to record *Tamburitza Boogie* on organ. It was such a hit that he went out with Jordan on a road tour for several months, and during this period the band's pianist, Bill Doggett, was so impressed by the Davis performances that he decided to invest in an organ himself. At the end of his third summer season at Grace's Little Belmont on Kentucky Avenue in Atlantic City, Davis opened in Washington with Bill Jennings on guitar. Three months later, Chris Columbus joined them on drums in Philadelphia.

"We opened at Birdland at the end of December," Davis continued, "and they were very skeptical about the organ at first, but during the first year we were in there sixteen or eighteen weeks, in and out. It was a little harsh to begin with, until the house became extremely crowded. We alternated with one or two small groups, but when there got to be a crowd in the place the other groups seemed to be lost, whereas we were always more at home. In other words, we could really get the pulse of the crowd, command their attention, and get them going. It was a big-band sound. After we had been in there a few weeks, they called in some acoustical engineers and revamped the place rather than keep us out. Acoustical tiles and drapes went up in certain places so that it dampened and absorbed the harshness and made a good, compact sound. As a result of that, they later started putting big bands in there. Before that, they hadn't had big bands. Very few people will admit this, but I know it to be a fact, and it's very gratifying to me.

"One reason I went into organ was that I don't like to do what everyone else is doing. I like a challenge and it was a challenge to me to get on Broadway, downtown, with an organ group. Another challenge was to get into the Savoy Ballroom in Harlem. We went in there in 1953 and made a very favorable impression. In fact, I think we were the only trio that went in there and made it. We were on one bandstand and the Erskine Hawkins band was on the other, and we swung 'em out of there! We went back several times and I used two Leslie speakers with a Hammond speaker in the middle there, because there was room for the big sound and a crowd to absorb it.

"After the Birdland period, I ran into some business problems I

240

don't want to go into, but they involved traveling at the time of year when there's a lot of ice and snow on the highway, which I dislike very heartily. I usually try to be in another part of the country then! So we got off at a bit of a tangent and since then I haven't worked very much in New York—every now and then in Smalls' and recently at Basin Street East. I work in Atlantic City during the summers, at the same place I began as a single. It's not big, but by being able to stay in one place all summer we were able to work out an agreeable deal.

"I've adjusted to doing a lot of one-nighters rather than subjugate myself, but I'd still rather work clubs. You have to carry the organ around with you, as well as the rest of the group, and there is never enough money to ship it by rail. I can get a trio in a station-wagon, but not a quartet. A trailer not only slows you up but costs extra money in tolls, plus inconvenience. If you're traveling five or six hundred miles with a single car and a few pieces, you can do it so much better. You can afford to give the promoter a break, maybe play for more promoters, and still come out further on top. This is the economics of the business. A competitor and friend of mine who saw the organ in the station-wagon suddenly visualized all the dollars with wings that had been flying away from him, because he had been renting a trailer to make his dates and carry the organ. There's also more wear and tear on the automobile with a trailer. The fellow I was talking about had burned out two transmissions in the course of a year pulling his trailer, which would cost $250 or $300 each time.

"During the last few years, I've had a number of tenor players with me, like George Clark, Jimmy Forrest, Crawford Wright, and Bob Brown. After Floyd Smith and Chris Columbus left, I had an interest in a Los Angeles club called the Wild Bill Davis Morocco, where I opened in February, 1957, for seven or eight months. After that, I decided to work as a single and pick up musicians as needed. Besides the tenors, that was how I ran into Grady Tate, the drummer. He's very versatile and I consider him one of the best. Al Aarons was with me a few weeks. Basie came by and heard him with me, but he had been hearing about him before that. This summer, I had Dicky Thompson on guitar—he's been working around New York a long time; Bob Brown, a schoolteacher from Philly on flute and tenor; and Jimmy Hopps from Washington on drums. This was the group I used for part of my first Victor album, *Free, Frantic, and Funky.*"

Apart from his own albums, those of several other artists have benefited from the organist's talent. His collaborations with Johnny Hodges, for instance, have proved singularly popular.

241   "I don't suppose there is anybody in the business," he said, "who

can do more with a melody than Johnny Hodges. Although I'd known and admired him for a long time, I'd never had the pleasure of working with him before we made that *Blue Hodge* album for Verve. You find out so much more about a musician when you work with him and I soon realized this was one time when melody wasn't going to be neglected, so I decided to do all I could to enhance what he was doing. I believe that you've got to tell a story in any kind of music, too. It should have a beginning, continuity, climax, and an ending."

The Bill Davis arrangement of *April in Paris* gave Count Basie one of his biggest hits and its genesis was unusual.

"When I first recorded it," he remembered, "I paid for the session and the engineering myself. Then I had a change of personnel and wasn't ready to record when the recording company called, so I offered them the version I had on the shelf. They put it out, but it wasn't any great big thing and didn't have the one-more-time bit that we started to do later. Then we were playing Birdland opposite Count Basie and some of his musicians had been at Tennessee State, Nashville, and had played some of my arrangements that had gotten around up there from Texas, Tuskegee, and Chicago. They knew I used to do a lot of writing, so they—not Basie himself—said, 'Why don't you do *April in Paris* for us?' I felt this was a good chance for me to try to adapt an arrangement from the organ to a band and I really did it without any thought of monetary gain, but rather as a challenge. So I went home one night when we finished work at three thirty and sat up until seven. When I went to work the next night, the fellows had talked to Basie about it.

" 'You got it ready, Bill?'

" 'Yeah, let's make it.'

"One of those things. No rehearsal. We sat down and played it in the next set and everybody liked it. So we played it again. We were there three weeks together and every night of the last two weeks we did it three or four times. I played organ with the band and I was supposed to record it with them, but my recording company wouldn't let me. After Basie's was issued, they put mine out again, but this time with 'One more time!,' and with Floyd Smith on guitar instead of Bill Jennings."

Bill Davis looked at the time. He had to return to a smoky nightclub, but he had a coda ready.

"Besides being a musician," he said, "if I had time to study, I would like to be an engineer. I wish I had an engineering degree. I love anything to do with electronics and engineering. I work on my organ and my automobile. I have my own airplane and I work on that, too. I use it for pleasure and business, and I've flown it to every big city in the country. When I flew it to California, someone else drove the car. I made it in four or five jumps and the distances depended on the weather. I don't like flying—I love it! I have enough experience for a commercial license and if I could make a good living out of it, I'd be in that instead of music. No joke. I like outdoor life."

Fortunately, he remained in music and, in 1969, the associations referred to earlier with Ellington and Hodges led to his becoming a part of the band. While it was performing in Atlantic City, Davis was in his usual haunt, Grace's Little Belmont, and Ellington persuaded him to write arrangements for the numbers to be sung by Joya Sherrill at a forthcoming engagement in New York at the Rainbow Grill. Davis rehearsed with Miss Sherrill and wrote so effectively for the smaller band required at the club (Willie Cook, Lawrence Brown, the five reeds, and rhythm section) that, on opening night, Ellington had him play piano as accompanist to the singer.

Shortly after this, a recording project for *Reader's Digest* called for a dozen arrangements of recently popular hits, and Ellington delegated the responsibility to Luther Henderson, Ron Collier, and Davis. The last was not only the arranger of *Alfie, Summer Samba, Mr. Lucky, Soon It's Gonna Rain, Moon Maiden,* and *Walking Happy,* but a participant on organ (and piano) at all the recording sessions.

The combination was so much to Ellington's liking that, when the band left New York for a cross-country tour, Davis was a part of it. After a month's engagement in Las Vegas, the whole company left at the end of October, 1969, for five crowded weeks in Europe, the first part of an around-the-world tour.

In view of Davis' potential as arranger, organist, and pianist, it was easy to foresee his assuming some of the additional burden that fell on Ellington's shoulders when Billy Strayhorn died.

[*1965 & 1969*]

A dance in West Germany

EVENTS & OCCASIONS

Every decade of Ellington's long career has contained great events and occasions. Hearing the band at the Palladium and Trocadero in London, at the Cotton Club in New York, and at the Palais de Chaillot in Paris were my personal highlights of the 1930s. The 1940s saw the remarkable series of Carnegie Hall concerts, the 1950s the greatest of all jazz festival triumphs at Newport, and the 1960s . . .

The following selection seems almost arbitrary from such an eventful decade, but Ellington himself regards the Sacred Concert as his greatest achievement. The White House dinner party was certainly an honor without parallel. The Latin American tour—a first—was viewed by the musicians themselves as one of the most exciting and successful they ever made. As for Suite Thursday, its quality was rather underappreciated at the time of its Monterey Festival première, but with its quiet strength and integrity it seems destined to live as one of the maestro's most accomplished suites. In any case, here are four aspects of an active ten years.

Festival: Preparation and Aftermath

The sea tumbled the drowned man up on the sandy beach. A suspicious character emerged from the fringe of tropical undergrowth and carried the body away. He was observed through the binoculars of the Border Patrol, vigilant in their launch a convenient distance offshore. He was observed, too, by Duke Ellington across a table strewn with manuscript paper. Ellington was modifying a section of the score of a new work to be presented at the Monterey Jazz Festival. He sized up the coastal situation and from then on looked up only to follow the action when the TV characters stopped talking.

Whenever he was long enough in one hotel, a piano had been moved into his suite. At Camden, it hadn't been possible, and he had worked alone in the hotel's empty ballroom, all lights on, until dawn. Here in Boston, the piano was conveniently situated opposite the TV and near the doors of the adjoining rooms. He could step out of the shower, play a chord or a phrase, and step back in again. He could swing around during a meal, a conversation, or a TV shoot-'em-up to try out an idea as soon as it occurred to him. There were constant interruptions during the irregular hours of his working day by friends, musicians, and journalists, but in between there was intense concentration, and *Suite Thursday* had begun to take shape.

Music was handed to Tom Whaley to copy, and at night in Storyville the band would play it, unannounced to the crowd. Sometimes it sounded right to its maker, but when it didn't, it was taken back upstairs for revision.

Soon there was enough music for a regular rehearsal. At the appointed hour, the piano player and a small and somewhat dejected proportion of the band were gathered together. The punctual musicians did not feel themselves obliged to wait on latecomers, and several wandered out of the hall and disappeared. Ellington, meanwhile, worked on the score at the piano, and played over some of the music previously found satisfactory.

Quite suddenly, without any signal or band call, the whole group was on stage and Ellington was bringing it to order with piercing whistles. The sax section began to run through the first part, now known as *Misfit Blues*. Its infectious character and wonderful tempo seemed to put everyone into a good humor. Ellington was listening intently, pulling at his ear lobes.

"Did I write that?" he asked Tom Whaley, pointing to a bar on the score.

"I copy what you put down," Whaley expostulated.

"Oh, I don't know. Sometimes I wonder . . ."

One phrase particularly intrigued Johnny Hodges.

"Hey, Duke," he called, "repeat that one more time. Be-boom-de-dey. See what I mean?"

"This is my this year's stuff," Ellington answered, "that I got from your last year's stuff, that you got . . . Bones right in!"

Hodges grinned and shrugged.

The band swung into *Schwiphti* with a considerable degree of confidence, having run it through twice the previous night. Until now, who would have thought that this behatted and casually attired group of men was the finest jazz orchestra in the world? Sam Woodyard there, superb big-band drummer, his cap on back to front, was mischievously discussing the vintage years with Matthew Gee while maintaining a vigorous, driving beat. Fats Ford wore a jaunty, semi-Tyrolean hat that suited him better than the tin derby he donned each night during performances of *Rockin' in Rhythm*. Johnny Hodges, his hat pulled well down over his eyes—was he meditating on the sounds around him or the Yankees' chances in the World Series? Jimmy Hamilton, slouched beneath a floppy cap appropriate to a golf course of the '20s, was playing now the pretty clarinet part of *Zweet Zurzday*, immaculately. Even Ellington was wearing a hat, a weatherproof model with a gay band. As his barber entered the hall, he cried:

"Everything is going to be all right, fellows. Billy Black is here. Have no fear!"

"Where are you going now?" asked Lawrence Brown gravely.

There was a great sorting of music and they were just ready for *Lay-by* when a waiter brought in the leader's breakfast-lunch.

"I'm too busy. Can you eat my steak?" he shouted to the musician who had been mildly reproved the night before.

Getting a negative reply, Ellington began to eat—steak, grapefruit, and black coffee with lemon. Aaron Bell eyed the spread a little hungrily from the stand as the band ran through *Lay-by*. Ellington looked up at him and said:

"I'm playing the part mentally if not physically, you know, and it's just as strenuous."

248

After a last sip of coffee, he took his seat at the piano again. A slightly heated discussion was developing within the band as to how one phrase should be interpreted.

"Don't let emotion interfere with our progress," Ellington called.

Ellington was talking about the work in hand after the rehearsal.

"Yes, I've been burning the midnight oil, drinking coffee with lemon, smoking cigarettes, chewing gum, walking the floor, humming, tinkling the piano, and so forth.

"What you've heard are little phrases, some of which will be used, some of which will not, and some of which will most likely be added to. Some are short and some are long. Some have to be pruned and some have to be extended. They have to be dramatically routined. We've been writing parts, passing them out, and trying them on the stand. If we didn't like them, we'd tear them up and rewrite them, and then pass them out and re-routine them. All I can say specifically at this point is that we expect to have a rehearsal when we get to Monterey, a final rehearsal. The thing that is about to take place is the adjustment of my perspective. The story is quite involved, you know. It's set in Monterey's Cannery Row after World War II."

Ellington picked up his notes on Steinbeck's *Sweet Thursday* and began to read, with humorous inflections and interpolations:

"After the pilchards have been caught, the canneries shut down, and the characters, judged by conventional standards, are a lot of social misfits who stay on for lack of anything else to do or any place to go. Steinbeck brings them alive and the mood evoked here is, I would say, gay and funny, sad and tragic, conveying through simple people and incidents the essence of, eh, human nobility touched with the ridiculous, which gives it reality. Yes, really.

"The main characters are Doc, a high I.Q. type from the University of Chicago, who makes a shaky living in his pad by catching and selling specimens of marine life to college and research laboratories. Then there's Susie, who is a crude, proud little girl, kind of down on her luck, who briefly inhabits the bar—the Bear Flag, I mean—and who is just a little too frank and hot-tempered to make a very successful lady of ill repute.

"Doc, of course, is beloved by all the folks of Cannery Row because of his natural and instinctive kindness, and the slight plot centers on their efforts to help him when they sense his depression is not really caused by his inability to write a research paper on the emotional manifestations of the octopi, but by the mere fact that nothing so big can be accomplished by a man so obviously in need of a woman.

Composer at work

"Doc and Susie are destined to really get together, but on Page 1 they have trouble. They are not able to get together, because both are proud and defensive, and seemingly incompatible by reason of wildly different backgrounds, mental capacities, and aspirations, if any. But they can't stay apart either, because—well, you dig? So on Page 273 they drive off to La Jolla in Doc's old car to catch the morning tide. Now I think that's where we are going to begin the last part, when we swing out.

"Doc has a theory that the octopus changes color according to his mood, emotions, etc. Now I'm just pulling this out of my head, but we sort of feel the people in Cannery Row change their colors, too. You look at a man, you think he's a bum, but it turns out he's a real angel. Or you think he's a horrible guy, but inside he's—well, dress him in some clean clothes and you find he's a real right guy, and so forth."

Ellington laid the notes down and continued:

"It's a very, very interesting thing to do. I don't know that we're going to be able to say very much about the story, because you can only parallel so much of it in music. The most we're going to be able to say, I imagine, is that on Page 1 Doc and Susie are not going to get together. Then we turn to the other people, looking for a story, and we find these different changes of color. Finally, we jump to Page

273 when the two drive off in Doc's car, and they're swinging, man! "The titles we have are just references. For instance, *Schwiphti* —well, there's one in every town.* *Lay-by,* you should know, is the official name for an emergency parking lot alongside the highways of England. We saw a lot of them when we were riding around over there in 1958."

A couple of days later, Ellington left for California. There was a final rehearsal, and then came the première performance at the Monterey Jazz Festival. The pattern of critical reaction was all too familiar.

Time found the work "considerably less intriguing than the titles" and spoke patronizingly of what "Ellington too often uses as a substitute for invention." when "he tries for concert length." To the reviewer in *Metronome,* it "seemed to be a hastily concocted group of independent statements without a substantial theme" and one that lacked anything more than "superficial musical content." *Down Beat's* man in Monterey got "the impression there was not the least intent to produce a work of the stature of, say, *The Liberian Suite,*" and he decided that "the four sections of *Suite Thursday* are separate entities, good musically and quite interesting in many places, but bearing no discernible relationship to each other, much less to John Steinbeck's works and Monterey."

Such criticism was almost completely contradicted subsequently in enthusiastic reviews of the recorded version, a fact which suggests that though jazz critics often lead the clamor for "extended works," they are not yet equipped by experience to judge them on one hearing. What was also indicated was a misconception of the musical meaning of that word "suite."

A suite is a series of short pieces which may be of quite varied character or linked together as parts of one idea. In the days of Bach, Handel, and the Elizabethan composers, the suite frequently consisted of different dance forms. The advantage of contrasting movements was thus recognized centuries ago, but some jazz critics seem to have in mind either the kind of formal development and variation which properly belong to the sonata and symphony, or the most banal kind of program music.

Ellington's suites usually consist of contrasting movements, mostly in dance style. However, quite apart from the recurring minor sixth interval referred to in the album notes, there is here an obvious melodic relationship between *Zweet Zurzday* and *Lay-by,* a relationship entirely undisguised by the switch from beguine rhythm to four-four. The loose and often subtle connection between the music

251　*Pronounced "Swifty," sibilantly!

and the Steinbeck book has been indicated earlier, but it should be noted that the suite as a whole, in keeping with a tale of "simple people," has an outward simplicity. With the exception of the fast-stepping *Schwiphti,* even the tempos are relaxed and easy. There is nothing pretentious, nothing highly colored or dramatic, and Ray Nance's fiddle is properly expressive of gaiety and happiness when they swing out to La Jolla. This, in fact, is the most consistently swinging of all Ellington's long works.

By the time the band had returned East and Johnny Hodges had rejoined, its interpretations were even more exciting than that on the record. All four movements were played, night after night, in clubs and at dances, and the entry of the saxes after the pace-setting piano in *Misfit Blues* was always an electric moment. The emphasis on the saxes throughout is worth remarking. This sax section has worked together with the same personnel longer than any other in the history of jazz. Each man in it is an individual with exceptional gifts, and together they form an incomparable team, especially since Ellington writes with so full an awareness of their every quality.

Complimented after a particularly brilliant performance, Ellington was asked how he himself felt about *Suite Thursday.*

"Well, I must admit I'm rather pleased with the way it turned out," he answered.

[*1961*]

The Ecumenical Ellington:

THE FIRST SACRED CONCERT

"Every time God's children have thrown away fear in pursuit of honesty—trying to communicate, understood or not—miracles have happened."

Thus Duke Ellington in his program notes to the concert of sacred music which he presented in San Francisco's Grace Cathedral on September 16th, 1965.

It certainly seemed like a miracle to see the famous faces of his famous orchestra looking down the nave from the chancel in the big, proud church on top of Nob Hill. Yet it was not without precedent of a kind, for that summer Catholic priests and a Negro choir had celebrated mass at the Antibes jazz festival. And it was no more incongruous than, say, the annual visit of a London symphony orches-

252

tra to the fifteenth-century church in the little town of Thaxted, England. For these were musicians offering what they did best—better than any others in the world—to the glory of God, the principal being, after all, the same as that of the harvest festival, when the finest fruits of the field are brought thankfully into church.

"Every man prays in his own language," Ellington explained, "and there is no language that God does not understand."

The language was perhaps not always fully understood by the well-dressed audience which packed the cathedral, for it was the Ellington language undiluted. In the "pursuit of honesty," fear of scandalizing had been put aside. So Cootie Williams spoke starkly with plunger-muted trumpet, Cat Anderson's high notes echoed around the high, vaulted roof, and Paul Gonsalves' tenor saxophone drove as excitingly as ever beneath a chanting choir.

Ellington knew, too, about the medieval *jongleur* who expressed his gratitude with a performance before the statue of the Virgin Mary. The evening's visual climax came when tap-dancer Bunny Briggs stepped forward to illustrate an up-tempo variation on Ellington's *Come Sunday* entitled *David Danced before the Lord with All His Might*. Briggs danced with all his might, spurred on by soft unison saxophone, by an Anderson trumpet obbligato, and by Jon Hendricks, who sang first the lyrics and then in scat.

"In the beginning God . . . ," the four words which open the King James Version of the Bible, provided the program's main theme and the title of an inspired Ellington composition. The six syllables were symbolized by a "phrase with six tones," which was used "many times . . . many ways." Harry Carney introduced the work on baritone saxophone, and the full, majestic sound this musician produces with his instrument—not to mention his finely nuanced phrasing—can seldom have been employed to better effect. It expressed awe and reverence, as if at the beginning "before all worlds," and none of the subsequent statements that were allotted to Jimmy Hamilton, Jon Hendricks, Paul Gonsalves, Cat Anderson, and Louis Bellson matched it in terms of dignity and feeling. A choir was also employed here to declaim the names of the books in the Old and New Testaments, Ellington having tutored its members in the matter of accent, so that they now sang "Corrr-*inth*ians!" and "Eee-*phes*ians!" to obtain the desired rhythmic impact.

Two choirs were, in fact, used in the course of the concert: one from San Diego, directed by Herman McCoy, and the other consisting of cathedral choristers. The former sang a selection of traditional spirituals as well as three from Ellington's musical production, *My People*, on which they were joined by Jimmy McPhail. The major vocal triumph, however, was achieved by Esther Merrill, a young gospel singer from Detroit with something of Mahalia Jackson's power and fervor. Her interpretation of *Come Sunday* gained the approval of even Johnny Hodges, who had played it earlier with serene artistry in the overture to *Black, Brown, and Beige*. A completely new arrangement of the number had been specially written for the concert, and following the singer the reed section made an exquisite final declaration. The score called for two clarinets (Procope and Hamilton), bass clarinet (Carney), alto saxophone (Hodges), and tenor saxophone (Gonsalves), and the resultant sound might justly be described as ethereal. Then an astonishingly joyous fusion of jazz and religious sentiment occurred when Miss Merrill sang *The Lord's Prayer*, the whole orchestra swinging enthusiastically behind her. Here the spiritual and the temporal came together in a thrilling affirmation of belief.

In this arresting performance, Ellington played an extremely important role at the piano, urging on his forces with authoritative, well-placed chords. Previously, all alone, he had played his *New World a-Comin'*, a work descriptive of a place "where love is unconditional and no pronoun is good enough for God."

Since he had done so much to make the occasion a success—by his own intensive work, by bringing in additional talent from all over the country regardless of cost, and by playing for scale—it was only regrettable that the cathedral's acoustics and sound system failed to do the concert justice. Indeed, it was a case of the last shall be first, for those at the back heard much better than those in front.

Two nights later, Ellington and his company were at the Monterey Jazz Festival. It was the big night, Saturday night, and the huge audience had already been brought to a peak of excitement by the magic of Earl Hines, to whom it gave a standing ovation. Ellington went on soon after eleven o'clock and played for an hour and a half, until the police began to make pointed references to the time.

He presented a fine program of new and old material. There were exhibitionistic vehicles for Cat Anderson (*El Viti*) and Buster Cooper (*El Busto*), and for Paul Gonsalves an excellent piece at medium tempo that had served as the background for the Old Testament chanting in the cathedral. Johnny Hodges had a new one, too, *When I'm Feeling Kinda Blue*. Written by Gerald Wilson, this had a catchy melody and a rock-'n'-roll gait. Hodges knew just what to do with it, and within eight bars he had the crowd wholly in his hand.

Then it was Sunday, and Esther Merrill came out to sing *Tell Me It's the Truth*, *Come Sunday*, and *The Lord's Prayer*. She touched the emotions just as surely and deeply as she had done in the cathedral, but now she sang with even more gospel fire and confidence. She exhorted the audience as a congregation—"Let me hear you moan, let me hear you moan!"—and she ended with a series of passionate and irrefutable amens.

That should have concluded the program, but Ellington could not beg off. Bunny Briggs danced as Jon Hendricks sang about David, and then, finally, there was *Rockin' in Rhythm* with Dizzy Gillespie, Rex Stewart, and Clark Terry supplementing the band's regular brass.

Northern California, many claimed, never had it so good.

[*1965*]

THE SECOND SACRED CONCERT

When the Duke Ellington band returned to New York after a long sojourn in the hinterlands, it promptly went into rehearsal for the Ed Sullivan Show, on which the nation was introduced to *Acht O'Clock Rock*, the leader's electric piano, and the new bassist, Jeff Castleman.

It was after one of these rehearsals that the band began work on the second Sacred Concert in a small hall off Eighth Avenue. There, the astonishingly beautiful voice of the Swedish soprano, Alice Babs, was heard for the first time in Ellington's new compositions, and Benny Green and Steve Little were added to the trombone and rhythm sections, respectively.

From Monday to Friday (January 15–19, 1968) of the following week, right up to an hour before the première, there were long and patient rehearsals in a large room alongside the Cathedral of St. John the Divine on 112th Street and Amsterdam Avenue. With a thousand details to attend to, and scores of officials, visitors, and reporters to speak to, Ellington himself was consistently the most relaxed and good-humored person present. He maintained a flow of encouraging banter with the band.

"Then you blow it," he said, after imitating the sound he wanted from the horns. A musician suggested that since he did it so well, he should leave it in the concert.

"I wasn't born to do that," he replied. "After *you* get through blowing, I bow."

At the end of a particularly arduous rehearsal, there were some long faces as instruments were packed.

"You've had a rough time today," Ellington announced cheerfully, "but there's reward in sight for you!"

This brought the expected reaction: expressions of scornful disbelief, ironic laughs, and incredulous smiles. Spirits rose, however, at the prompt realization that adversity was not personal, but something shared. The final dress rehearsal came all too quickly. At one point, Ellington was lying full length on his back, on the red-carpeted stand, calmly considering his band's performance. Tom Whaley and young Roscoe Gill had been deputed to rehearse choirs, but the whole responsibility remained his. No one else knew how the various pieces of his huge mosaic were to be fitted together. The score sheets were marked with abbreviations characteristic of his private code, and sometimes even his musicians seemed to find them mysterious. A worksheet produced during the last afternoon nevertheless accorded in all essential details with the program sent to the printers four days earlier.

The concert presented on January 19th, 1968, in the Cathedral of St. John the Divine, the largest cathedral in the world, was an occasion in every sense of the word. Any review of it would necessarily be subjective, since the huge building's huge echo made for an acoustical nightmare. The painful glare of TV lights was a further handicap to appreciation, but the audience of over six thousand people seemed to get its collective kicks, and a useful sum must have been raised for Exodus House and the cause of rehabilitation from drug addiction.

The Bishop of New York spoke well in introduction, and Alec Wyton played a formidable organ piece, *Praise Him in the Sound of the Trumpet*, before Ellington got his forces under way. The organ sound, projected at the high gothic roof, rolled around with noticeably less distortion than the band was subjected to down on the floor at the crossing.

All this served rather like an extra dress rehearsal for the performance the following night at the much smaller church of St. Mark's in New Canaan, Connecticut. The acoustics and sound system in this modern building were excellent, and the church's own admirable choir (partly rehearsed by Roscoe Gill) was mounted right behind the band, and on the same platform. (At St. John's, the A.M.E. Mother Zion Church Choir and the men of the cathedral choir were seated to the left of the band, and the youngsters of the St. Hilda's and St. Hugh's School choirs to the right. As at the original concert in San Francisco, there were problems in relating the choirs to the whole, and it seems that the contrasting effect Ellington wants from young and adult voices can best be realized when the choirs are close together, which was the case at the A.M.E. Mother Zion Cathedral in Harlem last April.)

In addition to the superior acoustics, St. Mark's had gone to the trouble of printing most of the lyrics in the program, a valuable help at any time, and especially at a concert where *nearly all the compositions were entirely new*. This fact, along with the originality and quality of the music, was what made the concert a landmark in Ellington's career. He had undoubtedly profited from his experience with the original sacred concert, and he had clearly been able to devote more time to the preparation of this one, although the words he had addressed to a zealous member of the "advisory committee" a few months earlier, in the writer's presence, kept coming to mind:

"I don't need time. What I need is a deadline!"

The concert began with a solemn theme, *Praise God*, which was largely entrusted—as was the opening statement of the original sacred concert—to Harry Carney and his baritone saxophone. The noble and reverent sound Carney produced from his instrument triumphed over even the acoustics of St. John's. The trombones and Jeff Castleman's bowed bass also contributed very helpfully to this appropriate introductory piece.

99% Won't Do, with Jimmy McPhail as vocal soloist, Cootie Williams as a stimulating commentator, and the choir weighing in enthusiastically, brought an optimistic gospel flavor to what is basi-

The art of relaxed conducting, 1968

*Jeff Castleman, Jimmy McPhail, Alice Babs, Tony Watkins,
Devonne Gardner, Sacred Concert, 1968*

cally a cautionary sermon. This, incidentally, was the only music used
from the original sacred concert, and it was first heard in *My People*.

Supreme Being was in many respects the musical peak of the
program. It represented a real extension of Ellington's range—perhaps inspired by the subject. The scoring created an impression of
brooding majesty via harmonies that were unworldly in their implica-
tions of infinity. Exactly how this impressive effect was achieved with
just thirteen horns (twelve at New Canaan, Benny Green having
fallen victim to flu) remains an Ellington secret. The impact of the
performance was certainly felt by musicians and non-musicians alike.
"When the classical people hear *that*," Alice Babs said afterwards,
"they will marvel." And "marvel" is the right word. The choir, and
soloists from it in speaking roles, were used in the description of the
Creation and the coming of responsibility to Man.

Something about Believing was a long and striking affirmation of
faith that embodied a refutation of the absurd *God Is Dead* cliché.
The Ellington lyrics were very free, maintaining a surprising im-
provisatory feeling as the band completed lines in the way cornetists
used to do for blues singers. The choir took to the catchy melody and
swinging medium tempo with gusto, and it was assisted by the solo
vocalists and a great beat from the band. The reed section also had
a stirring passage to itself, and Ellington egged them all on, standing

Sacred Concert, Cathedral of St. John the Divine, New York, 1968

in front at his electric piano. The variety of sounds this instrument was capable of—organ-like and guitar-like among others—became an important factor, quite apart from the convenience of its size in enabling him to work while facing his musicians.

The programing throughout was masterly. After this vigorous performance, Ellington introduced Alice Babs, whose voice, ease, and accuracy were thrilling whenever she sang. *God Has His Angels* had a recognizably traditional base, but new intervals elevated it to "where there's no sulphur smell." The soprano gave it a remarkable aerial quality, serene as a skylark. When Russell Procope took over, clarinet on mike, for a gentle variation, she stepped in occasionally with affecting embellishments.

Ellington had gone up on stand to the regular piano for this, and remained there for *Heaven,* another attractive melody, which Alice Babs invested with memorably supple lyricism—sweet but not sugary, moving but not sentimental. The perfect complement was the alto of Johnny Hodges, in solo and obbligato, as Sam Woodyard's hands moved softly on the cymbals.

Freedom was a long performance in eight segments that used all the resources. Alice Babs, Jimmy McPhail, Tony Watkins, Devonne Gardner, Roscoe Gill, and Trish Turner formed a vocal group separate from, but accessory to, the choir. The sixth section *Sweet, Fat,*

259

and That, was suggested by an old lick played by Willie "the Lion" Smith, who was credited in the program with having helped Ellington on his first visit to New York. In the seventh section, the leader recited the four freedoms by which Billy Strayhorn had lived, as the choir sang softly behind. In the eighth, individual members of the choir shouted "Freedom!" in some seventeen different languages.

After this, contrast again: *Meditation* by Ellington at the piano and Jeff Castleman on bass. Well titled, it was an effective, quiet duet, in which the two musicians demonstrated a warm rapport.

Then the leader returned to the floor and the electric piano as Tony Watkins came on for *Don't Get Down on Your Knees to Pray Until You Have Forgiven Everyone,* a piece of gospelry with droll lyrics to which Watkins did justice.

The preaching was even more earnest in the next selection. *The Shepherd* is a number Ellington subtitles *A Portrait of Pastor Gensel.* On it, the impassioned eloquence of Cootie Williams, open and muted, stirred the audience at both concerts, and he returned to his seat amid great acclamation.

The Biggest and Busiest Intersection was descriptive, according to the composer's amusing notes, of the last intersection before the Golden Gates, "down at the end where all ends end." There, apparently, the Opposition has cats who come up at the very last moment and say, "Baby, I know it looks pretty in there, but you should see how the chicks are swinging down where we are!" The rivalry in this "fire-and-brimstone sermonette" was expressed by Sam Woodyard and Steve Little, who duelled with disarming subtlety or hellish cunning, depending on the viewpoint.

T.G.T.T. brought back Alice Babs. The title, Ellington explained in the program, "means *Too Good to Title,* because it violates conformity in the same way, we like to think, that Jesus Christ did. The phrases never end on the note you think they will. It is a piece even instrumentalists have trouble with, but Alice Babs read it at sight." The program note was necessary, because she sang the wordless music with such extraordinary facility that the mind did not dwell until afterwards on the art and technique involved.

The finale was *Praise God and Dance,* based on the 150th Psalm and using—at a faster tempo—the same theme as the opener. Here the whole company was used, and after an impressively sincere introduction by Alice Babs the performance proceeded in a series of joyful explosions, like a Roman candle. Paul Gonsalves, Jimmy Hamilton, and Cat Anderson were the chief soloists. At St. John's, two sets of dancers had surprised the audience by erupting down the center aisle. The first, colorfully dressed, and coached by Geoffrey Holder, moved with gestures symbolic of worship in the idiom of modern dance. The second, issuing from behind the band, was swinging all the way with steps and rhythms right out of the Savoy ballroom. At New Canaan, the long-limbed Geoffrey Holder danced alone, exhibiting superb muscular control and causing tremendous excitement. It was a dance of praise, as by one possessed, while band and choir hammered home the message.

Tumultuous applause swelled until the entire audience rose to its feet in a standing ovation, and, significantly, remained standing throughout Tony Watkins' *a capella* delivery of *The Lord's Prayer* as in the original concert. It was a sober reminder that, for all its entertainment values, the concert was an act of faith. Ellington sees himself at these concerts as "one who tries to bring messages to people, not people who have never heard of God, but those who were more or less raised with the guidance of the Church."

Since Alice Babs had to return to Sweden after a third concert in New Britain, it was imperative that the music be recorded before she left. Ellington had expressed the wish that this concert not be recorded live, but in a studio. This was duly done in two sessions at the Fine studio in the Great Northern Hotel on January 22nd, where the A.M.E. Mother Zion Church Choir, directed by Solomon Herriott, Jr., assumed the choral duties. By midnight, all the new music had been recorded, except for those numbers on which neither Miss Babs nor the choir was employed. Details emerged even more clearly here than at the concerts, among them the stimulating effect Benny Green and Lawrence Brown seemed to have on one another. The former played brilliantly on *Something About Believing,* and the latter on *Freedom.*

[*1968*]

In Latin America

DIARY OF A TOUR

Some months before Duke Ellington's first visit to Latin America in 1968, I expressed a wish to accompany him. I had been concerned by the inadequate documentation of his previous foreign trips, and realized that an extensive tour in this part of the world had special significance.

"So you'd like to come with us," he said, with a quizzical smile. "Then we'll have to arrange it."

261

Nothing more was said until a few weeks before the tour began.
We were in his dressing room between preparations for a television
appearance in New York.

"Who's going on this tour?" his manager, Cress Courtney, wanted
to know.

"Eighteen musicians, two wives, and Stanley," Mercer Elllington
answered positively.

The wives were Mrs. Mercer Ellington and Mrs. Johnny Hodges.
The eighteen musicians included the singers, Trish Turner and Tony
Watkins, the band personnel being: Duke Ellington, piano; Cat An-
derson, Willie Cook, Herbie Jones, Mercer Ellington, Cootie Williams,
trumpets; Lawrence Brown, Buster Cooper, Chuck Connors, trom-
bones; Russell Procope, Johnny Hodges, Harold Ashby, Paul Gon-
salves, Harry Carney, reeds; Jeff Castleman, bass; Rufus Jones, drums.

Sunday, September 1st.

It is a pleasure and a good musical omen to find Willie Cook
rejoining the band at Kennedy Airport. Nobody is surprised to see
me, because I have often been here before to bid the band goodbye.
As farewells to wives and friends are made, the musicians board the
plane casually, one at a time. It is all routine to them.

"I'm giving up a lot of my virginity on this trip," Ellington observes as the big Aerolineas Argentinas jet heads south. "I've never
been in South America or below the equator before."

We enjoy our dinner: caviar (for which Ellington has never forgotten Iran) and paté; filet mignon; chocolate cake and ice cream;
champagne; an excellent Argentinian red wine; tea; and petits fours.
The movie which follows is *How to Save a Marriage—and Ruin Your
Life* with Dean Martin.

"You fell asleep," Ellington says reprovingly some time later. "It
was a pretty good movie, too."

Monday, September 2nd.

He does not sleep much during the night. Periodically, he hums
a few bars of a new number he is structuring in his mind. Sometimes
he gets up, jokes with the stewardess, and returns with more petits
fours. The sun begins to come up red and orange on the left, while
night remains in black command on our right—a novel experience to
people more accustomed to flying the Atlantic. We land at Rio de
Janeiro, where musicians, baggage, and instruments are cleared
through customs pleasantly. Harry Carney comes over.

"I told Procope, 'That fellow over there looks just like Stanley Dance,'" he says. "I didn't know you were coming with us."

While we wait for the plane that is to take us to São Paolo, Paul Gonsalves, who meets old friends and makes new ones everywhere, gets into animated conversation with a group of Englishmen.

"Hey, meet a countryman of yours," he says, and introduces the singer, Georgie Fame.

It is still early in the morning when the plane takes off, and most of the musicians miss a magnificent view of the crescent bay, because they are already dozing. I have not yet learned the necessity of relaxing and resting at *every* opportunity.

São Paolo is a bustling and surprising city. A high proportion of the automobiles are Volkswagens with impetuous drivers. In the city center, where traffic is heavy, the pedestrians treat them with disrespect, and thread their way across the streets as though through a herd of tin sheep. There is an amazing and apparently harmonious mixture of races, but we are soon made aware of the city's contempt for Rio de Janeiro and its cariocas: "They only get up to play there. *We* get up to work."

At the comfortable Othon Palace Hotel, some of the musicians go to bed; others go to eat, drink, or shop; still others are seized by earnest enthusiasts who have come to discuss Jazz with men they have previously known and heard only on records. Paul Gonsalves, with his bonhomie and knowledge of Portuguese, is a logical target for their attentions.

The Teatro Municipal is filled with an appreciative but not notably hip audience. We learn that the theatre's regular ticket holders are, for the most part, formidably in position. The program is much as usual, opening with the medley of "oldies," *Black and Tan Fantasy, Creole Love Call,* and *The Mooche.* Gonsalves takes Jimmy Hamilton's place on clarinet in *Creole Love Call,* and on tenor saxophone is the concert's most featured soloist (*Soul Call, Mount Harissa, Up Jump,* and *Diminuendo and Crescendo in Blue*). Harold Ashby plays clarinet in the ensemble behind Cat Anderson on *Salome,* and is featured on tenor in *B.P. Blues.* The heaviest applause follows the Rufus Jones drum solo.

Tuesday, September 3rd.

A reception at the Binational Center organized by Miss Caroline Millett of U.S.I.S. is attended by about five hundred people. Goodwill flows abundantly, and it is interesting to see how well the musicians behave in "diplomatic" roles. Music is only intermittently the subject.

263

Harry Carney strikes up an acquaintance with Denis Clare of the British Council in Sao Paolo, and Clare is obviously a little envious of the success of this American affair, and equally obviously impressed by Ellington's ease and bearing. "He's so composed," he says.

The guest of honor's attention is drawn to the piano on stage, and he obliges with *Satin Doll* and *Take the "A" Train* before getting Tony Watkins to sing the blues. A file of admiring ladies provides a background to these performances.

Since this is a free night for the band, many of the musicians accept more hospitality at the Totem Club, where a jam session goes on until the early hours. Television cameras are on hand and the indefatigable Paul Gonsalves is again the star, exaggerating close-ups by swaying towards the cameras as they move in on him. Ellington, who is relaxing in front of his television set at the hotel, is astonished by the uninhibited spectacle.

Wednesday, September 4th.

The second concert at the Teatro Municipal is completely sold out and a huge triumph. It is difficult to get through the crowds to the stage door. Ellington feels the warmth of a more perceptive audience and makes appropriate changes in the program. Ashby plays *I Can't Get Started* as well as *B.P. Blues,* and Gonsalves gets *Chelsea Bridge* and *Cottontail.* Johnny Hodges moves *these* people with *Passion Flower* and *Things Ain't What They Used to Be.* The mayor of the city presents a handsome trophy. It is late when the concert ends, and the musicians quit the stage quickly. Tumultuous and unabating applause makes an encore essential, and Ellington returns with just Castleman and Jones. Seeing Willie Cook still in the wings, he beckons him to the microphone down front. Cook's "chops" are still being built back to normal strength, but he takes a cup mute and plays *Tea for Two* with the bell of his trumpet practically touching the microphone. It is a pretty, dancing sound, and Ellington digs in at the piano. Another storm of applause, and then the quartet bows off after an interpretation of *St. Louis Blues* notable for a long and excellent piano solo.

Although tired, Ellington goes as agreed to a little club where folk musicians have been gathered together by Peter Solmssen, the United States Cultural Affairs Officer, to give him the opportunity of hearing authentic Brazilian music. The first person we see on entering is Russell Procope, very much at home, and very happy, The place is jammed, but room for us is found at a table where we are introduced to a number of important but remarkably unstuffy government officials. The absence of class and racial distinctions is again very noticeable. The Brazilian band is rhythmically exhilarating, its most fascinating feature being the *cuica*. This open-ended drum has a string fastened to its single head, and by stroking and dragging on the string the player increases and decreases tension, so that the drum virtually becomes capable of melodic expression. Ellington and Procope both try their hands at it, with moderate success. One of the guitar players also proves an extremely convincing ballad singer. The audience joins in his choruses with gusto. Afterwards, Ellington mimes approval and asks to be translated.

"Tell him," he says, "that I don't understand a word of what he sings, but I *believe* him."

Thursday, September 5th.

We are by now aware that Alejandro Szterenfeld of Buenos Aires is a jewel among impresarios. Responsible for organizing the whole tour, he is unfailingly polite, considerate, and marvelously efficient. Airline schedules in South America, however, result in certain inconveniences. After getting to bed at four, it is necessary to leave the hotel at 8 A.M. for a long drive to an airport much farther from the city than that at which we had arrived. Nevertheless, this provides the only real opportunity we have of seeing the Brazilian countryside. It is not strikingly tropical on this plateau route, but the bright red soil makes a sharp contrast with the vegetation.

On the way, we look through the São Paolo newspapers, which have devoted a great amount of space to Ellington and the concerts. There are many photographs, and big headlines: *Liberdade de Expressao, A Musica Negra No Municipal, Un Artista Sempre Atual, Papa do Jazz,* and *Mister Jazz.*

At the airport, a section of our plane is being loaded with crates of melons. When this is completed, it is proposed that another section be loaded with musicians. I am stopped courteously but firmly at the exit gate by an official. Having checked his bass through, Jeff Castleman, the only other white in the party, now witnesses my predicament with a great deal of amusement. "That's happened to me several times," he says, "and for the same reason." We call on interpreter Gonsalves and are permitted to pass.

After stopping briefly in Montevideo, we arrive in Buenos Aires at 6 P.M. A bus is ready, and the journey into this huge, very European city begins. "I don't see any soul brothers here," Buster Cooper observes, after studying the people on the street. There is barely time to check into the hotel and grab a *jamon y queso* sandwich before the bus returns to take the musicians to the Gran Rex, where the first concert in Argentina begins at 10 P.M. It is a tremendous success. The audience is discerning and the reaction warmly emotional. Of the soloists, Johnny Hodges gets the biggest response. The roaring applause after his *Things Ain't What They Used to Be* contains the same feeling, the same need to express passionate approval, that greeted the band in London in 1933. Harry Carney notices this, and remarks that he can remember nothing quite comparable to it since that time. The narrow backstage passageway and the foyer are jammed with admirers afterwards. Ellington and his men autograph their way out to the street patiently, good-humoredly, and obviously touched by the warmth of their reception.

Friday, September 6th.

We leave the hotel at 6:30 A. M., although the plane is not scheduled to depart until nine. There is time to spare at the airport, but the checking and loading of baggage and instruments consume a good deal of it. We arrive in Cordoba at ten-thirty. Johnny Hodges becomes enthusiastic about the food, and announces his intention of writing a number in tribute to the excellent Rio Segundo beer. There is some fruitless discussion about why honest, palatable beer can be made in Europe, Canada, Mexico, Brazil, and Argentina, but not in the world's wealthiest country.

Presentation of the concert in the Gran Cine Mayo has been very capably prepared by Hugo Allocati. There are handsome displays in store windows, a striking program, and at the airport Ellington records are being played continually. The concert is a long one and the audience again very enthusiastic. Ellington detects a difference between the Argentinians and the Paulistas in Brazil. "They enjoy melody here," he says. "In Brazil, they went for the rhythm numbers more."

An intermission exchange is the cause of amusement backstage. "Is he white man?" a lady had asked diffidently, pointing to the bassist. "No, ma'am," she was told. "That's Castleman."

Back in the hotel, Johnny Hodges is wandering about in the lobby disconsolately. His wife, Evelyn Ellington, and Trish Turner had spent most of the day shopping to good advantage. "I had a dream," he says, waving a few Brazilian *cruzieros* in the air. "I had a dream I had some money!"

Saturday, September 7th.

Early to rise again, this time for a journey to Tucumán farther north in Argentina. Spirits are good, in some cases because the airline regards scotch whiskey as an appropriate breakfast beverage. "Does your contract with the airline stipulate that you must be this pretty?" Ellington asks the attractive stewardess. We look at newspapers and magazines from Buenos Aires. The cover of *Primera Plana* shows a sign-painter painting the Stars and Stripes over the blue-and-white flag of Argentina. Inside, however, Ellington is warmly welcomed. "*Es un hombre que habla poco,*" it adds, "*y no gusta hacer declaraciones espectaculares.*" "That's right," he says. "I have a tendency to tepidity."

Buster Cooper has persuaded Trish Turner to sit on his lap, and Ellington teasingly draws Jeff Castleman's attention to this untoward occurrence. "I love peace and smiling faces," he says in a mischievous aside.

Press conferences are the rule in every city visited, but that in Tucumán is more provocative than most, partly due to the able interpretation of Dr. Max Torres, an expatriate American. Ellington's answers to questions include the following:

"Musicians of the past have influenced all musicians of the present."

"The throes of composition . . . ? All I need is a deadline. As a matter of fact, I'm a frustrated newspaperman."

"A good musician is a good musician no matter where he comes from."

"No, I haven't seen much ballet or opera recently. I work. I'm a laborer."

"What is the greatest danger to civilization? That we don't appreciate enough our natural heritage."

"All musicians who write reflect their time."

"I live by room service. The phone rings at seven o'clock, and a man knocks at the door with a sirloin steak and hot tea."

"Do I think of Charles Mingus as a disciple of my school? Well, that's what *he* says."

"The ultimate in art is self-expression, not escape."

The Tucumán concert is in a basketball arena jam-packed with some three thousand people. The excitement is intense and Cat Anderson's high-note trumpeting brings the crowd to its feet. Afterwards, it takes Ellington forty-five minutes to get from the dressing room to his car. He autographs programs, scarves, handkerchiefs, napkins, photographs, and scraps of paper with infinite patience.

A plane from the interior has been detained four hours to enable the band to get back to Buenos Aires tonight. The passengers in it were offered free seats at the concert, and we hope they came and enjoyed it. Meanwhile, Ellington has heard of a restaurant in the city where especially fine creme caramel can be obtained, and we make a long detour to prove the truth of this report before going to the airport.

Sunday, September 8th.

Back at the Gran Rex at the ungodly hour of 10:30 A.M., we encounter the same fanatical *porteños* we had met before. There is a hard core of enthusiasts here, just as determined, knowledgable, and discerning as those found in Paris before World War II. In the circumstances, the performance reaches a surprisingly high level. Harold Ashby is the soloist on *Just Squeeze Me.* "I like that," Ellington says after his first chorus. "Take another!" He takes two and, when the applause mounts, sits down with a puzzled, modest look on his face, as much as to say, "Can you really like *that?*" After intermission, and before Johnny Hodges works his magic, he is featured again on *I Can't Get Started* and *B.P. Blues.* Long after the curtain descends, persistent, disciplined clapping and shouts of *"Otra! Otra!"* continue.

Monday, September 9th.

Tonight's concert is in La Plata, about an hour away from Buenos Aires. On the bus are some newly made friends, among them Eddie Fiore, who displays more true insight into jazz than all but a few non-musicians of my acquaintance. He speaks English well, has a dry sense of humor, and ought to write publicly about the music. There are a few program switches: Cooper and Gonsalves are heard in *Mr. Sippi*, and Hodges answers a request for *Prelude to a Kiss*. At the concert's end, there are again uproarious demands for encores. The rhythm section answers them with *Latin American Sunshine*, a catchy number Ellington is working on for the band, and then an improvised blues.

Tuesday, September 10th.

There is an enormous crowd at the United States Embassy in Buenos Aires for a reception given by Ambassador and Mrs. Carter Burgess. The musicians take the formalities in their stride, and act as though they had been accustomed to receiving-lines all their lives.

268

Guitarist Oscar Aleman, last seen in Paris before World War II, is photographed with the Ambassador and Ellington. Both the latter and his son express gratitude in poised, articulate speeches. Then, with Castleman and Jones, Ellington plays *Satin Doll* and *Take the "A" Train*.

A romance has been blossoming, and Jeff Castleman and Trish Turner announce their engagement today. At the concert at the Gran Rex after the reception, it is appropriate, perhaps, that Trish should sing *Heaven*, the beautiful song from Ellington's second sacred concert. Hodges backs her superbly, and Paul Gonsalves excels himself on *Body and Soul*. It is after one o'clock when the concert ends.

Wednesday, September 11th.

Although the flight to Montevideo is short, the bus leaves the hotel at 6:30 A.M. By now, a routine is established. After the phone rings at five, the awakened one stumbles around, washes (doesn't shave), packs his bag, and blunders blindly along to the elevator. There is always someone he knows in it, also on his way down, mute, and similarly numb. Whether or not the bus has arrived, bags are stashed in the lobby and investigations opened as to the morning kitchen's resources. Admirable Spanish issues from Willie Cook,

Ellington in Montevideo, 1968

while Harold Ashby, after much thumbing of his phrase book, summons *el mozo*. Rudimentary demands for *café solo*, *té y limon*, and more *jamon y queso* are satisfied with varying degrees of promptness. Herbie Jones is reading *Inside South America*. Mercer Ellington is bravely coping with hotel bills at the desk, battling patiently in the local currency, and telephoning laggards in their rooms from time to time. Eventually, his repeated cries of "Rollin'!" start a reluctant movement towards the bus. There he counts heads. One missing! Tony Watkins, alias Toney, alias Stoney, disappears into the hotel, to emerge again with a musician who was perhaps leisurely finishing a second cup of coffee, or saying a fond farewell to one of his overnight fans.

In Montevideo, Ellington confronts the press again in the U.S.I.S. library, Biblioteca Artigas-Washington. The session goes comfortably enough, and everyone repairs to the Victoria Plaza Hotel, where the Leather King is lying in wait. This gentleman has a store nearby, and he soon persuades the musicians and ladies that his bargains are unbeatable. After Cordoba, there has been much wearing of ponchos, but late this afternoon nearly everybody suddenly appears in soft leather coats that have been made to measure. Another fast salesman somehow talks Paul Gonsalves and Willie Cook into letting him paint their portraits. They are satisfied with his artistic ability, but dismayed by his prices.

The evening concert is at seven, in a theatre somberly described as S.O.D.R.E. Nobody takes time to discover what the initials stand for. During intermission, there is general astonishment on finding that *all* the sandwiches in a snack bar across the street are made with ham and cheese. There are many varieties of bread and rolls, but none encloses beef. We morosely decide that Uruguay, like Argentina, must export most of its beef, because we are simply not getting it frequently enough. Curious-looking—and curious-tasting—meat in the hotel, the band's authorities determine, can be nothing else but buffalo!

The concert is another great success, although we are told tickets have been priced too high. Afterwards, the backstage corridors are made completely impassable by people waiting for Ellington's autograph. One of the theatre officials suggests letting him out a back door to avoid the crowd, but he refuses. "I can't let these people down," he says, and signs himself steadily through and out into the street. This makes him late for the reception at the Residence of Ambassador Robert M. Sayre, where he meets many important figures in Uruguayan society. The ambassador and his wife impress everyone with their sincerity and kindness.

Thursday, September 12th.

Back in Buenos Aires for another concert at the Gran Rex, Ellington is conscious that many people are attending every concert, so this time changes in the program bring *C Jam Blues* and *Rockin' in Rhythm*, two strong features for Cootie Williams in *Tutti for Cootie* and *The Shepherd,* and a long, up-tempo ride for Paul Gonsalves on *How High the Moon. Latin American Sunshine* is explored again with increasing confidence by the rhythm section.

Because of the enthusiasm in Buenos Aires, impresario Szterenfeld has decided to put on an extra concert here, although tomorrow the band must leave for Santiago in Chile. At 2 A.M. this night, when Ellington wants to speak to him, he is outside the theatre, personally supervising the loading of the band's instruments on a truck. He makes light of the work, for he is accustomed to moving symphony orchestras and ballet companies across continents.

Friday, September 13th.

At 2:45 A.M., half of the musicians are in the hotel lounge, surrounded by the idolatrous fans they have made in the city, fans who are still there at five-thirty when the bus leaves for the airport.

Crossing the Andes, Ellington remembers the date. It is not a superstition he personally respects, but he turns around in his seat with his widest smile and shouts to his men; "It's Friday the Thirteenth, you know!" Outside, there is nothing to be seen but wild, bleak, snow-crested mountains.

After arriving in Santiago at 9 A.M., there is another full-scale press conference at the Hotel Crillon. Fortunately, reporters tend to ask the same questions, so Ellington's intellectual capital is not always severely taxed.

"I wrote *Mood Indigo* in fifteen minutes while my mother finished cooking dinner," he says. *"Black and Tan Fantasy* was written in a taxicab on the way to a recording session. I'd been in an after-hours joint—Mexico's—all night long, shootin' 'em up. In each case it was a matter of deadlines. When I did *Solitude*, I was one number short, and I wrote it in twenty minutes standing up against the glass enclosure of RCA Victor's record studio in Chicago."

Santiago is a very interesting city, but for the wiser heads sleep has to come before sightseeing. The exacting schedule and somewhat dirty weather have resulted in exhaustion and numerous colds. Johnny Hodges is very sick with swollen glands, and unable to play.

271

The only musician who accompanies Ellington to the reception given by Ambassador Korry in honor of the orchestra is the indomitable Russell Procope, who has the kind of cough that Scotch can alleviate.

Before tonight's concert begins in the Gran Palace at ten o'clock, Ellington announces cheerfully that there will be a rehearsal at 1:15 A.M. to prepare for the performance of the extended work, *Harlem,* at the farewell concert in Buenos Aires. This provokes the only display of artistic temperament so far witnessed on the tour. One overtired veteran refuses to stay and stomps out in a fury. Unruffled, Ellington proceeds to conduct and play with his usual vigor and humor. "Hey, I got the tempo here!" he shouts from the piano as the tempo gets out of hand elsewhere. Harold Ashby is doing his best with the unfamiliar clarinet part, and at the end of the rehearsal Ellington sits down and counsels him on it.

Saturday, February 14th.

At 4 A.M., several of the musicians are still sitting around in the hotel, eating ham sandwiches with Coca Cola. The nightlife of the city, its costs and hazards, are the subject of grave discussion.

The concert at night is made unusual by the absence of the nonpareil Hodges. Willie Cook takes his place in the reed section, playing mostly into a derby. Cat Anderson gets an ovation for his work on *El Viti, Birth of the Blues, Basin Street Blues,* and *Things Ain't What They Used to Be.* Harold Ashby, who has studied the clarinet part and practiced it all day, copes skillfully with the demands of *Harlem.* The audience is rapturous, and two awards are made to the leader on stage, one from the *Comite de Jazz del Instituto Chileno Norteamericano de Cultura*, the other from the *Sociedad Chilena de Jazz.*

Sunday, September 15th.

It is not worth going to bed in Santiago, because departure time from the hotel is 4 A.M. A party has been organized by José Hossiason for the joint benefit of Ellington's men and a band of touring jazz musicians from Germany. Those who attended are full of glowing but rather inarticulate praise of the hospitailty.

We are back in the Continental Hotel in Buenos Aires at 8:45 A.M., and the last concert at the Gran Rex begins two hours later. The theatre is full, the atmosphere highly emotional. Hodges is still absent and Chuck Connors arrives late, but everything is ecstatically approved. Jeff Castleman's solo on *Satin Doll* gets a big hand. There is an ovation for Cat Anderson as in Chile, and for the same numbers. When one of Rufus Jones' sticks flies downstage, Ellington catches it and returns it to him backhanded. *Harlem*, a tightly interwoven work, is hard to appreciate fully at one hearing, but the audience is deeply impressed by it. Finally, Ellington is saying goodbye with *Latin American Sunshine*. Cheers of football-crowd intensity, and insistent, deep-throated shouts of *"Otra! Otra!"* are unavailing this time, because of other demands on the theatre.

A huge crowd waits for Ellington outside. The last autographs are signed. People are actually crying, and trying to touch him. Others are thrusting gifts on him, gifts that don't bear the donor's name. Hands clutch at the car as it draws away. Rarely has he been so moved.

The rest of the day isn't free, however. He has agreed to a radio interview, and he expresses himself freshly on a wide range of subjects:

"Improvisation? Anyone who plays anything worth hearing knows what he's going to play, no matter whether he prepares a day ahead or a beat ahead. It has to be with intent."

"We've all worked and fought under the banner of jazz for many years, but the word itself has no meaning. There's a form of condescension in it."

"The cooler or more intellectual forms mean reversion back to the original African. It's like modern painting and sculpture. The same thing with bop—Charlie Parker, Dizzy Gillespie, and those people—that was in the direction of Africa."

"Many musicians acquire great technique, but taste is the final thing. I think taste is something you're born with. Acquiring the skills is a matter of handling the tools. Even a great hack has to have good taste, because he has to know what to steal."

"Daybreak Express? I was crazy about trains, but I wasn't influenced by Honegger, who was writing about European trains. There was great romance in the sound of the old U.S. trains. And it was what it meant to the guys who built the railroad. They'd been diggin' and diggin', and swingin' a hammer for six months, and then the train goes by—swish! . . . *whoo-oo-oo . . .*"

"A jam session is a polite encounter—an exchange of compliments. In the old days, they had cutting contests where you defended your honor with your instrument."

"Sometimes I think a piano limits you when you're writing.

You employ what you can play when you use a piano. Otherwise, your mind is much broader."

Paul Gonsalves and Willie Cook work, too. They had earlier met the pianist, Enrique Villegas, and a record date for the Trova label begins at 7 P.M. The music is of an impromptu nature, but there are several very successful performances, the titles recorded being *Tea for Two, I Cover the Waterfront, I Can't Get Started, Perdido, Blues for B.A., Just Friends, St. Louis Blues*, and a medley notable for Gonsalves' interpretation of *Ramona*.

Monday, September 16th.

We leave the hotel at 5 A.M. There is little talk on the way to the airport as the sun comes up. Heads nod, and the famous faces all around quickly crumple in repose. The bus stops, and the baggage is already disgorged on the sidewalk by the time the first passengers begin to straggle out in the direction of the restaurant.

Ellington has prepared a statement for Señor Szterenfeld to give to the press. In part, it reads:

"My first visit to South America has been a tremendous experience, far greater than I ever anticipated, and one that I can never possibly forget. The generosity and enthusiasm of the audiences were together the inspiration of a lifetime—a virtual summit in my career. Everything and everyone have been so completely and warmly attuned that I am truly overwhelmed, and at a loss to express my appreciation. Perhaps I can do so at a later date, in music.

"We spent the most time in Argentina, but we were made to feel equally at home in Brazil, Uruguay, and Chile, and we leave all four countries with emotion and the deepest feelings of friendship."

It is seven-fifteen when we leave Buenos Aires airport. We stop at Santiago, Lima, Quito, and Bogatá. Meals are served between each city, but attractive open-faced sandwiches and liquor are waved aside somewhere between the last two, limits having generally been reached. We arrive in Miami at 10 P.M., happy in the prospect of a good night's sleep.

Tuesday, September 17th.

It is 11:30 A.M. in the restaurant at the Miami airport. The plane to Nassau will leave in a half-hour. Ellington and I are drinking tea, Paul Gonsalves and Buster Cooper, coffee. Chuck Connors is seen approaching, and it is obvious that he has not spent the night wisely.

"Here comes Black Power!" Ellington says.

By evening, the sun and sea have reinvigorated several jaded bodies. The audience in Le Cabaret on Paradise Island is typically American gambling crowd. It has to be shown, but it warms to the music, particularly to Hodges' *I Got It Bad, Things Ain't What They Used To Be*, and *Jeep's Blues*. Some invidious comparisons are made with the South American audiences, but what is familiar and what has never been experienced before will always evoke different responses.

Wednesday, September 18th.

I fly home as Ellington and his men begin a brief series of single engagements in the United States. There is no respite for them after what seems to me an exhausting tour. Flying has merely changed the perspective, and they have adjusted to it, but the pattern of their lives is not much different from that which prevailed when they traveled long distances by bus.

Monday, September 23rd.

Reunion at Kennedy Airport. "You must like the road," Johnny Hodges says, a trifle sardonically. This trip is complicated by the film unit which impresario Gary Keys is taking along with the backing of the Council for Latin America. The crew immediately proves itself flexible and resourceful, but the amount of equipment is staggering, a problem in itself. When we arrive in Mexico City at 11:25 A.M., it is all laid out on the sidewalk alongside the band's baggage and instruments, and then it looks like an insoluble problem. The mariachis outside the airport, we are somewhat amused to find, have not been assembled to serenade us. They are there to welcome the national teams as they arrive to compete in the Olympic Games. When a group of healthy-looking athletes appears, they break out with animated music, and then loll patiently back against the wall until the next team arrives.

After checking in at the very modern Aristos Hotel, we leave by bus for Puebla and its impressive new concert hall. The scenery en route is picturesque, but the females on the street are studied more attentively by the musicians.

"That lady is over for the day, I'm telling you."

"I'm hip," says Buster Cooper.

The concert has apparently been inadequately publicized, and the hall is only half full. Even the refreshment vendors seem to have been taken by surprise, and their service and stock likewise prove inadequate. But the concert is a good one, and Ellington tries out several sections of his *Mexican Anticipación*, the suite which in-

275

Arrival in Mexico, 1968

cludes *Latin American Sunshine*. The latter, now scored with striking passages for the reeds, assumes richer dimensions. The concert
is filmed and recorded, the complications of lights and cables being
overcome with little fuss. We arrive back in Mexico City at 2:30 A.M.

Tuesday, September 24th.

We set out in the afternoon for the Hacienda Vista Hermosa at
Tequesquitengo, sixty miles away. The hacienda, which was first
established by Hernán Cortés in 1529, is a building of fortress-like
proportions, excellently preserved, and now run as a first-class hotel.
The guest rooms are furnished in colonial style with antiques, and
everywhere are objects of historic interest.

The band performs in the dining room, where massive walls and
archways create a medieval impression. This is enhanced by the dogs
that come through the open doorways to explore beneath the dining
tables. There is nothing medieval about the music, however, and
more sections from the new suite are performed under the code
names of *Roma* and *Gaye*. A cockfight that had been promised as an
interlude does not take place, and nobody seems to care.

Ellington had intended to return to Mexico City and fly to Acapulco next day, but he now changes his mind and decides to ride with

276

Harry Carney surveys the baggage,
Mexico City, 1968

Ellington in Merida

the band in the bus overnight. It is a long journey through mountains, where it rains heavily, and there are occasional hazards on the road in the forms of pigs and cows, but nearly everyone manages to sleep. From time to time, people sit up to light cigarettes.

"How're you doin'?" one asks, when his neighbor stirs.

"I'm hangin' on."

Wednesday, September 25th.

There is a stop at dawn for a general stretching of legs. The scenery, which has changed completely, is much more tropical, and the soil rose-colored in the morning light. Ellington, first out of the bus from his "navigator's seat," exercises on the lonely road by sparring like a boxer.

We reach the Hilton Hotel in Acapulco at 8 A.M. The younger members of the group decide that the beach looks more inviting than bed, but a joint descent cannot be made until the stores have opened and Paul Gonsalves has acquired bathing trunks. After this purchase has been made, with great care and deliberation, it is discovered that the way to the beach lies through an outdoor bar full of friendly people having fun, so a long delay ensues for the intake of liquid breakfast. The beach, in fact, is not reached until the afternoon,

277

everyone being well aware of the danger of the noonday sun.

Harold Ashby enjoys the beach very much. "I'd never even been to Atlantic City before I joined this band," he says appreciatively. Chuck Connors is the first to try the spectacular flight around the bay on a parachute towed by a motorboat. He is followed by Jeff Castleman, Trish Turner, and Tony Watkins. Buster Cooper assists the departures.

"It's very enjoyable, " he is told by his close friend, Connors.

"I'm hip," he says, but he doesn't go.

When we leave the beach, Paul Gonsalves is still at the bar, entertaining and being entertained, still in his bathing trunks. Several of the older musicians are resting here, too, and everybody warmly approves of Acapulco.

At 10:30, there is a dinner dance in the hotel. Ellington himself is restricted by a piano as bad as that encountered the previous night. The first set of "dinner music" features Cat Anderson on *Perdido* and Paul Gonsalves on *Laura*. Ava Gardner has brought a party, and a very happy atmosphere prevails, expecially since she has known Ellington and several members of the band for some time. *The Mexican Suite* (to use its alternative title) is played in its entirety, and the ensembles begin to show creditable polish. The rhythms suit the wealthy-looking patrons, many of whom are dancing barefoot.

Thursday, September 26th.

"Where've you been?" Ellington asks at Acapulco airport. He had taken a cab at 7:30 A.M., assuming the bus had left, but it is one of those mornings when his son has considerable difficulty in rooting out his charges.

"Acapulco is the place for me," Paul Gonsalves announces. "I'm going to have a house here one day."

No one is in peak condition, and no one seems to relish the thought of breakfast until it is learned that beer will be served. *"Aeronaves de México* is a good airline," affirm those who need the hair of the dog.

On arrival in Guadalajara, we find that a party of attractive college girls, supervised by two attractive matrons, have been assigned to guide us about the city. Willie Cook declares with an air of great sincerity that the company of young girls is just what his doctor recommended for him. Mercer Ellington, however, nominates him for a television appearance that afternoon. The M.C. knows little English, and Mercer and I stumble in Spanish, but Cook talks fluently and steals the show when he borrows a trumpet and plays *Stardust* with the studio orchestra.

Earlier parts of this diary must have shown that the hardest worker in the organization is Ellington himself. He carries the main responsibility at every performance, and is at press conferences, official functions, and radio stations when his men are relaxing. In this case, his son has taken a television appearance off his shoulders, but Mercer also has many extra duties. Immediately after the television show, for example, he must go to the Teatro Degollado to see that the stage is properly set up for the band. Here there is an excellent piano. The beautiful old theatre has five balconies and a pictorial representation of the Divine Comedy in the dome. As we leave, we note advertising for the same German group that we encountered in Chile, They will be here in a few days.

At each of the two concerts tonight, the new suite is performed. Harry Carney's importance in the ensemble is constantly audible. The work is still being modified by its composer, who shouts instructions during each performance. At the second concert, Paul Gonsalves makes a daring descent from the stage to serenade with *In a Sentimental Mood* a young lady he insists is the mayor's daughter. When he is safely back in position, the leader calls on him for *Happy-Go-Lucky Local*.

Between concerts, several of the musicians with their girl escorts are taken to a sidewalk café for refreshments and a sampling of Mexican popular music. Guadalajara's hospitality is considered exemplary.

Friday, September 27th.

Leaving the hotel at 7 A.M. and the airport at eight thirty, we arrive in Mexico City again at nine thirty. There are problems about transportation to Mérida in Yucatán, but the musicians are happy in Eastern Airlines' V.I.P. lounge, where everything is done for their comfort. In fact, when it is announced that half the band can leave on a mid-morning flight, the priority of Ellington and the seniors goes completely unchallenged. As Mercer Ellington shepherds the rearguard aboard an aged DC-3 at one thirty, he has a question for the impresario:

"Will there be a bus?"

"Absolutely."

"Absolutely what?"

"I absolutely don't know," Gary Keys confesses.

It is a long, slow flight. The cheerful stewardess has a limitless supply of beer, Coke, and fritos, but nothing else. When we stop at Veracruz, she will not allow us to disembark.

279

"Why'd we stop there, senorita?" Buster Cooper asks when we take off again.

"To refuel."

"I didn't see any gas trucks."

"Maybe they forgot."

"I'm hip," Buster says, closing the subject.

The DC-3 drones across the Bahía de Campeche. Over the darkening land of Yucatán, it is cold in the unpressurized cabin, quite unlike the steamy jungle we imagine below. Five hours after Mexico City, the lights of Mérida are very welcome, and on landing, the air is soft and balmy.

There is no bus, and everybody sags limply on the airport steps with hand luggage, waiting to see what baggage and instruments come off the DC-3. The locals inspect us with polite curiosity, and the musicians eye the chicks with increasing appreciation. Five minutes later, the five o'clock jet from Mexico City arrives—a ninety-minute flight—bringing with it the rest of the instruments and the camera crew's equipment.

"Hurry, thirteen thousand people are waiting for you in the ball park!" urges Keys.

It is nine instead of seven when the concert begins, and some of the thirteen thousand have clearly not waited. The band emerges from the dugout into the tropical night in shirtsleeves and crumpled traveling clothes. The crowd is stupefied by the music, as well it might be, for the sound system is atrocious, Piano and drums are presented at overwhelming strength, with thirteen violently distorted horns, and no bass. The leader's vocal instructions issue from the speakers with unprecedented power. Solos by Cat Anderson and Rufus Jones communicate, however, and there is an orderly dispersal when the concert ends.

A handsome bus arrives to transport us to a luxurious country club, the Club Campestra de Mérida. One of the maestro's stage suits has materialized, and he succeds to a large extent in diverting attention from his disheveled flock, whose uniforms have not yet been located.

The elegant crowd dances energetically to the Golden Jets, a talented local rock group, but Ellington's sets progressively turn into concerts as listeners crowd around the band and stand about all over the dance floor. Requests are readily answered, and Harold Ashby is called forward for *Hello, Dolly*, which he swings with relaxed phrasing and smooth tone that partly mask his very firm intent.

Back in the hotel at three, Ellington finds there is no room service. He decides on sleep and folds up the score of the new suite, which he had been revising again that afternoon. "Meet you in the lobby at six thirty," he says.

Saturday, September 28th.

We lead the field by cab and are at the airport a long time before the bus arrives. Aero Mayo, we discover, has laid on a special flight for the band—the same DC-3 and the same stewardess—which will leave at nine. There are signs of life in the restaurant, and *El Rey de Jazz,* as he is properly billed in Mexico, orders a well-done filet mignon and drinks the first of three bottles of Carta Clara, a highly rated Yucatán beer which we find pleasant, but inferior to Bohemia. As the room fills with musicians, Johnny Hodges patrols the tables to decide which dish looks the most appetizing, muttering the while about nonexistent pork chops.

A new baggage problem causes delay, and Tony Watkins is ultimately left behind to follow with the balance of the suitcases—most of them never opened in Mérida—in another plane. Ellington, Gonsalves, Cook, and Ashby pass the time bargaining at the gift counter for bracelets, necklaces, and rings. Sombreros are now being worn, but at this unshaven hour banditry rather than music would appear to be more appropriate to the wearers.

Departure is eventually at nine thirty. More beer and chips. Ellington, who is riding at the front of the plane, turns around at one point to ask his men, "Doesn't this remind you of when we went to Kabul?" At Veracruz, this time, everybody scrambles rebelliously out onto an empty oil drum, and the plane is kept waiting until substantial refreshments have been secured. We arrive in Mexico City at two thirty and leave the hotel at five for the first of two concerts at the Palacio de Bellas Artes.

Tonight is the official première, as promised, of *Mexican Anticipación,* alias *The Mexican Suite,* a part, as Ellington now recognizes, of what must become *The Latin American Suite.* "For years and years we have wanted to come to Mexico," Ellington explains, "and we thought of her as a beautiful woman. This is a musical reflection of our mental anticipation." The performance at the second concert is better than at the first, and the audience really savors the music. Encores are obligatory in each case. At the first, Ellington and Castleman play *Meditation,* followed by an improvised blues with drums added. Willie Cook joins this trio for *Stormy Weather* and *St. Louis Blues* at the second.

Sunday, September 29th.

There is a concert organized by Eastern Airlines at 12:30 P.M. in the small, intimate theatre of the Aristos Hotel. The hour and the altitude are unsettling. Paul Gonsalves and I, probably for the first time in our lives, drink whiskey for medicinal purposes. At least, it seems to assist breathing. "I don't like playing jazz at this time of day," he says seriously.

Ambassador Fulton Freeman is on hand to introduce Ellington. "We have no ambassador of goodwill better than the Duke," he says.

Standing between two charming stewardesses, the maestro is in sparkling form. "Here we are, in the reflection of the halos of Eastern's angels," he says, "but we have to be geographical at this point."

Take the "A" Train is thereupon played as representative of New York, *Chicago* as of Chicago, and *Creole Love Call* as of New Orleans. Nothing is specifically named for his own city, but presumably any or all of his compositions can be taken as saluting Washington.

The Ambassador later borrows Lawrence Brown's trombone to play a very creditable version of *Stardust*, and the concert ends on a euphoric note.

In the evening, there are two concerts in the huge Auditorio Nacionál, where the seats are priced low enough to permit the city's poor to hear *El Rey de Jazz*. At the first concert, Jorge Rojas substitutes for Jeff Castleman, who has been suddenly felled by a mysterious virus. Hours later, Rojas is still so elated with the experience that one of the musicians feels compelled to ask him:

"Are you high, man?"

"Everybody is high in Mexico City," Rojas replies.

While drinking with friends who arrived from California yesterday, so Ellington claims, he made the mistake of putting *plain* water with whiskey. The power of his medicine bag, which proved so efficacious in South America, was briefly challenged by the proverbial curse of the Aztecs. Luckily, the medicine bag and his constitution soon triumph.

Monday, September 30th.

All are sorry to be leaving Mexico City. But here, as in South America, the musicians have been dogged by jazz fans with the question: "What do you think of Ornette Coleman?" Russell Procope found the answer that precluded argument, even if it did not always turn away wrath. "I don't," he said simply.

At the airport, where the Eastern Airlines people by now seem like personal friends, all loose change is spent on sombreros and tequila. The flight home is uneventful except for one incident.

"We are just passing over Atlanta, Georgia," the pilot announces with a southern accent.

"Keep going," Tony Watkins shouts. "Don't stop now!"

[*1968*]

282

At the White House

Duke Ellington's international fame is securely based on his achievements as a composer, bandleader, pianist, arranger, and lyricist. A musician who typifies this century as none other, he has been assessed and analyzed many times in the course of his long career. His wit, highly charged personality, originality of mind, undeviating loyalties, and belief in God—all have been often examined and discussed. What has never been stressed is his devotion to his country. He is proudly an American, a patriot.

It was therefore altogether fitting that President and Mrs. Nixon should have honored him with a dinner at the White House on the occasion of his seventieth birthday. In the past, April 29th had been merely a milestone that he swept past annually in the course of his musical progress, but this year added significance was thrust upon it. When the President presented him with the Medal of Freedom, the highest civilian medal the Government can bestow, many of those in the East Room must have been reminded of how Ellington introduces a moving section of his new Sacred Concert.

"Freedom," he says, "is a word that is the foundation of our country."

Freedom is also the key to his music, and "freedom of expression" is the prerogative he claims for musicians of the milieu in which he works. So when President Nixon spoke of him as carrying "the message of freedom" throughout the world, he spoke a double truth. Ellington has been—and is—a magnificent ambassador unofficially for his country, and officially for the music of which he is today the supreme exponent.

In the two weeks before the White House dinner, his working routine was disturbed by the needs of the national and foreign press. He gave the considerable time they required with varying degrees of cheerfulness and patience, in varying attire, in varying situations, and in varying positions. Some of the more self-important reporters could not believe that an interview would take place with their subject lying on his back in bed, facing the headboard, his feet high on the wall in front of him. Whatever the effect on the circulation, the reversed posture seemed to have a stimulating effect on the ensuing conversation.

Special TV and radio programs were also made for European

networks. The BBC filmed him at the piano in the trophy room of his New York offices, where the walls are lined with cups, plaques, awards, and significant memorabilia. The Danish Broadcasting Corporation caught him at work in National's big new record studio, where he was trying out vehicles for his new singer, Shirley Witherspoon.

In between these activities, and desperate attempts to keep dentists' appointments ("It's the root-and-canal man's turn today!"), he repeatedly turned to his piano and a major concern, the music for a provocative new film called *Change of Mind*. In hotel suites, there would always be an electric piano capable of soft-toned utterance during the night. "You have to write it down when it comes to you," he said. "You can remember the notes next day, but not the values and rhythm." The music was no sooner written, and the parts of the score copied, than it had to be heard, and where better than in the record studio again? This, in fact, had been his practice for many years: to record new music, to take home a reference tape for consideration, and to revise next day if necessary.

In this case, an unusual band was gathered together, for his regular group was supposedly enjoying a lay-off, and several of its members were far from New York. The backbone remained, however, and it was satisfactorily reinforced with veterans from the Count Basie and Earl Hines bands.

"Are you sober?" he asked with mock fierceness as one wayward musician entered the studio a little late. "I understand you were all 'tore up' yesterday."

The music included several items originally recorded in the '30s. *Wanderlust* was a down blues for the "visit to Soulville". *Creole Rhapsody*, revered by the more scholarly Ellington followers as his first "extended" work, was incidentally updated by the sound of the Fender piano that its composer chose to play it on. "Keep it soft and round-toned," he reminded the four-piece brass section, which, with its foreign elements, was showing some divergence of opinion on tonal values. For the nightclub scene there was *What Good Am I Without You*, and this occasioned another gentle directive: "This is a love song, boys, played with heart." For the opening hospital sequences in an operating theatre, there was original dissonant writing that required accuracy to be effective, so after tentative attempts at an "ensemble" statement, each man was required to play his part separately, paying particular attention to time. When they all played together again, the music was immediately satisfactory, and the leader indicated satisfaction by finishing the session with a kind of *feu de joie*, an up-tempo piano solo accompanied only by bass and drums.

284

Ellington constantly reiterates his disapproval of categories in music. He views them not as a convenience to listeners, but as a restriction on artists. Although the fifteen-piece band of brass, reeds, and rhythm is his normal instrument, he writes confidently for the bigger ensembles films often require, for symphony orchestras, for octets (as on his Rainbow Grill engagements), for choirs and choruses. His confidence and energy rub off to some extent on associates, but none can keep his pace for long. "*You* are tired!" he repeated ironically to a wilting aide at four in the morning. "Do you know I had only three hours' sleep last night?"

The transitions he makes and the pace he maintains in music have their counterparts in his social life. Seeing him next on the steps of his Washington hotel, promptly on time for his appointment with the President, but concerned about transportation for his party, was to be reminded of his evenness of temper and of a comparable occasion, when he was presented to Queen Elizabeth II at the Leeds Festival eleven years before.

At the White House, he and his sister, Ruth Ellington, were received by President and Mrs. Nixon on the second floor, where the President showed his guests his private quarters and demonstrated the stereo equipment. Meanwhile, the dinner guests were gathering in the Cross Hall as the Marine Band played appropriate selections. There were Ellington's son, Mercer, his daughter-in-law, his two grandchildren, and a nephew, who had flown in from London that day. There, too, were three of the people on whom he most relies: Dr. Arthur Logan, his physician; Harry Carney, who has been a member of his band for over forty years; and Thomas L. Whaley, choirmaster, copyist, and arranger. Besides government officials and Ellington's personal friends, a formidable cross-section of the music profession included Harold Arlen, Mrs. Count Basie (her husband was, unfortunately, in Europe), Dave Brubeck, Cab Calloway, Billy Eckstine, Dizzy Gillespie, Richard Rodgers, and the two "jazz priests," Father Norman O'Connor and Pastor John Gensel. Ellington's performances in churches and cathedrals also explained the presence of prominent clerics from New York, Toledo, and San Francisco.

When the President and Mrs. Nixon had made an elegant descent of the grand staircase with Ellington and his sister (the two ladies wore pale shades of green, which by good fortune did not clash), the four of them stood on a reception line to greet the guests. The passage to the dining room was then somewhat delayed as Ellington greeted each of his intimates with four kisses, two on each cheek, according to his custom. This certainly helped establish the atmosphere of happy informality that was to prevail all evening.

285   Inside the State Dining Room, the company was seated at round

tables, husbands and wives being separated from one another. The President, with Miss Ellington on his right, was joined by, among others, Benny Goodman, singer Lou Rawls, and Dizzy Gillespie, the last of whom reportedly took the opportunity to speak to the President about conditions in South Carolina, where he was born. At the opposite table, Ellington and Mrs. Nixon had the company of Billy Eckstine and Richard Rodgers.

Animated conversation broke out on every side as the attraction of both common and uncommon interests made itself felt. At Table Eleven, Daniel P. Moynihan, Assistant to the President, discussed books and publishing with Mahalia Jackson, while the veteran Thomas L. Whaley explained the peculiarities of the music business to Mrs. George Shultz, wife of the Secretary of Labor. The Rev. Bryant Kirkland, who was much responsible for the presentation of Ellington's Sacred Concert at the Fifth Avenue Presbyterian Church in New York, got an affirmative answer to the suggestion that Miss Jackson should sing there. And how had she enjoyed recording that Columbia album with Duke Ellington?

"He didn't rehearse me nothin'," she replied forthrightly. "He said, 'Just open the Bible and sing!'"

Just then, a dozen or so violinists—the United States Army Stroll-

Ellington and President Nixon in the White House, 29 April, 1969

ing Strings— came briskly into the room. Taking up positions among the tables, they created an exhilarating effect with performances of some of Ellington's most famous compositions.

In proposing the toast, the President spoke warmly of the guest of honor's Washington background, and Ellington concluded an urbane reply on a note of simple, moving sincerity. "There is no place I would rather be tonight," he said, "except in my mother's arms."

After dinner, and after a hundred more guests had been welcomed, the Medal of Freedom was presented in the East Room. Reading the recipient's name, the President paused humorously after "Edward Kennedy," drew a big laugh, and concluded with "Ellington." "In the royalty of American music," he added, "no man swings more or stands higher than the Duke."

Ellington showed his gratitude characteristically by kissing the surprised President twice on each cheek. Then he recited the four freedoms by which his friend and writing colleague, the late Billy Strayhorn, had lived: "Freedom from hate unconditionally; freedom from self-pity; freedom from the fear of doing something that would help someone else more than it does me; and freedom from the kind of pride that makes me feel I am better than my brother."

"It did occur to me," the President said, returning to the bandstand, "that one number was missing from the program. Please don't go away. And everybody sing, please—in the key of G." Then he sat down at the imposing, eagle-legged Steinway and proceeded to play a very positive version of *Happy Birthday* as everyone sang heartily and joyfully.

The concert that followed was produced by the Voice of America's Willis Conover, who acted as M.C. The handpicked band, representative of the profession at large, consisted of Clark Terry and Bill Berry, both formerly with Ellington (trumpets); Urbie Green and J. J. Johnson (trombones); Paul Desmond (alto saxophone); Gerry Mulligan (baritone saxophone); Hank Jones (piano); Jim Hall (guitar); Milt Hinton (bass); and Louis Bellson (drums). The ninety-minute program was made up entirely of numbers written by, or closely associated with, Ellington, and the unusual instrumentation often revealed unsuspected qualities in the material. Generally, the treatment was of the "concerto" type pioneered by Ellington, a different soloist being featured on each number. The selfless rhythm section acquitted itself well throughout, and among the horns Clark Terry was outstanding. Without ever seeming to exert himself, he established an easy authority that dominated the ensemble. The President was apparently much taken by his use of the plunger mute, a perennial Ellington device that was employed with marked success by both trumpets on *Just Squeeze Me*.

287

Three pianists appeared as guests. Billy Taylor played a medley that introduced the seldom-heard *All Too Soon*; Dave Brubeck played *Things Ain't What They Used to Be* with assistance from Desmond and Mulligan; and Earl Hines brought the concert to its peak in three thrilling choruses of *Perdido*. Such excited, shouted approval as greeted this performance can seldom have been heard in the White House before.

The first of two singers was Mary Mayo, who did *A Prelude to a Kiss*, *I Didn't Know About You*, and *Praise God*. Joe Williams, who is experienced in singing Ellington, brought depth and conviction to *Come Sunday* and *Heritage*. After these, he gave the concert a swinging climax with *Jump for Joy*, the lyrics of which, written in 1941 but as relevant today as then, were wittily expressive of the composer's social philosophy.

After Willis Conover had introduced each musician individually, and Ellington had risen from his chair to bow or blow kisses as each name was called, the President returned to the microphone and said he felt they ought to hear from at least one more pianist.

"It is the greatest compliment ever paid me," Ellington replied, "to suggest that I am eligible to follow such artistry as we have heard tonight. However, I am of a somewhat courageous nature, and I shall pick a name, and see if I can improvise on it, something very gentle and graceful—something like Pat."

His improvisation at slow tempo was indeed gentle and graceful, with serene melodic and harmonic qualities not entirely to be grasped at one hearing, as is so often the case with his piano solos.

It was now after midnight, and to the general surprise the President announced that refreshments would be served in the adjacent hall while preparations were made for a jam session in the East Room. After he and Mrs. Nixon had retired, Ellington listened to Vice-President Agnew play *his* Ellington favorites on the Marine Band's piano.

Friends from his Chicago years meanwhile converged on Earl Hines to congratulate him. Mahalia Jackson, who had been excited by his *Perdido*, embraced him and reminded him of when he tried to get her to sing blues. Billy Eckstine, whom Hines originally brought to fame, came to bestow a jazz encomium.

"You *dirty* old man," he said admiringly. "I told Lou Rawls one number was all you needed. 'Let him alone and you'll see,' I said. And one number did it!"

Hines was called to participate in the jam session, but he begged off because he was leaving for a South American tour a few hours later. There was no shortage of pianists, however. At one time or another Willie "the Lion" Smith, George Wein, Marian McPartland,

Dave Brubeck, Billy Taylor, *and* Duke Ellington took their places at the keyboard, sometimes two together, as the musicians heard earlier jammed with musician guests and members of the Marine Band. The joys of the jam session were evident enough on the participants' faces, but it perils were also shown when Lou Rawls, Hollywood's conception of a blues singer, elected to sing the blues. Joe Williams and Billy Eckstine joined him and they had forgotten nothing. After *Every Day* and *Stormy Monday*, *It's a Lowdown Dirty Shame* seemed extremely appropriate.

Chairs were pushed back and spirited dancing took place, led by Ellington and a radiant Carmen de Lavallade. Freedom was again the operative word as members of the clergy joined in with energy and surprising ability. "This must be that *Ecumenical* Strut," a musician observed thoughtfully.

It was after two o'clock when the party broke up. The White House staff seemed to regard it as an exceptionally enjoyable occasion, and even those of differing political beliefs gave ungrudging credit to President Nixon for personally having done so much to ensure a relaxed, informal, and friendly atmosphere. Show business people were particularly appreciative of the smoothness with which everything had been conducted.

Back at the hotel, Ellington quickly changed into his traveling clothes. While making his farewells in the crowded suite, he was stuffing telegrams and birthday cards into his coat pockets. He had a plane to catch. He would get a little sleep in Oklahoma City, where he and the band had an engagement the very next night.

[*1969*]

The band in 1948: Ellington, piano; Wendell Marshall, bass; Sonny Greer, drums; Lawrence Brown, Quentin Jackson, Tryee Glenn, trombones; Jimmy Hamilton, Johnny Hodges, Ben Webster, Russell Procope, Harry Carney, reeds; Al Killian, Shorty Baker, Francis Williams, Shelton Hemphill, Ray Nance trumpets.

Recording "Afro Bossa," 1963

**DISCOGRAPHY
CHRONOLOGY
INDEX**

Duke Ellington's Recordings

293

Greatest Hits	Reprise 6234
Hi-Fi Ellington Uptown	Columbia CCL-830
Hits of the 60's	Reprise 6122
Hodge Podge (with Johnny Hodges)	Encore (CBS) 22002
Hot in Harlem (1928–29)	Decca Dl-79241
In a Mellotone	RCA LPM-1364
Indispensable Duke Ellington, The	RCA LPM-6009 (2 discs)
In My Solitude	Harmony 11323
Jazz Piano, The (with Earl Hines, the Lion, etc.)	RCA LSP-3499
Johnny Come Lately	RCA LPV-541
Jumpin' Punkins	RCA LPV-517
Money Jungle (with Charles Mingus and Max Roach)	Solid State 18022
Music From "Mary Poppins"	Reprise 1641
Music of Duke Ellington	Columbia CCL-558
My People (Original Cast Recording)	Contact 1
North of the Border (In Canada)	Decca DL-75069
Nutcracker & Peer Gynt Suites, The	Odyssey (CBS) 321-60252
On the Cote D'Azur (with Ella Fitzgerald)	Verve 64072 (2 discs)
Popular Duke Ellington, The	RCA LSP-3576
Pretty Woman	RCA LPV-553
Rockin' in Rhythm	Decca DL-79247
Seventieth Birthday Concert	Solid State SS-19000 (2 discs)
Side By Side (with Johnny Hodges)	Verve 6.8345
Soul Call	Verve 6.8701
Symphonic Ellington, The	Reprise 6097
Things Ain't What They Used to Be (with Johnny Hodges and Rex Stewart)	RCA LPV-533
Will Big Bands Ever Come Back?	Reprise 6168

Duke Ellington: A Brief Chronology

1899 Born in Washington, D.C., on April 29th

1906 First piano lessons with Miss Clinkscales.

1914 Wrote *Soda Fountain Rag.*

1919 Birth of Mercer Ellington.

1922 Joined Wilbur Sweatman in New York with Otto Hardwick and Sonny Greer.

1923 Returned to New York at instigation of Fats Waller. Band, including Hardwick, Greer, and Artie Whetsol, engaged first at Barron's in Harlem and then on Broadway at the Kentucky Club.

1924 Wrote score for revue, *Chocolate Kiddies.*

1925 Bubber Miley replaced Artie Whetsol, who returned later.

1926 Wellman Braud and Joe "Tricky Sam" Nanton joined band. Compositions: *East St. Louis Toodle-oo* (adopted as the band's theme) and *Birmingham Breakdown.*

1927 Band began engagement at the Cotton Club, New York, its expanded personnel including Harry Carney and Barney Bigard. Compositions: *Black and Tan Fantasy* and *Creole Love Call.*

1928 Johnny Hodges joined band. Compositions: *Black Beauty, The Mooche,* and *Misty Mornin'.*

1929 Cootie Williams replaced Bubber Miley, and Juan Tizol joined band, which appeared in Florenz Ziegfeld's *Show Girl* and a short film entitled *Black and Tan Fantasy.* Compositions: *Doin' the Voom Voom* and *Saturday Night Function.*

1930 Band went to Hollywood for first time to appear in film, *Check and Double Check,* and performed at Fulton Theatre, New York, with Maurice Chevalier. Compositions: *Old Man Blues, Ring Dem Bells, Mood Indigo,* and *Rockin' in Rhythm.*

1931 Ivie Anderson joined band. Composition: *Creole Rhapsody.*

1932 Concert given in Columbia University at Porter Grainger's request. Lawrence Brown joined band. Compositions: *It Don't Mean a Thing, Lazy Rhapsody, Ducky Wucky,* and *Sophisticated Lady.*

1933 First European tour. Compositions: *Merry-Go-Round, Drop Me Off at Harlem, Harlem Speaks,* and *Daybreak Express.*

1934 Rex Stewart joined band, which appeared in films, *Murder at the Vanities* and *Belle of the Nineties.* Compositions: *Stompy Jones* and *Solitude.*

1935 Wellman Braud replaced by Billy Taylor and Hayes Alvis. Band appeared in short film, *Symphony in Black*. Ellington's mother died. Compositions: *In a Sentimental Mood* and *Reminiscing in Tempo*.

1936 Recording of small units began. Compositions: *Caravan, Clarinet Lament (Barney's Concerto)*, and *Echoes of Harlem (Cootie's Concerto)*.

1937 Band appeared in Marx Brothers film, *A Day at the Races*. Compositions: *Azure, Diminuendo and Crescendo in Blue*, and *Harmony in Harlem*.

1938 Harold "Shorty" Baker joined band for first time. Ellington's father died. Compositions: *The Gal from Joe's, I Let a Song Go Out of My Heart, Jeep's Blues, Pyramid, A Gypsy Without a Song, Prelude to a Kiss, The Jeep Is Jumpin'*, *Wanderlust, Blue Light*, and *Boy Meets Horn*.

1939 European tour. Billy Strayhorn and Ben Webster joined band. Jimmy Blanton replaced Billy Taylor. Compositions: *Subtle Lament, Portrait of the Lion, Something to Live For, Solid Old Man, Serenade to Sweden, The Sergeant Was Shy, Weely*.

1940 Ray Nance replaced Cootie Williams. Compositions: *Jack the Bear, Ko-Ko, Morning Glory, Cottontail, Never No Lament (Don't Get Around Much Anymore)*, *Bojangles, Harlem Airshaft, All Too Soon, In a Mellotone, Warm Valley*, and *Day Dream*.

1941 *Jump for Joy* premièred in Los Angeles. Tom Whaley joined Ellington organization. Billy Strayhorn wrote *Take the "A" Train*, which was to become band's theme. Mercer Ellington wrote the enduringly successful *Things Ain't What They Used to Be*. Compositions: *I Got It Bad, Jump for Joy*, and *Subtle Slough (Just Squeeze Me)*.

1942 Jimmy Hamilton replaced Barney Bigard. Band appeared in film, *Cabin in the Sky*. Juan Tizol wrote *Perdido*. Composition: *C Jam Blues*.

1943 Series of Carnegie Hall concerts began. Band appeared in film, *Reveille with Beverly*. Composition: *Black, Brown, and Beige*, which includes *Come Sunday*.

1944 Cat Anderson joined band for first time. *Blutopia* premièred by Paul Whiteman. Compositions: *Blutopia* and *I'm Beginning to See the Light*.

1945 Russell Procope and Oscar Pettiford joined band. Compositions: *The Perfume Suite, New World a-Comin'*, and *I'm Just a Lucky So-and-So*.

1946 Compositions: *Esquire Swank, Rockabye River, Pretty Woman*.

1947 *The Liberian Suite* premièred at Carnegie Hall. Tyree Glenn joined band. Compositions: *The Deep South Suite* (including *Happy-Go-Lucky Local*), and *The Liberian Suite* (including *I Like the Sunrise*).

1948 European tour without band, but with Ray Nance and vocalist Kay Davis. Wendell Marshall, Jimmy Blanton's cousin, joined band. Composition: *The Tattooed Bride*.

1950 European tour. Paul Gonsalves joined band. Compositions: *Love You Madly* and *Harlem*.

1951 Willie Smith, Louis Bellson, and Clark Terry joined band, and Juan Tizol returned after several years' absence. Composition: *Monologue (Pretty and the Wolf)*.

1953   Sam Woodyard joined band. Composition: *Satin Doll.*
1955   Johnny Hodges rejoined band after four-year absence. *Night Creature* premièred at Carnegie Hall with the Symphony of the Air.
1956   Triumph at Newport Jazz Festival, following performance of *Diminuendo and Crescendo in Blue* which featured Paul Gonsalves extensively, resulted in Ellington's appearance on cover of *Time* magazine.
1957   Willie Cook joined band. Compositions: *A Drum Is a Woman, Portrait of Ella Fitzgerald* (including *All Heart*), and *Such Sweet Thunder,* the Shakespearean suite that includes *The Star-Crossed Lovers* and *Half the Fun.*
1958   European tour. Ellington presented to H. M. Queen Elizabeth II at Leeds Festival. Compositions: *Happy Reunion* and *Mr. Gentle and Mr. Cool.*
1959   European tour. First film score, for *Anatomy of a Murder.* Booty Wood joined band. Compositions: *Toot Suite* and *Idiom '59.*
1960   Music written for the film *Paris Blues* and a play, *Turcaret,* performed at the Palais de Chaillot, Paris. Compositions: *Suite Thursday, The Queen's Suite* (including *The Single Petal of a Rose) 'Asphalt Jungle Theme,* and *Paris Blues.*
1962   European tour. Buster Cooper joined and Cootie Williams returned to the band. Piano recital at Museum of Modern Art, New York. Compositions: *Self-Portrait of the Bean, African Flower, Money Jungle,* and *The Feeling of Jazz.*
1963   European tour. Ellington wrote and produced show, *My People,* for the Century of Negro Progress Exposition in Chicago, with Jimmy Jones as conductor of specially organized band. Tour of Near and Middle East for U.S. State Department. Compositions: *Afro-Bossa* (a collection of original compositions incorporating Latin rhythms) and the music for a production of Shakespeare's *Timon of Athens* in Canada.
1964   European tour and first tour of Japan. Mercer Ellington joined band as road manager and member of the trumpet section. Compositions: *The Far East Suite* (including *Mount Harissa* and *Isfahan*).
1965   European tour. Performances in Festival of the Arts at the White House and with Boston Pops at Tanglewood. First Sacred Concert at Grace Cathedral, San Francisco. Compositions: *The Virgin Island Suite, The Golden Broom and the Green Apple,* and *A Blue Mural from Two Points of View.*
1966   European tour with Ella Fitzgerald. Music written for film, *Assault on a Queen,* and Milton College production of *Murder in the Cathedral.* Sacred Concert performed in Coventry Cathedral, England. President's Gold Medal presented in Madrid. Ellington opened restored wing of Château de Goutelas in France, and represented the United States at the World Festival of Negro Arts in Dakar, Senegal. Compositions: *La Plus Belle Africaine, Swamp Goo, Drag, Rue Bleu, The Shepherd.*
1967   Jeff Castleman joined band. Ellington given honorary degree, Doctor of Music, at Yale University. Billy Strayhorn died.

1968   Second Sacred Concert at the Cathedral Church of St. John the Divine, New York, with Alice Babs as chief vocalist. Tour of South America and Mexico. Score for film *Change of Mind* written and recorded in New York. Ellington appointed to National Council of the Arts. Harold Ashby replaced Jimmy Hamilton. Compositions: *The Second Sacred Concert* (including *Heaven, God Has Those Angels, Too Good to Title, Supreme Being,* and *Freedom)* , and *The Latin American Suite* (including *Latin American Sunshine)* .

1969   Birthday party at the White House and presentation of Medal of Freedom by President Nixon. Tour of West Indies and performance of Sacred Concert in Kingston. European tour with first performances behind the Iron Curtain (in Prague). Sacred Concerts in Stockholm, Paris, and Barcelona. Wild Bill Davis joined band.

1970   Tour of the Far East and Australasia. Johnny Hodges died.

Besides collaborating with Duke Ellington on many of the compositions mentioned above, Billy Strayhorn was solely responsible for numerous contributions—compositions and arrangements—to the band's book, among which should be noted: *After All* (1941), *Clementine* (1941), *Passion Flower* (1941), *Raincheck* (1941), *Chelsea Bridge* (1941), *Johnny Come Lately* (1942), *Midriff* (1946), *Overture to a Jam Session* (1946), *Smada* (1951), *Boo-dah* (1953), *All Day Long* (1954), *Snibor* (1956), *U.M.M.G.* (1956), *A Midnight in Paris* (1962), *Absinthe* (1962), *Tigress* (1962), *Charpoy* (1964), *The Intimacy of the Blues* (1967), and *Blood Count* (1967).

Index

299

303

307

311

PICTURE CREDITS

Other DA CAPO titles of interest